Java and JavaScript Programming

Peter Wayner

AP PROFESSIONAL

AP Professional is a division of Academic Press, Inc.

Boston   San Diego   New York
London   Sydney   Tokyo   Toronto

AP PROFESSIONAL
An Imprint of ACADEMIC PRESS, INC.
A Division of HARCOURT BRACE & COMPANY

ORDERS (USA and Canada): 1-800-3131-APP or APP@ACAD.COM
AP Professional Orders: 6277 Sea Harbor Dr., Orlando, FL 32821-9816

Europe/Middle East/Africa: 0-11-44 (0) 181-300-3322
Orders: AP Professional 24–28 Oval Rd., London NW1 7DX

Japan/Korea: 03-3234-3911-5
Orders: Harcourt Brace Japan, Inc., Ichibunan

Australia: 02-517-8999
Orders: Harcourt Brace & Co. Australia, Locked Bag 16, Marrickville, NSW 2204, Australia

Other International: (407) 345-3800
AP Professional Orders: 6277 Sea Harbor Dr., Orlando FL 32821-9816

Editorial: 1300 Boylston St., Chestnut Hill, MA 02167; (617) 232-0500

Web: http://www.apnet.com/

United Kingdom Edition published by
ACADEMIC PRESS LIMITED
24–28 Oval Road, London NW1 7DX

Library of Congress Cataloging-in-Publication Data
Wayner, Peter, 1964–
    Java and JavaScript programming / Peter Wayner,
        p.   cm.
    Includes index.
    ISBN 0-12-738769-2 (alk. paper)
    1. Java (Computer program language)   2. JavaScript (computer
program language)   I. Title.
QA76.73.J38W39   1996   96-38447
                                                                          CIP

Printed in the United States of America
96 97 98 99   IP   9 8 7 6 5 4 3 2 1

Contents

Preface

The team of people at AP PROFESSIONAL were incredibly gracious with their time and encouragement. I'm glad for all of their support throughout this project. They are Jeff Pepper, Mike Williams, Barbara Northcott, Tom Ryan, Josh Mills, and Gael Tannenbaum. Thanks also to Don DeLand of Integre Technical Publishing.

There were others who helped in the world beyond the text. The staff at Tax Analysts were kind enough to coordinate my consulting schedule with the demands of putting out a book. Anyone would be lucky to work for a company that was so understanding. Finally, I want to thank everyone in my family for everything they've given through all of my life.

Peter Wayner
Baltimore, MD
pcw@access.digex.com
http://access.digex.net:/~pcw/page.html

Book Notes

The copy for this book was typeset using the LATEXtypesetting software. Several important breaks were made with standard conventions in order to remove some ambiguities. The period mark is normally included inside the quotation marks, like this: "That's my answer. No. Period." This can cause ambiguities when computer terms are included in quotation marks because computers often use periods to convey some meaning. For this reason, my electronic mail address is "pcu@access.digex.com". The periods and commas are left outside of all quotes to prevent confusion.

Hyphens also cause problems when they're used for different tasks. LISP programmers often use hyphens to join words together into a single name like this: Do-Not-Call-This-Procedure. Unfortunately, this causes grief when these longer words occur at the end of a line. In these cases, there will be an extra hyphen included to specify that there was an original hyphen in the word. This isn't *hypercompatible* with the standard rules that don't include the extra hyphen. But these rules are for readers who know that *self-help* is a word that should be hyphenated. No one knows what to think about A-Much-Too-Long-Procedure-That-Should-Be-Shortened-For-- Everyone.

Chapter 1

Java, JavaScript, and Beyond

This chapter provides a basic introduction to both Java and JavaScript. The basic structures of the languages are covered at a general level so you can understand how they were designed and how they are used.

First there was the concept of the *agent*—a neat idea about what could happen if programs could roam freely throughout the Net. Sun Microsystems decided to take this concept and make it real—at least for the Web. Sun created the Java language to make it easy to safely exchange software without worrying about viruses or malicious intent. In the early days of development, Sun intended the language to support the explosion in sales of Personal Digital Assistants that many people imagined was just around the corner. More recently, the rapid growth of the World Wide Web and HTML made it obvious that there was a desperate need to be able to ship programs across the Net to run in distant Web browsers. Everyone wanted to dress up their Web pages with slick animations, smart forms, or locally responsive interfaces. This could only be done if the browser could give incoming software the ability to do neat things without allowing it the power to cause trouble.

Meanwhile, there was HTML. Everyone wanted to juice up their Web pages to be slicker, faster, and more responsive. So Netscape, the browser company, created a small scripting language originally called

LiveScript that was intended to give Web page designers a way to embed simple functions directly inside HTML. It is a scripting language that is a cousin to the C-shell script from UNIX and the AppleScript language from Apple. Since the word "Java" was a public-relations gold mine, the project was renamed JavaScript with the blessing of Sun Microsystems.

In the most abstract sense, both Java and JavaScript can be used for the same purpose: to provide a way to execute local code that will allow sophisticated Web pages. The languages, however, take very different approaches and so each may be better for different projects. Java is a full-function language that has almost every feature available. Sun has built an extensive Java compiler and a large toolkit for constructing elaborate user interfaces. The Java code isn't limited to Web browsers because there are many system-level classes that allow programmers to do all system work on their own local, trusted machines.

JavaScript, on the other hand, is more limited because it will only run on a Web browser. The language is simpler and it doesn't offer many of the more complicated structures that make it easier to create complex programs. There are some provisions for creating a user interface, but they are tightly integrated with HTML. For the most part, you use JavaScript to extend HTML and add local customization to the look of pages or the behavior of forms.

One simple rule that you might use to choose between the two languages is that Java is good for big problems and JavaScript is better for little problems. This may be generally true, but there are many exceptions. Building small animated icons is easy to do in Java, but not possible in JavaScript. Some complicated problems are much easier to solve in JavaScript because the language is so tightly integrated with HTML. You can easily spit out HTML code from JavaScript and the browser will do the work of formatting it. Java is not as tightly integrated. In many cases, both languages and their tools would do fine and so the choice is one of personal preference.

Java by the Buzzword

Many parts of the Java language should be familar to programmers who work with the very popular C or C++, but there are significant changes made in the internal structure to support the goal of a virus-free environment. Since Java comes from the computer industry, it is only natural that these differences be described through a list of buzzwords and acronyms. Here's a tour of some of the major buzzwords that are used to describe Java as well as an explanation of how they affect the performance of the code:

Object-Oriented Every computer language can be called "object-oriented" in some sense or another. The term is very broadly defined and overused. Java itself emerges from the tradition of Smalltalk, which is a language that forced everything to be an object. Other object-oriented languages weren't so demanding or as doctrinaire. In Java, everything begins as an object. Constants, types, records, and data structures all begin as objects.

Strongly Typed Not only must everything be an object in Java, but every bit of code must specify the type of the object that it will work upon. This strong typing follows the tradition of Pascal, which enforces the same discipline for variables in order to identify potential problems at compile time. The rigor is also necessary for security. If the type of every object is known and checked, then it is not possible to exploit a loophole by switching objects on a function.

Dynamically Linked Programs are created out of a number of different subroutines or methods. Each time one method calls another one, the flow of execution must jump. In statically linked languages, the jump can be evaluated during compilation and an absolute jump can be placed in the code. Java is dynamically linked, which means that it will not try to locate a particular method until it is run. This is an important feature because it allows Java programs to use local methods that are kept at the browser. This shrinks the size of code that must migrate over the Net. The code can arrive and link itself when it begins to run.

Garbage-Collected If you need a slice of memory in a langauge like C, you must allocate it yourself and then return it to the machine when you're finished with it. Although this feature can be quite powerful and efficient, it is also the source for many of the most troublesome bugs in the world. This problem is even greater for Java, which aspires to keep the browser's computer free from trouble. A program doesn't need to be malicious to suck up memory and not release it. So Java controls all of the memory. Every once in a while, it will scan through all of the objects in a process known as "garbage collection" to see if any of them are not used. The obsolete objects are reclaimed from the memory. The user never gets direct access to the memory at all.

Pointer-Free Many languages like C or Pascal give the programmer the ability to create pointers to memory and manipulate them freely. This can make it very efficient to program the computer because you can pack the data tightly. It can also be the recipe for disaster on many machines because all of the system information is kept in the same memory space. Any simple program can write over any part of memory simply by changing its pointers. This makes pointers dangerous. Java permits pointers, but it won't allow the user to manipulate them directly. You can, say, swap the pointers x and y, but you can't make the pointer x point to any place in memory that you choose.

Class-Oriented Each object is defined by its class. The first thing you do in Java is build a class. This is a list of data elements and methods that are associated with the class of objects. These classes can inherit behavior from one another. That is, you can develop a general class like car that contains data and methods that will work for all cars. Then you can create more specific examples for more particular types of cars like station wagons. These more particular classes can *inherit* their general behavior from the general class, while defining more specific behavior that applies only to them.

The structure of the Java class system and the mechanism for inheritance can be found in Chapter 5.

This structure can make life easier for programmers because they only have to do the general parts of the program once. It is also an important part of Java's strategy to make it easy to ship code across the Net. Java programs are just objects from a class that inherits its behavior from a more general class known as `Applet`. Most of the important general software for this class is kept locally at the browser. Any new applet that comes over the Net must only carry along the new code. If it needs any general functions, it can rely upon the local code it inherits.

Weak Multiple Inheritance Some object-oriented languages like C++ allow a class of objects to inherit its behavior from many different classes. This can make it easy to add features to classes, but it can be a nightmare if these classes start overlapping. Debugging can be very confusing. Java allows each class to descend from only one parent class, but it also allows a weak form of inheritance it calls "implementation." This compromise should provide programmers most of the flexibility they need.

Compiled Many programming languages like C are compiled, that is, translated into a set of simpler instructions that are fed directly into the CPU. Java code is compiled, but it is converted into *byte code*. This is a processor-independent set of instructions that is quite similar in structure to machine code. The Java compiler may use many of the more complicated techniques used by many compilers for optimizing the final output to make it run faster.

Interpreted Although Java code is compiled, its byte code must eventually be interpreted by the host machine. That is, the host machine does not feed the byte code directly into the CPU—it just simulates a virtual machine operating on the code. This is a requirement of dynamic binding that forces the running machine to look for objects and methods at run time.

Architecture-Independent The byte code produced by the Java compiler can run on PCs, Macintoshes, Sun workstations, or any other major computer. This is one of the best features of the virtual machine.

Secure The Java interpreter enforces security and prevents Java code from causing damage by strictly watching the byte code. It makes sure that all of the objects that are created are of the right type and ensures that all of the methods only work on these objects. Although some people have discovered minor bugs in this model, all of them have been fixed at this time.

Multi-threaded A program is a list of instructions, and the path through the list of instructions is often called the *thread of execution*. In some cases, a single path makes sense because all of the items in the list must be done in order. In many other cases, though, multiple paths make more sense because they can be more efficient. Imagine that your program needed to open a file, draw something on the screen, and print out something else. Each of these requires waiting for access to a resource. A multi-threaded program can, in effect, start up three different threads of execution for these three tasks. If the printing thread is waiting for more paper to be loaded in the printer, then the file thread and the drawing thread can continue operating.

Java's threads are discussed in Chapter 7.

Java is multi-threaded. That means that the interpreter can keep track of multiple threads and jump among all of them, giving each a fair share of the processor's attention.

Efficient Java was designed to run on a machine without much memory; 4 megabytes of memory is enough to support it and a minimal operating system. The byte code for a program is often much smaller than the corresponding machine code that would be generated by a C compiler, but the database needed for dynamic linking can wipe out this advantage.

Extensible Java can link in local source code modules written in languages like C. This means that it stands a good chance of becoming a major system programming language used for all tasks—not just for creating flashy Web pages.

Error Friendly By this, I mean that Java comes with a built-in error-handling mechanism that can corral errors and help you solve them. You can still create the errors, but the applet will not crash immediately. If you add your own code to grab the errors and filter them out, the code will function quite robustly. They're called *exceptions*.

Exceptions are discussed in Chapter 8.

Fast Java is much faster than a basic scripting language like JavaScript because the first stage of compilation has streamlined the code. The dynamic linking and the rest of the interpretation, on the other hand, slow down the execution. Native C code is often 20 times faster. This may change in the future when recompiling interpreters become available. These will take the byte code and convert it directly into native machine code. The dynamic linking will still slow down the process, but these systems have the potential to come close to the speed of native C.

Toolkit-Enabled Many of the better compilers come with their own collection of object-oriented tools that you can use to build a complete program very quickly. PowerPoint comes with the Metro-werks compiler. Other languages like Visual Basic have a strongly integrated collection of widgets for building interfaces. Java is no different. It comes with a large selection of tools known as the Abstract Windowing Toolkit (AWT) that allows you to create almost every type of gadget possible.

The Abstract Windowing Toolkit (AWT) is described in Chapter 11.

Each of these buzzwords describes a feature of the Java language. When they're added together, you get a language that offers many of the modern conveniences that programmers expect, but in a package that is secure enough to run on a distant machine without the opportunity to cause trouble. The language has traded off some execution speed for security and the small size of the dynamically linked executable. This makes it an ideal language for programming migrating applets that travel the Net.

JavaScript by the Buzzword

The JavaScript language is a scripting addition to HTML. It is not so much a programming language as a mechanism for allowing HTML creators to execute a function if a user activates some part of the page. Many of the more advanced HTML pages include forms or collections of links. JavaScript code can manipulate the contents of these forms or links and react to mouse or key events.

JavaScript is also often described with a collection of buzzwords. Here is a list followed by an explanation of how they apply:

Object-Oriented JavaScript is also object-oriented, but it is not as strict or as sophisticated about it as is Java. The basic data about a browser, its window, the document displayed in it, and the forms or links within that document are all arranged in a big hierarchy that appears very object-oriented. There is no greater class structure, however, nor any provisions for inheritance.

Basic JavaScript programming can be found in Chapter 15.

Interpreted JavaScript is 100% interpreted. You can define new variables or functions on the fly and use them several lines later. There is no compiler or preprocessor that checks to uncover the most flagrant errors.

Event-Ready JavaScript includes many built-in event-handling routines that can be attached to events that might be generated by some HTML code. You can easily create a script and attach it to the event handler. When that key is typed or the mouse is clicked, the script will be executed.

Toolkit-Ready JavaScript doesn't really have a toolkit of its own in the same way that Java has AWT. It picks up most of that functionality from HTML and Web browsers. JavaScript is more an extension to HTML than a language on its own.

Easy to Use Many simple JavaScript programs will only add a few lines to an HTML file. There is no need to get a separate compiler as there is with Java. You can certainly make JavaScript programs that are very complicated, but you don't have to.

Secure Although many people don't think of JavaScript as being secure, there is no reason why it can't be as secure as Java. The language is entirely interpreted, and JavaScript code can't touch any important data except the information that is used to fill the browser's page. However, there is a basic problem with being able to peek at people's past history and watch which pages they turn. This information can be transmitted back across the Net. This type of intrusion may be unstoppable unless you further restrict the information available to JavaScript programs. It is unclear how people feel about the tradeoff of power versus security in this case. In most cases, though, JavaScript programs can't read general files or install viruses.

Persistent That is, JavaScript provides a mechanism for a JavaScript program to write information to the local disk. The amount of data is strictly limited to only 4K, but it can provide an ideal mechanism to customize forms. If a person's orders or access data can be stored locally, then an incoming form or HTML page can customize itself using this data.

JavaScript is a simple language without many of the extra tools that you might want or desire. You can't use it to draw arbitrary lines on the screen, but you have all of the simple power of HTML. If the structure of HTML is good enough for you, then JavaScript may be just the ticket.

Choosing between Java and JavaScript

There are some tasks that can only be done in Java and there are others that can only be done in JavaScript. Some can be done as easily in one as the other. Here's a list of several hypothetical project ideas and my opinion on which would be the better tool:

Simple Spreadsheet-like Form *JavaScript.* You can easily create form elements in HTML and attach JavaScript code that will be processed whenever the user changes the form. This makes it easy to, say, create a simple form that will take the basic tax information and calculate the right numbers to put in your tax form.

Slick Spreadsheet-like Form *Java.* Let's say you want to do something complicated with the form. You might want to display an actual image of the IRS form and let the user click on the right place to input data. This requires a much lower-level approach and only Java lets you interpret mouse clicks and draw information with the precision necessary to achieve this end.

Customized Shopping *JavaScript.* If you're happy with HTML, then it is quite easy to use JavaScript to change the layout of the forms. JavaScript offers the cookie, which makes it simple to leave a small amount of data on each user's local disk. This is a great tool for customizing data and remembering a person's past history.

Animation *Java.* Java lets you draw arbitrary things to a box in the browser. You need to be able to do this if you want to animate something.

Three-Dimensional Worlds *Java.* Sun distributes a neat application with the Java Development Kit (JDK) that plots three-dimensional models of molecules. It's great, and Java provides all of the low-level routines you might need to calculate the positions and display the information on the screen.

VRML Worlds *JavaScript.* You can easily create a VRML description of a world and pass the information to the VRML plug-in that some versions of the Netscape browser support.

As you can see, there are many differences between the two languages and you can solve some similar problems with both. In most cases, your decision may be based upon graphical output. If HTML in a browser suffices, then JavaScript is a great choice. If you want more, then Java is the solution.

How to Use This Book

Marginal notes give pointers to other locations of the book that might be important to understanding a current example.

Chapters 2 through 13 will concentrate on Java, its class structure, and its collection of libraries and tools. Chapters 14 through 17 will focus on JavaScript and describe how to use it effectively to solve many basic problems. Both sections will offer many examples that you can borrow and use.

Most readers will want to begin with Java. The language is the most sophisticated approach to distributing code across the network. Chapter 2 begins by showing a simple section of Java code and then describing its action line by line. The basics of Java syntax are covered in Chapter 3; you won't find many surprises if you're a C programmer. Class structure and the details of inheritance are covered in Chapter 5. The rest of the chapters describe how to deal with more prosaic topics like interfaces (Chapter 6) and threads (Chapter 7). The AWT is covered in detail in Chapter 11.

JavaScript is covered in Chapters 14 through 17. Chapter 14 explains the contrasts between Java and JavaScript. You can learn JavaScript from this introduction if you don't know Java, but you may miss some of the nuances that are explained in the comparison. The remaining chapters describe how to create your own JavaScript code and access the guts of documents so you can build a customized interface.

For the most part, you will want to move through the book in order. The beginning chapters on Java cover the most important details first. The later chapters build upon these details, but many of them can stand independently. You can learn threads, for instance, without understanding interfaces. The same progression holds for the chapters on JavaScript.

Chapter 13 offers a collection of longer Java examples that you might want to look at. They can provide good inspiration and you are free to use them as the beginning for your own projects. Chapter 17 offers some JavaScript samples for the same purposes.

Good luck, and have fun!

Chapter 2

A Short Java Program

This chapter presents a short Java program and explains how it works line by line. The program creates two objects and passes messages between them. Objects are the basic format for Java, and learning to use them is essential. This example also uses the standard Java class structure to produce an applet that will run on browsers or Sun's Applet Viewer. Most programmers want to create code that will run on distant machines linked through the Internet and HTML. Although Java may be used as a standard system programming language, experimenting with applets is the best way to begin.

The best place to begin with a new language is with a short example. Although you might not know anything about Java, you can still learn a great deal by examining a short program in detail. This can give you a high-level orientation to how the language is structured and how a program can be created. The details will follow in the other chapters.

Here's a short program that creates two objects and shows how they can interact:

```
import java.applet.*;
public class Kids extends Applet {
    int boredomFactor = 3;
```

```
     // How long until they quit.
   String message = "";
     //What they normally say.
   String quitMessage = "";
     //What they say when they quit.
   public void MyTurn(Kids WhozNext){
      if (boredomFactor-- <= 0){
         System.out.println(quitMessage);}
      else {
         System.out.println(message);
         WhozNext.MyTurn(this);
      }
   }
   public  void init(){
      Kids Bobby,Kenny;
      Bobby = new Kids();
      Bobby.message="Kenny, you did it.";
      Bobby.boredomFactor = 4;
      Bobby.quitMessage="Fine.";
      Kenny = new Kids();
      Kenny.message="Bobby, you did it.";
      Kenny.quitMessage="Fine.";
      Kenny.MyTurn(Bobby);
   }
}
```

The output from the program looks like this:

```
Bobby, you did it.
Kenny, you did it.
Bobby, you did it.
Kenny, you did it.
Bobby, you did it.
Kenny, you did it.
Fine.
```

Here's a line-by-line description about what is going on in the program:

`import java.applet.*;` The Sun implementation of Java comes with a toolkit filled with many predefined classes. These classes are defined hierarchically and the periods separate each level of the hierarchy. In this case, the program wants access to all of the classes that are part of the distribution for applets.

The definition of Java is very broad and it may be used as a general system programming langauge in the future, but now almost all of the interest in the language comes from people who want to use it to provide flexible programs that can travel the Net successfully. Most people will want to use the language to develop applets, a standard Java class that is already accepted by WWW browsers like Netscape.

This program will be inheriting some behavior from the basic Java `Applet` class. This allows it to be very small, yet still provide all of the functionality of a full-fledged program. The information in `java.applet.*` is already stored locally with the browser. Anyone who wants to download the class defined here, `Kids`, will only need to download the small amount of information that defines the class and its particular methods. The other classes and definitions are already there ready to run.

`public class Kids extends Applet {` This line is the start of a new class called `Kids`. It extends a predefined class called `Applet` that just happens to have been loaded into the compiler's environment by the previous line. The verb `extends` means that `Kids` will inherit much of its behavior from `Applet`. Any methods defined to work with objects from the class `Applet` will also work with objects that are created with this new class `Kids`.

Java is case-sensitive. This means that `Applet` *is different from* `applet`*. This can be confusing at times. The current convention is to capitalize the first letter of classes.*

The word `public` is a modifier that means that the class will be available to other programmers who want to use the class to create objects. (The opposite of this is `private` and it is mainly used to prevent others from accessing certain methods or classes.)

The curly bracket, "{", begins the definition of the class, `Kids`. Everything contained between the two brackets falls within the class. The curly brackets are used in Java to define the layers of control or scope. They're also used, as you can see in this program, to delineate the beginning and end of the branches of an `if-then-else` statement.

`int boredomFactor = 3;` This line defines a new integer variable called `boredomFactor`. Every time a new object from the class `Kids` is created, it will contain one slot to hold an integer and this slot will be referred to as `boredomFactor`.

At initialization, the slot will hold the number 3. The initialization is optional here, but it must be done somewhere in the program. The compiler checks to make sure that every variable is initialized to prevent both random errors and security problems.

One standard hacking trick is to create a new variable, but leave the old value left in memory in place. This can allow you to sneak in data around filters that would normally prevent their passage.

The semicolon is used to terminate statements, just like in C. It is not a statement separator as in Pascal. It must end all statements in a block.

`//` `How long until they quit.` This is a comment that is ignored by the compiler. A pair of slashes signals the compiler to ignore everything until the end of the line. If you want to block out large comments, place the symbol "`/*`" at the beginning of the block and the symbol "`*/`" at the end.

`String message = "";` Java contains several base types like `int`. Here `String` is actually a class, not a data type. You're not just creating a slot for an integer, you're creating an object from the class `String`. You wouldn't know that from the syntax. One clue is that the first character is uppercase. This is a convention that is fairly standard in Java, but it is not required or checked by the compiler.

The `String` class is one of the few that is folded into the basic Java syntax for convenience. Many of the less commonly used classes must be accessed through their own methods like `setDataElement(blah)`. The Java compiler automatically handles these details when the double quotes are used to signal a string.

`public void MyTurn(Kids WhozNext){` This creates a new method from the class with the name `MyTurn`. The method takes one parameter, `WhozNext`, which must be an object from the class, `Kids`.

When this method is called, the statements in between the curly brackets will be executed in turn. These statements will have access to the three locally defined variables for the object, `boredomFactor`, `message`, and `quitMessage`.

The modifier `public` in the front of the definition specifies that the method is available to other objects outside of the class. This is not strictly necessary in this example because the method is only invoked in the `init` method, which is part of the same class.

Finally, the modifier `void` tells the compiler that the method will not return any information. If it was going to return, say, an integer, then the type `int` would be placed here.

A cleaner class structure might have created two different classes here. One would hold the kids and the other would be a subclass of `Applet` *responsible for interfacing with the browser. This was not done in the interest of simplicity.*

`if (boredomFactor-- <= 0){` This is the beginning of an `if-then-else` clause. The code between the normal parentheses must evaluate to a boolean. If it is `true`, then the first branch between the curly branches is taken. If it is `false` and there is an `else` clause as there is here, then that branch is taken. Although it is not obvious here, Java requires that the decision clause must produce a boolean. You cannot use integers or pointers as shortcuts as you can in C or LISP. If your program defines the variable `i` to be an integer, then the clause `if (i) {` will generate a compiler error.

This example shows one of the shortcuts that is left over from C. The variable `boredomFactor` is decremented by 1 after the decision is made. There are also post-action increments as well as versions that do their work before the data in the variable is accessed. This shortcut was kept because there is no known way to use it to breach security. It is just a syntactic substitute.

`System.out.println(quitMessage);}` Java was created at Sun and Sun is the land of UNIX. It should not be surprising that the creators included a few methods for spitting out text. In this case, the `System.out` class has a method called `println` that will pass a `String` object out. If you're running Java on a UNIX box, then it will appear as `stdout`. If you're using a Mac, a browser, or a Windows machine, it will appear in a separate window.

This technique for outputting information is not a good long-term practice. The Sun class libraries come with extensive methods for drawing information on the screen. When you develop actual applets for public consumption, you'll want to use these methods. For now, this is a simpler approach that is easier to use in a text-based book. It is also one of the only ways to debug programs. At this writing, there are several Java compilers, but there are no truly effective debuggers. This is sure to change with time, but early readers will want to use these classes extensively.

See page 150 for a complete description of what an applet is.

else { This starts the other branch of the if-then-else construction.

WhozNext.MyTurn(this); This line is a bit complicated. WhozNext is
an object from the class Kids. This line invokes the method MyTurn
on the object WhozNext. This method also requires an object from
the class Kids to be passed into it. Here the word this means pass
along a reference to the currently running object itself.

This creates the ping-pong effect that is seen in the output of the
program. The two objects that are created later, Kenny and Bobby,
will alternate in the positions of WhozNext and this.

public void init(){ This is the beginning of a new method, init,
that takes no parameters and returns no data. It is made public so
other objects outside of the class can access it.

What is not apparent here is that the method init is *overriding* a
version of init that is defined inside of the superclass, Applet.
When Sun created the Applet class, it provided a certain set of
methods that make it easy for you to control how your own applet
starts, runs, and finishes its job. Normally, a browser will receive
the Java code and start it up by invoking the init method. There
are also other classes like start and stop that are used in the same
way, but they're beyond this introduction. To some extent, this is
not an ideal use of the method init, but it serves its function here.

Java also contains the ability to fire up a program by looking for
the one method, main. This code would start and stop like the
binary code produced by a C compiler and it would not need to
inherit any behavior from a class like Applet. Although that may
be a better way to write a simple program that outputs text, it was
not used in this example. Most people will be using Java to create
applets for the near future so it makes more sense to create code in
this realm.

Kids Bobby,Kenny; Two variables from the class Kids are created
that will be referred to by the names Bobby and Kenny. They are
not initialized on this line.

Bobby = new Kids(); This is where a new object is created. The word
new indicates that a new object should be created. The word Kids
here starts up a method that was implicitly created when the class
Kids was created. This method, which is often called a *constructor*,

is responsible for allocating the memory for the object and filling it with any initial values.

In this case, the code does not define an explicit constructor, but many classes will do that. Such a program could do additional calculations to fill up the object with the correct data. In this version, the next several lines do the same job. Many classes will contain explicit constructors that will take values as parameters and assign them to the object's variables.

`Bobby.message="Kenny, you did it.";` The `message` string that is part of the object Bobby is assigned this value. The basic syntax is the same. The first word is the object and the period after it says "access a part of the object."

`Kenny.MyTurn(Bobby);` This starts up the action. The method `MyTurn` is invoked for the object `Kenny`. It takes the object `Bobby` as the parameter. The ping-pong effect begins.

That's the program. If you wanted to run it, you would first compile the file `Kids.java` using the Java compiler. This would produce the output file `Kids.class` that would be the byte-code equivalent of the code. This is shorter and easier to run. You would run the program by loading an HTML file into your Java-compatible browser. Here are the HTML tags that would tell the browser to load up the code from `Kids.class` and invoke its `init` routine:

```
<applet code=Kids.class width=200 height=200>
</applet>
```

Note that there are several differences between Java and other languages, and these can have subtle effects. For instance, the Java compiler will turn Java code into binary data known as *byte code*, but it will not produce binary information that can be fed directly into a CPU. That's the main difference between a `.class` file and a `.exe` file on an MS-DOS machine. The `.class` file has to be loaded into a Java environment that has all of the support files that can be linked to it.

If you've been paying attention, you should have numerous questions that are unanswered. This example has glossed over many important details about just what an applet is and how rich its life can be. The `init` routine is used as a substitute for `main` because it allows the applets to be run in browsers and Sun's Applet Viewer. This leaves details hanging. For instance, how does the application terminate? Normal programs will end when `main` ends. This one will only end when someone switches to a new page or shuts down the Applet Viewer. Chapter 9 covers the basics of applets to make this clear.

Summary

This chapter presented a basic Java program that created two objects and passed messages between them. It showed:

- Some basic details about the syntax for creating objects, adding variables, and using `if` clauses. More information about the syntax can be found in Chapter 3.

- The creation of one new class that was descended from another class. This class had two methods and several instance variables. Information about classes and building class hierarchies can be found in Chapter 5.

The data presented here was simple. There were integers, strings, and objects from classes. The way that Java handles data is explained in Chapter 4.

Chapter 3

Java Syntax

This chapter explores the syntax of Java and describes all of the details that you must know in order to program correctly.

The Java programming language is a combination of many parts of different languages like C, C++, Pascal, LISP, and ML. Although each of these has contributed some part to the final confection, the syntax is largely that of C and its close cousin C++. Variables, branches and loops, and functions are defined in almost identical fashion. This makes it much easier for C programmers to pick up the basic details of Java.

Here are some notable distinctions of the Java syntax:

Simplicity Many extra details that are part of the full-fledged C development systems are gone. There are no define files, header files, structures, or macros to juggle. There is usually only one way to accomplish a certain task and this streamlines the coding process. Although there are times that it may be inconvenient, this simplicity is usually a net win.

Strong Typing Java forces every data element to have a type, just like Pascal. The types are not optional like many of the C compilers that preserve the ability to process old code. This allows the compiler to detect many potential errors when the program is compiled instead of later when it may be running on a distant machine.

Completely Object-Oriented The language itself is completely object-oriented. The fundamental construction is the class, which has data and methods that process the data. There are no programs or units. If you want to use a structure, you simply create a class and add the different elements as data.

Uses Some Shortcuts Although Java does not have many of the extra constructs of C or C++, it is not as spartan as LISP. LISP and its cousin Scheme have a very simple syntax that make them simple to learn, but that can lead to complicated-looking programs because the programmer only has a limited way to express what should happen. In Java, many of the simple C/C++ shortcuts are preserved. You can still use i++ to mean "use i and then increment it by one." Also, functions for handling strings are built into the syntax even though they may be implemented in different ways. Java's designers made many practical concessions to working programmers.

This chapter will describe the details of Java syntax so you can read basic Java programs and construct your own. It will show you how to create classes, fill them with variables, and produce methods for changing the data. It will also show you how to design the control structure of the program so you can create loops, if-then blocks, or case statements.

This treatment, however, is just an examination of the surface of Java. A thorough exploration of the insides of the system is necessary to understand how programs operate. Although there are many similarities between C++ and Java syntaxes, the insides often handle operations completely differently. You should bear this in mind when you read through this chapter. Most of the details will become more apparent in later chapters.

Names

The basic building blocks of any program are the names that are given to the classes and variables and the numbers that are used as constants.

Java names can be any combination of characters and numbers that starts with either a letter, a dollar sign ("$"), or an underscore ("_"). So Route66, Route_66, ROUTE_66, and route66 are all acceptable variables. 23SkiDoo and 8_2_much are prohibited. Java distinguishes between upper- and lowercase letters, however, so each of these four names for Route 66 would be treated as distinct values.

Some Java compilers recognize UNICODE, a 16-bit extension of the 8-bit ASCII that was designed to include symbols for all of the languages throughout the world. Most of the important international glyphs are represented in UNICODE, including those common in America. Accents aigu ("é") are just one example. At this writing, most Java users will be creating their programs using simple text-editing programs like emacs, BBEdit, or perhaps even Microsoft Write. ASCII works fine.

If you need to include a strange UNICODE value in a program, use uXXXX where XXXX holds the four hexadecimal digits.

Many Java programmers, or at least the original masters at Sun, use a few standard conventions when choosing their variable names. Classes usually begin with an uppercase letter. Methods and variables usually start with a lowercase letter. If you want to use a multiword phrase to name a variable, you often run the words together, but capitalize only the interior words like this: secretPassword or badKarmaAndDogma.

Finally, there are 47 words that are reserved by the compiler to indicate operations: These words can't be used as names for classes, variables, or constants. Here they are with a short description of what they normally do:

abstract Classes and methods can be defined as abstract if the definition of some method isn't found in the current class. It will be forthcoming in a subclass. See page 95.

boolean This is one of the basic class types. It is either true or false. Note that Boolean is a class while boolean is a type! See page 46.

break This jumps out of a loop or case statement. It is used instead of goto. See page 39.

byte One of the basic types. It holds 8 bits. See page 25.

case The first word of a case statement that is used to combine several if-then blocks into one statement that is easier to read. See page 38.

catch Java supports an error-containment concept known as *exceptions*. catch marks the beginning of the error-handling code. See page 132.

char One of the basic types used to hold a character. See page 46.

class This keyword marks the definition of a class, the basic foundation of object-oriented Java programming. See page 65.

const This is apparently an undefined keyword that is still on the reserved list. Constants are defined in Java with the final keyword, which also marks classes, methods, and variables that are not changed by a subclass.

continue This keyword is a complement to break. If it is encountered, the execution immediately jumps back to the top of the loop. See page 41.

do The basic loop constructor. See page 41.

double One of the basic types used to store double-precision, floating-point numbers. See page 25.

else The second half of the if-then clause. It indicates the branch to take if the statement is false. See page 37.

extends A modifier for the class keyword. It indicates that a particular class is a subclass of another. See page 65.

final Used by classes, methods, and variables to indicate that something is not changed later. It is also a substitute for constants. See page 92.

finally Part of the case definition.

float One of the basic types used to hold single precision numbers. See page 46.

for The beginning of a simple loop. See page 39.

goto This keyword is currently not implemented. You should use either break or continue. See page 39.

if The first keyword in a branch decision function. See page 37.

implements A modifier of the class definition. It indicates that a particular class inherits behavior from another superclass. See Chapter 6.

import Used at the top of files to include class definitions from other files. See page 101.

instanceof A test function that checks to see whether a particular object is a member of a certain class. See page 89.

int One of the basic types. See page 25.

interface A more restricted version of a class. It is used to allow multiple inheritance. See page 97.

long One of the basic types. A longer integer. See page 25.

native Used to link in code compiled for the native machine. This might be done with C, Pascal, or Fortran.

new Indicates that a new object is to be constructed. See page 67.

null The null pointer.

package Classes can be grouped together in a package to make handling easier and help control access. See page 100.

private A modifier for methods and variables that indicates that other classes and methods will not be able to access them. The alpha version of the Java compiler from Sun also allowed you to use this modifier on classes. See page 89.

protected Like private, but it allows subclasses to access the methods or variables. See page 89.

public Explicitly modifies a class definition to allow others to access the class. Also used with variables and methods. See page 89.

return Exit a method and return a particular value. See page 67.

short Another basic data type. A 16-bit integer. See page 46.

static Used to modify a variable definition in a class when one location should serve all instances of a variable. See page 73.

super Refers to the method of the superclass that a current method used as its model. See page 85.

switch Part of a case statement. See page 38.

synchronized Used to define a thread that must not conflict with another. See page 120.

this The current object. Used in statements or expressions. See page 81.

throw The complement to catch that is used in the Java exception mechanism. This is used to indicate an error has been found. See Chapter 8.

throws Indicates what types of exceptions are thrown. See Chapter 8.

transient Persistent objects are objects that may be stored to a file. If a variable is marked transient, then it doesn't need to be kept around. You might mark some semitemporary variable to be transient to save disk space.

try Used in conjunction with catch to set up exceptions. See page 132.

void When a method returns no information, the definition line uses void to represent this nothingness. See page 67.

volatile This keyword means that a variable can be changed by more than one thread. When this happens, the compiler must take special precautions. The alpha version of the Java compiler used a different keyword, threadsafe, to designate which variables were safe from multiple interference.

while A loop constructor. See page 40.

Numbers and Other Literals

Numbers begin with one of the ten digits. Integers like 1,1432 and 1134224 are treated as integers without any extra characters. Long integers, floating-point numbers, and octal and hexadecimal values need extra letters to help the compiler interpret them. The compiler won't recognize that 3.1415 is a floating-point number. You must use a trailing f, like this: x = 3.1415f. Double-precision floating-point numbers end with a d. Numbers in exponential notation use either e or E to join the mantissa up with the exponent, like this: x = 6.023e23f. Long integers are followed by an l or an L, like this: longvar = 132312312412L. Hexadecimal numbers begin with 0x or 0X and look like this: x = 0xDEAD14. Octal numbers merely begin with a 0, so this can cause confusion.

Here's the information about numeric syntax summarized in a table:

Type	Size	Range	Syntax
byte	8 bits	-2^7 to $2^7 - 1$	121
short	16 bits	-2^{16} to $2^{16} - 1$	4023
int	32 bits	-2^{32} to $2^{32} - 1$	412235
long	64 bits	-2^{64} to $2^{64} - 1$	62231288288L
float	XX bits	$-$Inf to Inf	6.023e23f
double	XXX bits	$-$Inf to Inf	1.234142343242D

Note that sizes and ranges of numbers are defined throughout the Java world. Many languages like C or Pascal were not so fully specified, so versions for different machines would use different definitions for int, for example. In Java, the number of bits for an int is fixed.

There are also literal values that are used with characters and strings. Characters are compared with single quotation marks like this: charvar='a'. Strings are enclosed in double quotation marks like this: stringvar="Hello World". If you need to use special characters in a string, you can refer to this table:

Symbol	Character	Symbol	Character
b	backspace	'	single quote
n	linefeed	"	double quote
r	carriage return	\	backslash
t	tab	u	UNICODE version
f	form feed		

In Java, unlike C, there are no special characters for a bell or a vertical tab.

Some string literals might look like this:

```
message = "Bob was 'strange'";

message = "Name t Rank t Serial Number";

message = "Macintosh is a trademark (2122) of Apple.";
```

In the first example, single quotes are nested inside of a string; in the second, tabs are used to create column headers; in the third, a UNICODE character for trademark is included. Many systems can't display UNICODE, so you should be careful in adopting it.

The boolean literals are `true` and `false`. You cannot use zero as a surrogate for `false` or any non-zero number as a replacement for true. Booleans must be defined explicitly.

Expressions

When you combine a set of variables with a set of *operators*, then you create an *expression* that the computer will calculate. 2+2, `length * width`, and `(right - left) * (bottom - top)` are all expressions. The variables or literals on either side of an operator (2, `length`, `right`, and so on) are called the *operands*.

Here are the basic numerical operators:

Symbol	Action	Example
+	addition	$3 + 2$ or "pre-" + "fix"
−	subtraction	$12 - 3$ or -3
×	multiplication	length × width
/	division	miles / gallons
%	modulus	$10 \% 4$
&	bitwise and	num & mask
|	bitwise or	this | that
^	bitwise xor	tall ^ short
~	bitwise complement	mask = ~ item
<<	left shift	var << 3
>>	right shift	var >> 12
<<<	left shift with zero fill	arg <<< howMuch
>>>	right shift with zero fill	arg >>> howMuch

Note that the plus sign ("+") can also be used in string concatenation. Both the plus and minus sign do not need two operands. The caret ("^") does not stand for exponentiation. There are also two types of shifting here. The standard left shift is often called a left rotation. The bits that drop off the left (the most significant bits) are inserted on the right to replace those that are gone. The zero-filling shifts insert zeros instead.

Boolean Operators

Some operators are used for comparisons and only return boolean values. These cannot be mixed as freely as they can be in C. You cannot use the integer zero as a replacement for false and a non-zero number as a replacement for true. Java requires that types be preserved. Here are the basic operators:

Symbol	Action	Sample Expression
==	equal to	if (a == 41)
!=	not equal to	if (a != 14)
<	less than	if (a < 14)
>	greater than	if (a > 141)
<=	less than or equal to	if (a <= 1)
>=	greater than or equal to	if (a >= 14)
&	and	if ((a > 14) & (a < 17))
&&	and	if ((a > 14) && (a < 17))
|	or	if ((a == 16) || (a == 19))
||	or	if ((a == 16) |||| (a == 19))
!	not	if !((a == 16) |||| (a == 19))
^	xor	if ((a==16) ^(a == 19))

All but one of these boolean operators take two operands and return a boolean value. Only the not function ("!") takes one operand. The comparison functions are defined to take numerical arguments. Strings are not supported. The boolean combination functions take boolean operands.

There are important differences between the single (&, |) and double (&&, ||) versions of the and and or operators. The single version executes both sides regardless of the outcome. The double and operator (&&) evaluates the left side. If it is false, it returns false without evaluating the right side. If the double or operator (||) evaluates the left side and finds it is true, then it returns true without evaluating the right side. This point is important if the evaluation has side effects.

Here's a short program that illustrates how the side effects can be important:

```
import java.applet.*;
class InventoryItem extends Object {
  public int InStock= 0;
  public int OnOrder= 0;
  public boolean GetItem(){
    if (this.InStock>0){
      this.InStock--;
      return true;}
    else {
      return false;}
  }
}
public class Store extends Applet {
  InventoryItem Chicken, Egg;
public void init(){
  Chicken = new InventoryItem();
  Chicken.InStock = 2;
  Egg = new InventoryItem();
  Egg.InStock = 2;
  if (Chicken.GetItem() || Egg.GetItem()) {
    System.out.println("First Order Filled.");}
  else {
    System.out.println("First Order NOT Filled.");}
  System.out.println("Chickens Left:"+Chicken.InStock);
  System.out.println("Eggs Left:"+Egg.InStock);
  if (Chicken.GetItem() && Egg.GetItem()) {
    System.out.println("Second Order Filled.");}
  else {
    System.out.println("Second Order NOT Filled.");}
  System.out.println("Chickens Left:"+Chicken.InStock);
  System.out.println("Eggs Left:"+Egg.InStock);
  if (Chicken.GetItem() && Egg.GetItem()) {
    System.out.println("Third Order Filled.");}
```

```
  else {
    System.out.println("Third Order NOT Filled.");}
  System.out.println("Chickens Left:"+Chicken.InStock);
  System.out.println("Eggs Left:"+Egg.InStock);
  }
}
```

The output of this shows how the second half of the function is often not executed:

```
First Order Filled.
Chickens Left:1
Eggs Left:2
Second Order Filled.
Chickens Left:0
Eggs Left:1
Third Order NOT Filled.
Chickens Left:0
Eggs Left:1
```

The single operators (& or |) generate errors with the beta version of the MacJDK used when writing this book, so they are not illustrated here.

The Equality Operator and Objects

The equality operator ("==") can also be used to test whether two objects are equal. This can be deceptive. It doesn't test to see whether the *contents* are equal. It just compares the pointers and sees if they point to the same object. This example does a good job of showing a simple way to build structures by using a class without methods.

Remember that Java defines String to be a class of objects, not a basic type. If you use the "==" operator, it will only determine whether they are the same object, not the same string.

```
import java.applet.*;
class BallPlayer extends Object {
  float BattingAvg;
  int Errors;
}
public class BallPlayerLab extends Applet {
  BallPlayer Larry, Curly, Moe;
    //Three objects.
public void init(){
  Larry = new BallPlayer();
  Larry.BattingAvg = .305f;
  Larry.Errors = 400;
  Curly = new BallPlayer();
```

```
Curly.BattingAvg = .305f;
Curly.Errors = 400;
Moe = Larry;
if (Moe == Larry) {
  System.out.println("Larry equals Moe.");
} else {
  System.out.println("Larry doesn't equal Moe.");
}
if (Curly == Larry) {
  System.out.println("Larry equals Curly.");
} else {
  System.out.println("Larry doesn't equal Curly.");
}
if (Curly == Moe) {
  System.out.println("Moe equals Curly.");
} else {
  System.out.println("Moe doesn't equal Curly.");
}
}
}
```

This short program creates *three* pointers and *two* objects. When the value of Larry is assigned to Moe, they both end up pointing to the same object. The other pointer, Curly, designates a different object. Even though the contents of both objects are the same, they generate a false when they're compared. Here's the output:

```
Larry equals Moe.
Larry doesn't equal Curly.
Moe doesn't equal Curly.
```

Assignment Operators

Variables receive their values through assignment operators. The simplest version is the simple equals sign, "=", that tells the computer to evaluate the right side of the equals sign and stick the value in the variable named on the left, like this: x = 2 + 2.

Java borrows heavily from the C language, and its designers chose to keep many of the modified versions of the assignment operator which are used as shortcuts in C. Two of these are the prefix and suffix incrementors, that is, x++ and x--. These operators change the value of the operator at the same time that they make a copy. They are ideally used in code that jumps through an array.

The prefix operator increments x *before* the side is evaluated. The new value of x is what is passed along. In this code:

```
a = 5;
b = ++a;
```

b receives the value 6. The final value of a is also 6.

The suffix operator increments x *after* the side is evaluated. The *old* value of x is what is passed along. In this code:

```
a = 5;
b = a++
```

b receives the value 5. The final value of a is still 6.

The code x++ is really a syntactic replacement for x=x+1 so it can stand alone as a statement. There are also prefix and suffix decrementors: x-- and --x.

Java also contains the operators that mix assignment with more complicated arithmetic. If you want to increment x by a larger value like 5, then you can use the statement x+=5. This is equivalent to x=x+5. Here's a table with other equivalent operators that work with other functions:

Operator Use	Equivalent
a+ = b	$a = a + b$
a− = b	$a = a - b$
a* = b	$a = a \times b$
a/ = b	$a = a/b$
a% = b	$a = a \% b$
a& = b	$a = a \& b$
a| = b	$a = a\|b$
a^ = b	$a = a\hat{}b$
a <<= b	$a = a << b$
a >>= b	$a = a >>= b$

These shortcuts are perfectly nice, but they can be dangerous because they do not make the order of execution clear. Here is a bit of sample code that exposes this potential problem:

```
import java.applet.*;
public class ArithTest extends Applet{
  int x=2;
  int y=3;
  int z=0;
  int TripleAndAdd(int a){
    x=x+a;
    return 3*a;
  }
  public void init(){
    x++;
    System.out.println("x="+x+" y="+y+" z="+z);
    x+=y;
    System.out.println("x="+x+" y="+y+" z="+z);
    z=x+TripleAndAdd(y);
    System.out.println("x="+x+" y="+y+" z="+z);
    z=TripleAndAdd(y)+x;
    System.out.println("x="+x+" y="+y+" z="+z);
    x+=TripleAndAdd(y);
    System.out.println("x="+x+" y="+y+" z="+z);
  }
}
```

The output looks like this:

```
x=3 y=3 z=0
x=6 y=3 z=0
x=9 y=3 z=15
x=12 y=3 z=21
x=21 y=3 z=21
```

As you can see, the method TripleAndAdd has a side effect. When it is executed, it adds the value of a to the class's global variable x. This shows the order of execution. The first time it is executed, it falls on the left branch of a + operator. The code x+TripleAndAdd(y) becomes 6+TripleAndAdd(3) which becomes 6+9 or 15.

In the second occurrence, TripleAndAdd falls on the left of the + operator, so it gets evaluated first. This means TripleAndAdd(y)+x becomes TripleAndAdd(3)+x which becomes 9+x. Now x has been incremented by the function so it is 12, not the 9 when the evaluation of the line began. That produces the final answer 21.

What happens in the third case? First x is looked up. It has the value of 12. Then `TripleAndAdd` is executed, returning 9. The value of x has changed, but this change is ignored. Now the result, 21, is stored in x.

These side effects can cause plenty of grief when you program. Be careful.

The Conditional Operator

There is one operator that takes three operands, known as the *conditional operator*. You can use it as the shorthand for the `if-else` clause that is described on page 37. Here are some examples:

```
int PosValue = x>0 ? x : 0;
float Avg = num>1? total/num : num;
```

There are two symbols, the question mark ("?") and the colon (":"). An expression that evaluates to a boolean value must come in the first part. If it is true, the expression evalates to the value between the question mark and the colon. If it is false, the expression evaluates to the value between the colon and the end of the statement.

In the first example, if x is 10, then `PosValue` receives the value 10. If it is −15, then `PosValue` gets 0. In the second example, the division is only done if `num` is greater than 1. This could be used to avoid computation.

As you can see, the arithmetic operations and the comparison operations happen before the conditional operator is evaluated. The conditional operator has a low precedence.

Precedence of Operators

Most of the operators described in this chapter are binary operators. They take two operands and return one. In general, you can combine the results of multiple operations into one statement with parentheses. You might write x=(a+b)*c. In order to save space and respect the tradition of mathematical notation, parentheses are sometimes optional. For instance, x=a+b*c is the same as x=a+(b*c) because convention dictates that the multiplication is performed before the addition.

There is an established order of precedence that Java uses to break ambiguities and allow you to avoid using parentheses if you don't have to. While this shortcut may seem desirable, you should be aware that it is prone to errors if you don't remember the correct order of precedence. It is fairly easy to remember the algebraic rules that govern arithmetic and multiplication, but you may not remember where shifts fit in the hierarchy. It is often good practice to use parentheses to make sure that you and the Java compiler are speaking the same language.

Here's a table of precedence in order from highest to lowest. The operators on the top of the hierarchy are performed first. Items on the same level cannot conflict:

Operators	*Description*
. () []	The dot operator is described in Chapter 5, and is used to access subcomponents of an object. It's also been used in several programs in this book. The parentheses are used for grouping and the brackets are used to access arrays described beginning on page 53.
++ -- !~instanceof	++ and -- are the prefix and suffix operators. ! is the boolean not and ~ is its bitwise cousin, the complement. instanceof is described on page 89. You can use it to test whether an object is an instance from a certain class or one of its superclasses.
new (type)data	new is used to construct new instances of objects. See page 68. Typecasting is performed by placing the name of the type in parentheses before the data.
* / %	Multiplication, division, and modulo arithmetic.
+ -	Addition and subtraction.
<< >> <<< >>>	Bitwise shifts: left, right, left zero-fill, right zero-fill.
< > <= >=	Less-than, greater-than, less-than or equal to, greater-than or equal to.

== !=	Equals and not equal to. Note that these are one notch lower than the comparison functions so a>b==b<c is equivalent to (a>b)==(b<c).
&	And, usually bitwise. (Note that these three are not on the same level.)
^	Xor, usually bitwise.
|	Or, usually bitwise.
&&	Logical And. (Note that these two are also not on the same level.)
||	Logical Or.
? :	This is shorthand for if-then-else.
= += -= *= /= %= &= ||= <<= >>=	Assignment statements are at the bottom. Also the ^= command.

Note that all items that are on the same level are evaluated left to right. So x=y=z=21 will set all three variables to 21.

Statements, Expressions, and Blocks

So far in this chapter, we have described the basics of Java variables, literals, and the operators that can join them together into expressions. So x is a variable, 2 is a literal, and x+2 or x*(x+1) are expressions. If the expression contains at least one assignment operator, then it can be used as a *statement*. As you've seen before in some examples, Java statements are terminated by a semicolon.

Blocks in Java are groups of statements that are enclosed in curly brackets ("{" and "}"). Normally, these blocks are used as parts of loops, if statements, or the definition of a method. So an if-else clause will specify two blocks and execute one of them if the statement is true and the other if it is false.

Variables are defined in blocks. As you may have noticed in the examples, a new variable is defined with a statement that begins with the variable's type or class and ends with the name of the variable. These definitions may also include an equals sign that specifies the initial value of a variable.

Pascal uses the semicolon as a statement separator. You don't need one after the last statement in the block. Java is different. You need one to end each statement, even if a curly bracket is closing off the block.

The *scope* of a variable is an important concept to grasp. Variables are only defined in the innermost block in which they are defined. This allows you to define local variables that do not interfere with other definitions. It is quite easy, for instance, to use i over and over again in different blocks. Each of the instances will be separate and side effects will not affect each other.

The scope also allows Java to manage memory effectively through garbage collection. When a new method begins executing, Java can allocate memory for all of the local variables defined within the scope of the method's block of statements. When the method ends, it can de-allocate them in one operation. This can separate the run-time garbage collection from the persistent objects.

Here's a simple illustration of scope:

```java
import java.applet.*;
public class ArithTest2 extends Applet{
  int x=2;
  int y=3;
  int z=0;
  int TripleAndAdd(int a){
    System.out.println("  Beginning TripleAndAdd:
                        x="+x+" a="+a);
    x=x+a;
    System.out.println("  After TripleAndAdd:
                        x="+x+" a="+a);
    return x*a;
  }
  public void init(){
    int x = 5;
    x++;
    System.out.println("x="+x+" y="+y+" z="+z);
    x+=y;
    System.out.println("x="+x+" y="+y+" z="+z);
    z=x+TripleAndAdd(y);
    System.out.println("x="+x+" y="+y+" z="+z);
    x+=TripleAndAdd(y);
    System.out.println("x="+x+" y="+y+" z="+z);
  }
}
```

Here is its output:

```
x=6 y=3 z=0
x=9 y=3 z=0
  Beginning TripleAndAdd: x=2 a=3
  After TripleAndAdd: x=5 a=3
x=9 y=3 z=24
  Beginning TripleAndAdd: x=5 a=3
  After TripleAndAdd: x=8 a=3
x=33 y=3 z=24
```

It is clear that there are two versions of x at work here. One is part of the variables defined for the class ArithTest2 and the other is a local variable for the method init. They both point at different locations.

You should always aim to keep variables as local as possible. You should also note that there is a major functional difference between variables that are local to classes and those that are local to method blocks. Class variables stick around until an object is destroyed. Method variables are initialized each time. Java requires that all variables be initialized so you probably won't have trouble with this caveat. It isn't possible to generate method code that will try to use an old version of a variable. This is a potential security hole.

Finally, you can declare variables inside of blocks that are part of if-else clauses or loop statements. These remain local to the block and can't be used in other parts of the method.

Classes offer two types of variables: static and instance. Static variables are shared by all objects of a certain class. Instance variables are different for each object. These variables are described in Chapter 5.

The if **Statement**

An if statement consists of the keyword if, an expression that must evaluate to a boolean, and then another statement that will execute if the boolean expression turns out to be true. A block of statements enclosed with curly brackets is also acceptable. For consistency, most of the examples in this book include the curly brackets even when there is only one statement.

If you want something to be executed in the event the boolean expression turns out to be false, you can add a second statement or block of statements with the keyword else. Here are some examples:

See page 33 for a shorthand expression for if-else.

```
if (x>10) y=x+y;
if (y<=14) {
  x=x+10;
}
if ((a>10) && (b <11)){
  x++;
  y++;
}
if ((a == 10) && (b ==11)){
  x++;
} else {
  y++;
}
```

Each of these is a valid expression. The greatest difference that C programmers will notice is that the test expression *must* evaluate to a boolean value. You cannot use zero as a shorthand for `false` and a non-zero number as a shorthand for `true`.

The `switch` Statement

Many programmers find themselves linking together several `if-else` statements in long chains. These are necessary when you want to choose the right solution from a number of choices. Some people find this unwieldy, so many languages include a `case` or `switch` statement. Here's what they look like in Java:

```
switch (kids) {
  case 0:
    FinancialAid = 0;
  case 1:
  case 2:
    FinancialAid += 10000;
    break;
  case 3:
    FinancialAid += 15000;
    break;
  case 4:
    FinancialAid += 17500;
```

```
    break;
  case 5:
  case 6:
    FinancialAid += 20000;
    break;
  default:
    FinancialAid +=25000;
}
```

This code tests the variable kids and starts execution at the statement with the corresponding case tag. If kids was 3, then execution would jump to the line FinancialAid += 15000;. If no statements match, execution jumps to the default tag. If there is no default tag, then the entire block of code is ignored.

Whenever a break statement is encountered, the execution jumps outside of the block and ignores the rest of the code in the block. This allows you to mix several cases together with the same code.

The switch statement only works with the basic types byte, char, short, and int. If you want to use strings, objects, long or a float, you must use if-else statements.

Pascal programmers should beware. Pascal case statements automatically break. Java does not. You must insert your own break statements in Java just as in C.

The for Statement

The for statement is used to create a loop that executes a number of times. It is just like the C version of the for loop that is a nice abstraction of the for loops found in Fortran, Pascal, and Basic.

Here's an example:

```
for (int x=1; x<5 ; x++){
  System.out.println(x);
}
```

This loop will print the numbers between 1 and 4. First, x is initialized to 1.. Then the block of statements is executed. Then the increment is done (x++). Then the test condition, x<5, is checked. If the test is true, then the block of statements executes again. If it is false, it exits.

The for loop statement is nicely abstract. There are three expressions in the block: for (a ; b; c). You can place any statement in

Note: The variables declared in the for loop line are only local to the for loop block!

the first (a) and third (c) sections, but it makes sense to make sure that
c is changing something that will eventually make b false.

Arrays are defined in
Chapter 4.

If you want to scan an array of items, you might use the for loop
like this:

```
for ( i = 0; !IsThisIt(item[i]) ; i++) ;
```

There is no block of code. It executes the method IsThisIt until
it finds a true answer. The not operator ("!") inverts the result of the
method.

Scope and how it
affects blocks is
discussed on page 35.

There are two more subtle differences between these code frag-
ments. In the first one, the keyword int is found before the assignment
x=1. This is the first time that the variable is defined. The scope of the
variable is the pair of brackets that enclose the one println statement.
After the loop finishes, x is no longer defined. In the second example,
i must be defined earlier in the code or the compiler will generate an
error.

The while **and** do **Statements**

Java offers two basic loop constructs known as while and do. C programmers will recognize both of them immediately because both function just like their C equivalents with one exception: the test expression
must evaluate to a boolean. The only major difference is that the while
loop has the test at the top of the block of code and the do loop has
the test at the bottom of the code. In some cases, you will want to use
a while loop when you need to test the expression before executing
any code within the body of the loop. In other cases, you'll want to
automatically execute the loop once, and this is what the do loop offers.

A while loop looks like this:

```
x = 100;
while (x>0) {
  System.out.println(x+" bottles of beer on the wall.");
  System.out.println(x+" bottles of beer.");
  System.out.println(Take one down, pass it around."
  System.out.println(--x +" bottles of beer.");
}
```

This loop will start with the test (x>0) and if it is true, execute the body. Then it will return to the top and test again.

A do loop always executes the body of the loop before the test. Functionally, this only makes a difference on the first pass through the loop. This first pass will always happen. The test statement that guards the continuation of the loop will then work the same way.

Here's an example:

```
do {
  System.out.println("T minus "+time+ " seconds to liftoff.");
  Time--;
} while (time>0);
```

In this case, the statement will always be printed at least once.

The break **Statement**

Although Java reserves the goto statement for itself, the current implementations do not use it. Many programmers find that goto statements can be quite elegant when they are used in the middle of complex loop constructions. Java offers two other keywords, break and continue, that are designed to offer simple escape hatches for loop programmers.

The break command immediately exits the loop without executing the rest of the body or checking with the final test evaluation. Here's an example:

Some computer scientists maintain that it is better to set a "test" boolean and flip it off when necessary. As if!

```
i = 0;
while (i<100){
  if (ItemArray[i].FoundIt) break;
  i++;
}
if (ItemArray[i].FoundIt)
  System.out.println("It was found in slot:"+i);
else
  System.out.println("Not found.");
```

This loop will scan through the array, ItemArray, until it finds the first object with a boolean, FoundIt, set to be true. Then it jumps out of the loop.

The continue command simply skips the rest of the body and goes to the top. If the loop is a do loop, this means that it skips the test case at the bottom. If it is a while loop, then it returns to the top where execution begins again. In for loops, the incrementing expression is executed. Here's an example:

```
i = 0;
while (i<100) {
  if (ItemArray[++i].SkipMe)
    continue;
  ItemArray[i].DoStuff();
  ItemArray[i].DoMoreStuff();
}
```

Here execution begins scanning through an array, ItemArray. If a particular object in the array has its boolean, SkipMe, set to true, the loop returns to the top. Otherwise, the extra methods DoStuff and DoMoreStuff are executed.

If you're using multiple nested loops, the break and continue commands might not be strong enough. An ordinary break command would only jump out of the innermost loop. Java offers a label that will tell the break or continue command where to go.

Here's an example:

```
freedom:
  for (i=0; i<100; i++){
    for (j=0; j<200;j++){
      if ItemArray[i][j].FoundIt
        break freedom;
    }
  }
if ItemArray[i][j].FoundIt {
  System.out.println("It's at ("+x+","+y+")");}
else {
  System.out.println("Not found.");
}
```

This code scans through a 100×200 array, ItemArray, looking for the first object with FoundIt set to true. The break command will skip outside both loops when it executes and jump to freedom.

Summary

This chapter has described much of the basic syntax of Java including how names are chosen, how arithmetic expressions are created, and how control structure is built. C programmers should find much of the information here familiar. The greatest differences lie underneath the syntax.

Here's a summary of the most important facts in this chapter:

Names Variable names must begin with a letter, an underscore, or a dollar sign. Some Java systems recognize UNICODE so you can use a wide range of characters. The convention is to capitalize class names and use a lowercase first letter for variables.

Literals Numbers are numbers, characters are enclosed in single quotes, and strings are enclosed by double quotes. Some numbers need special character prefixes or suffixes to indicate their type. Floating-point numbers end with f. Long integers end with l. Hexadecimal numbers start with 0x.

Comments Double slashes (//) tell the compiler to ignore the rest of the line. A slash and a star (/*) tell it to ignore everything until it encounters a star and a slash (*/).

Expressions Variables and literals are combined into expressions for computation using standard arithmetic (+, -, *, /, %). There are also shortcuts for incrementing and assigning variables (i++, i--, ++i, --i and so on).

Branches Java offers an if statement and an else statement for choosing branches. The most important thing to remember is that the test statement must evaluate to a boolean. There is also a switch statement that can combine several if statements.

Loops There are three types of loops: for, while, and do. The for loop offers the most structure by asking for three expressions that allow you to specify the initialization, the test condition, and the increment evaluation. The while and do loops only ask for a test condition and leave it up to you to make sure the loops progress. The break command will exit a loop and the continue command will start the block again.

This chapter has not described the syntax of several other important parts of the Java language. The syntax for creating and modifying objects is described in Chapter 5. Arrays, vectors, and strings are discussed in detail in Chapter 4.

Chapter 4

Data in Java

*Java handles data differently than C. It provides rou-
tines that allocate the memory and automatically clean
it up after it is finished. This chapter describes how to
build data structures and arrays in Java.*

The syntax of the Java language is borrowed almost entirely from
C and its cousin C++. Although this may give the first impression
that the Java language is just like the C language, nothing could be
further from the truth. The Java run-time interpreter is significantly
different in the way that it handles data. It is closer to LISP than any
C implementation.

The biggest difference is that Java's run-time mechanism keeps
track of the use of memory for the programmer. This is both a convenience and a security measure. Programmers who can't access the
memory directly can't muck about in the system data to malicious
ends. But it should also make life simpler and perhaps faster for
programmers. Memory leaks brought about by incorrect memory
allocation are some of the most difficult bugs to fix. An automatic
garbage-collection mechanism that handles the memory should be
much more efficient.

There are a few other notable differences between Java and C. Java
is a much stricter object-oriented language. Some forms of data are
not available. If you want to create a structure, you can't do it directly.

45

You must create a class and add instance variables to it. This is largely a difference in sematics.

Other changes have create potential traps for unwary programmers. The keywords int and Integer are both used in Java for similar purposes, but there are big differences in the implementation. int is a basic type of data that is used for variables. Integer is a class that comes with a host of methods. If you're not aware of this difference you can easily be confused.

This chapter will describe:

- How Java handles basic types.

- What Java does with strings.

- How arrays are implemented.

- How the Vector class can store flexible arrays.

- What Java's Stack class offers.

The Basic Types

Java offers eight different *basic* or *primitive* types. Data that is stored in these variables are written directly into a memory location and there is no additional object information stored with them. You can't access the memory location directly, but the compiler will arrange for you to find it indirectly.

Here's a table with the eight types:

Type	Declaration Keyword	Size
byte	byte	8 bits
short integer	short	16 bits
standard integer	int	32 bits
long integer	long	64 bits
floating-point	float	32 bits
double-precision	double	64 bits
character	char	16 bits (UNICODE)
boolean	boolean	1 bit

These basic types can be converted from one to another with the simple typecasting mechanism. Here's an example:

```
int x = 1003;
float y = (float) x;
long z = (long) x;
```

You take your chances with precision when you use type conversion operators like this. If x was an int set to be 4023, then it could not be converted to byte without losing precision. Here's an example of what can happen when you use type conversion.

```
import java.applet.*;
public class NumberLab extends Applet {
    byte a;
    short b;
    int c;
    long d;
    float e;
    double f;
    char g;
    boolean h;
  public void init(){
    d = 9000000323;
    c = (int) d;
    System.out.println("c = "+c);
    b = (short) c;
    System.out.println("b = "+ b);
    a = (byte) b;
    System.out.println("a = "+a);
    e = (float) b;
    System.out.println("e = "+e);
    e = (float) d;
    System.out.println("e = "+e);
    f = (double) d;
    System.out.println("f= "+f);
    g = (char) d;
    System.out.println("g = "+g);
    g = 'a';
    b = (short) g;
    System.out.println("b = "+b);
  }
}
```

Here's the output:

```
c = 410065731
b = 6979
a = 67
e = 6979
e = 4.10066e+08
f= 4.10066e+08
g = C
b = 97
```

You can't cast a boolean into a numeric type. The compiler forbids it.

As you can see, the precision loss can be surprising. Even casting d into a `double` loses some value. This data was calculated on the beta version of the MacJDK 1.0 from Sun. Perhaps future versions will handle this better.

Data Objects

Booleans, characters, and numbers can also be stored as objects. Java provides these basic classes which also contain a wide variety of methods that can be quite helpful:

The Java documentation often refers to these data objects as wrappers.

Primitive Type	Associated Class
boolean	Boolean
char	Character
int	Integer
long	Long
float	Float
double	Double

You may often want to use numeric objects when you use some of Java's more abstract classes like hash tables. They take objects, not basic types.

The four numerical data classes are all subclasses of `Number`, a class that offers a number of basic methods. The methods, `intValue()`, `longValue`, `floatValue`, and `doubleValue`, return the value that is stored inside of the object in the appropriate type. Java will round off numbers if appropriate.

There are a number of different functions that are available in each of these classes defined to hold data. Some of them offer many practical alternatives to the parsing routines found in C's standard libraries. For instance, the `toBinaryString` method from the `Integer` class is static, so you can issue a line like:

```
String s = Integer.toBinaryString(i);
```

The integer, i, is then converted into a binary string.

    There are many non-static methods that must be called on objects that are of the correct type. For instance, hashcode returns a code that can be used to store Integer objects in hash tables. The method is also defined in many other classes as well. You might use it like this:

Static methods do not need to be called with a base object. You can just use the name of the class where they reside.

```
Integer I;
int   j;
int    hash;
j=14;
I = new Integer(j);
hash = I.hashcode();
```

    This section does not summarize all of the functions available to you. The API documentation distributed with the Java Development Kit offers the most up-to-date list of methods and their calling arguments. These lists are sure to grow with time.

Strings

It may be easier to define Java strings by what they are not. They are not basic types like integers, longs, or characters. Nor are they arrays of chars in the same way that they are in C. They are objects with their own class and collection of methods, but they are quite different from all of the objects you'll create. Many of the methods for creating and manipulating strings are part of the basic syntax of Java. So you can type "pre"+"fix" to concatenate two strings; you'll need to use a method to do something similar with your own objects: Foo.ConcatenateMe(Bar). Although this ambiguity may be a little bit confusing, it was created to make life easier for programmers. Adding all of the operational shorthand saves keystrokes because strings may be the most important data type.

    You can create a basic string by placing double quotes around the text you wish to represent as a string:

```
"I'm a string"
```

The string variables are defined with the type, String, with a capital letter that indicates that it is an object. So, you create a new string with code like this:

```
String s;
s="Transistor.";
```

Notice that the new operator was not used. Still, a new string object was created. If you need to use a new operator, then the standard constructors are also available, although the behavior might seem a bit circular. String is a method that will accept another String object. That doesn't mean that it needs another String object to create one. It merely allows you to pass in something in quotations. You can also pass in an array of characters:

Arrays are defined beginning on page 53.

```
char[] letters = 'l','e','t','t','e','r','s';
String s = new String(letters);
```

One of the most significant differences between Java strings and the strings that are used in C or Pascal is their immutability. You can't reach into a Java string and manipulate an individual character. If you want to change, say, the fifth letter of a string s, then you *cannot* type s[4] = 'a'. (The first letter is zero, the second letter is in position one.) You must deliberately convert it into a character array, like this:

```
char[] temp = s.toCharArray();
temp[4] = 'a';
s = new String(temp);
```

It might appear as if a new string is created and all of the old information is copied over. This is not immediately clear. The String can be a type that hides the internal operation of a character array.

The index of characters in a string begins with 0. The second character has index 1.

There is also another String function known as charAt that will return the character at a particular index in a string.

There are also String constructors that will take arrays of bytes with ASCII values or StringBuffers, a class of input/output tools.

Manipulating Strings

The equals sign (=), the plus sign (+), and the combination of the two (+=) are the basic operators used to manipulate strings. The plus sign is short for concatenation and you use it to join two strings together like so:

```
String a, b,c, d;
a = "alpha";
b = "beta";
c = a + " " + b;
d = a;
d += " ";
d += b;
```

In this example, both c and d end up with the same information in them.

You can also mix in numbers and Java will automatically arrange for them to be cast into the correct type. This behavior is somewhat unorthodox because Java normally insists upon explicit definitions of types and any typecasting between them. The requirement is removed here because the operation is so common and it has no security implications. Here's an example:

```
 int age = 10;
String message;
message = "Bob is "+age+" years old today. Happy
        Birthday.";
```

In these cases, the Java compiler is secretly arranging for a call to the method toString. This method is defined for many of the most common types and objects. In the String class, it will convert data into a string. In other classes, it will convert data into them. You could have easily typed:

```
int age = 10;
String insert,message;
insert = String.toString(age);
message = "Bob is "+insert+" year old today. Happy
        Birthday.";
```

You may want to include your own versions of toString so Java's internal compiler will allow you to call them automatically with the + operator. Here's an example:

```java
public class Thermometer{
  int temperature;
    //In degrees Fahrenheit.
  public String toString(){
    if (temperature >=85)
      return "hot"
    else if (temperature >=70)
      return "nice"
    else if (temperature > = 60)
      return "cool"
    else if (temperature > = 40)
      return "chilly"
    else
      return "cold";
  }
}
```

Now you can execute code like this:

```java
Thermometer t;
// ...
System.out.println("It is "+t+" outside today.");
```

Obviously, you might want to do something more elaborate. If you create complicated objects that contain many different data elements, you might want to define toString to pack these into an easy-to-read string. I've done this for debugging in many cases.

Common LISP offers a similar service with its defmethod *command.*

There are also several methods for pulling apart strings. These are:

```java
public String substring( int beginIndex);
  // This will return everything after beginIndex
  // including the character.
public String substring(int beginIndex, int endIndex);
  // This returns everything between the two indices.
public int indexOf(char c);
  // Find the first occurrence of c.
public int indexOf(char c, int beginIndex);
  // Find the first occurrence of c starting at
  // beginIndex.
```

These can be used to locate substrings and pull apart strings when you are parsing information.

There are also numerous functions that can be used to compare strings. These include:

```
public int compareTo(String anotherString)
   // Returns zero if the two strings are equal,
   // a positive integer if anotherString is less
   // than the string in the the basic object and
   // a negative integer if anotherString is greater
   // than the object's string.
public boolean startsWith(String prefix)
public boolean startsWith(String prefix,
                                int toffset)
   // Returns true if an object's string starts with
   // prefix. toffset is an optional parameter that
   // can be used if you want to start scanning in
   // the middle of the string.
public boolean endsWith(String suffix)
   // Returns true if an object's string ends with the
   // suffix.
public boolean equals(Object anObject)
   // Returns true if both objects hold the same strings.
public boolean equalsIgnoreCase(String anotherString)
   // Returns true if they're equal regardless of the
   // case of the letters.
```

Each of these functions is used as a method applied to objects. To compare two strings, you would type string1.equals(string2). You must always remember that the normal == operator is *not* the same as the equals function for the class of Strings. The double equals operator will check to see if two objects are the same, that is, if both pointers are the same. The equals method will actually compare them. So if you have two objects that contain the same string, the == will return false, but the equals method will return true.

Arrays of Data

Arrays are some of the most common data structures used in computer programming. Java's implementation of arrays is, on the face of it, not much different than C's. The syntax is identical, but there are several functional differences that can be quite important. The most important difference is Java's requirement that arrays have a fixed length that can never be violated. This is a very important security feature because the index to an array is something of an ersatz pointer. arr[i] means "start at the base of the array, arr, and move i units along." If the array is 10 units, but i is equal to 100, then you could access forbidden memory. Java watches the array bounds during run time and generates an error if it finds a problem.

The syntax is simple. You create an array by placing square brackets next to the name of the array: Here are some examples:

```
int a[] = new int[10];
String b[] = new String[10];
Foo[] c = new Foo[10];
Bar d[];
```

This code creates three new arrays and initializes them to hold ten units. The fourth example, d, is uninitialized for now. The indices 0 through 9 can be used to access the parts of a, b, and c. The first, a, is an array of basic integers. The other two arrays, b and c, are arrays of object pointers. The brackets that indicate an array can be placed in two different locations. The first location used in the definition of a and b points should be familiar to C programmers. The second location is intended to be more harmonious with the way that Java defines objects. You might define a method that returns a character array with this syntax:

```
char[] someLetters(){
}
```

Two-dimensional arrays are created as arrays of single-dimensional arrays. They can be created like this:

```
int ticTacToeBoard[][] = new int[3][3];
int AgeWeight[][] = new int[100][];
int AgeWeight[0][] = new int[3];
int AgeWeight[1][] = new int[5];
// ...
```

This code created two different two-dimensional arrays. The first, ticTacToeBoard is a three-by-three array of ints. AgeWeight is also a two-dimensional array, but only the bounds of the first dimension are specified in the first line. This example might be used to create a table of the weight of people at a certain age. In this example, there might be three people of age zero, i.e., less than 1 year old. The third line creates a new one-dimensional array with three slots to hold the weights of these three people. The fourth line creates a five-slot array for the people of age 1. The other 98 lines are left out to save space. This flexibility can save plenty of memory.

The previous examples of arrays have only created arrays and set their limits. You can also fill them with initial material like this:

```
int[] a;
a = {100,200,300,400,500};
int[] b = {3,2,1};
String s1 = "Lorraine";
String s2 = "Carol";
String s3 = "Gilda";
String c[] = {s1,s2,s3};
```

The array a gets filled with the five integers and b gets filled with three. The array c gets three strings that are defined on previous lines. This is the standard way to define multidimensional arrays.

You should only use the multistep array allocation routine if you need to do so. There are many opportunities for compilers to optimize code using multidimensional arrays. Java compilers may not take advantage of them now, but they could in the future.

Accessing the Contents of Arrays

Arrays are accessed with a syntax just like C. You place the index in brackets after the name of the array. You should also be aware that arrays, like almost everything in Java, act as objects from a class. One of the standard tools is length, an instance variable that is the number of items in an array. Here's an example of how this can be used:

In other classes like String, the length is a method, not an instance variable.

```
public int sumArray(int[][] theArray){
  // Adds up everything in the array.
  int total = 0;
  for (int i = 0; i < theArray.length(); i++)
    for (int j = 0; j < theArray[i].length; j ++)
      total+=theArray[i][j];
}
```

The code will add up all of the elements in a two-dimensional array. You should note that this will work with both `ticTacToeBoard` or `AgeWeight` that are defined above.

There is no other explicitly defined array class, however, that might contain extra methods and instance variables. You cannot explicitly subclass arrays either. There is only one function, `arraycopy` that can be used to copy one array to another. It is defined for most of the major types and the parameters set the starting positions and the amount to be copied.

Vectors

Vectors require objects. You must use an array if you want the efficiency of basic types like `int` *or* `char`.

Arrays are very useful for many activities, but they can grow to be problematic if you want them to grow and shrink. Once they are defined, their size is fixed. If you want to create a flexible class of arrays, the Java designers have spared you the work. *Vectors* are a class that keeps a hidden array of objects in order for you. After an initial amount of memory is allocated, the vectors will grow if you add more objects. The objects are kept in a list and you can insert or delete objects at any position.

Vectors are created and accessed like any standard class of objects. There are no special shortcuts built into the syntax to make them easier to use. You create them with the standard constructors:

```
public Vector()
  //Creates a vector.
public Vector(int StorageCapacity)
  // Creates a vector with StorageCapacity units at
  // the beginning.
public Vector(int StorageCapacity, int Increment)
  // Creates a vector with StorageCapacity units. When
  // it grows Increment new units are added.
```

You should only use the extra parameters if you need to control the growth later in the program. If you know you're going to use 1000 units, then start off with that many.

There are several functions that will add and delete elements from a vector. They are:

```
public final synchronized void addElement(Object obj)
   // Adds the object to the last slot in a vector.
public final synchronized void insertElementAt
(Object obj, int index)
   // Put the new object at location index. The objects
   // at index and after are pushed over one unit to
   // make space for it.
public final synchronized void setElementAt(Object obj,
   // int index) Replace the element at index with obj.
public final synchronized void removeElementAt(int index)
   // Get rid of the element at index.
```

The synchronized *keyword is used to prevent deadlocks between threads. See page 120.*

The first command, addElement, simply adds an element at the end of the list. The second, insertElementAt, places it at a particular location. setElementAt replaces one object with another. The last method here, removeElementAt, destroys an element. If new items are added to a vector or elements are destroyed, the other objects are bumped.

There are several methods that can be used to find elements in a vector. These are:

```
public final synchronized Object elementAt( int index)
   //Return the object at a location.
public final boolean contains(Object element)
   // Return true if an object can be found.
public final synchronized int indexOf(Object element)
   // Finds the index of an object.
public final synchronized int indexOf(Object element,
int start)
   // Finds the index of an object starting at position
   // start.
public final synchronized int lastIndexOf(Object element)
   // Finds the index of an object working backward.
public final synchronized int lastIndexOf(Object element,
int start)
   // Finds the index of an object working backward
   // from start.
public final synchronized Object firstElement()
   // Finds the first element.
public final synchronized Object lastElement()
   // Finds the last element.
```

These functions allow you to search through a vector for particular objects. You should be aware that they require you to pass in an object's pointer, not the data inside the object. That means you can't ask a vector for `myVector.indexOf("FindMe")`. This won't find the string because it is looking for an object, not the contents. You need to write your own loop to search through the vector.

There are three functions you can use to write a loop that will scan a vector. `size` returns the number of active elements in a vector. The `Enumeration` class also offers two functions, `hasMoreElements` and `nextElement`. The first returns a boolean function. The second offers the next element. If you use `hasMoreElements` in the test condition of a `while` loop, then you would use `nextElement` inside it.

Hash Tables

The standard Java classes also include *hash tables* for storing objects and finding them quickly. You'll want to use a hash table if you must keep a collection of objects in no particular order while still retrieving the one that you want without searching through all of them. If you need to keep the objects in a clear order, then you'll need to use vectors.

Hash tables work by using a *hash function*. Generally, this function takes an object and points to one of n "buckets." If you want to store an object, you use the function to choose a bucket and then you store the object in it. The "buckets" may be implemented as vectors or arrays. When you want to find an object, you compute the function and then begin searching in that particular bucket. The search should only take one nth of the time if the hash function does a good job of distributing the object over all n buckets.

Java's hash tables require you to identify a *key* that will be used to search for an object. The put method from the `Hashtable` class will take a key and the associated data and store them in a hash table. If you want to recover the data, you execute the get method with the key and it will return the associated data. In general, the speed can be quite impressive.

The `Hashtable` class uses the `hashCode` method defined by the base class of `object`. This method takes an object and returns an integer that should be relatively unique. That is, different objects containing different information should return different numbers. Naturally, there are limits to this. The hash codes are `ints`, which means that there are only 2^{32} different codes. There are many more objects, so it only follows that some will have the same code. Still, the function should do a reasonably good job of distributing them across the field.

There are three different constructors specified in the basic API:

```
public Hashtable()
  // Construct a hash table.
public Hashtable(int initialCapacity)
  // Construct one ready to accept initialCapacity
  // objects.
public Hashtable(int initialCapacity,
      float loadFactor)
  // Also rehash the table when a loadFactor is reached.
```

Hash tables start to fill up with time. If you start with *n* buckets, then soon after *n* objects, you'll start placing more than one object in a bucket. Performance soon drops. At this time, the hash table code can create an entirely new table with more buckets and redistribute the old objects into the new buckets. Performance increases again. When you set `initialCapacity`, you tell the hash table to be ready to handle that many objects. This can prevent several rehashing episodes along the way and so it is a good idea if you can predict the number of objects that will end up in the table.

Setting the `loadFactor` is trickier. This is a fraction between 0.0 and 1.0. The larger it is, the longer it is before the hash table is rehashed. You might want to set it high if you want to avoid rehashing. If you need to trigger rehashing on your own, you can execute the method `rehash`.

The routines for adding and subtracting elements from the hash table are:

```
public synchronized Object put(Object key,
      Object value)
  // Store value in hash table with key as search guide.
public synchronized Object remove(Object key)
  // Remove an object.
public synchronized void clear()
  // Remove all objects.
```

The class Dictionary *is the parent of* Hashtable. *It offers many of the same features without the ability to control the size or the growth of the database.*

You can control the behavior of the class Hashtable *by writing your own version of the method* equal *for the key objects. The code first uses the result of* hashCode *to identify a bucket and then* equal *to find the right answer in it.*

You can retrieve the objects with these functions:

```
public synchronized Object get(Object key)
  // Feed in a key and get back the associated object.
public synchronized boolean contains(Object value)
  // Returns true if an object is found.
public synchronized boolean containsKey(Object key)
  // Returns true if a key is found.
```

The containsKey merely executes a get and then checks to see if it is null. The contains function can be quite slow because it must search through all of the objects sequentially. If you need to do this on your own, you can use the Enumeration class in a loop. The method elements will return an enumeration of the values stored in a hash table while the method keys will return an enumeration of the keys. You use the boolean method hasMoreElements in the test clause of a while loop and you use the method nextElement to find the next item. Here's an example:

Vectors also implement the Enumeration class to scan the elements.

```
void ReportCodes (Hashtable h){
Object i;
int j;
  for (Enumeration e = h.elements() ;
  e.hasMoreElements() ;) {
    i = e.nextElement();
    j = i.hashCode();
    System.out.println("Code:" + j);
  }
}
```

Instrumenting Hash Tables

You could also simply execute the size method that is defined for the class Hashtable.

Here's an example of how you can subclass a Java class to add your instrumentation to the system. You might want to do this if you're curious about how some black box is functioning. It is also a good lesson of how object-oriented programming can be extended with little effort. In this example, a new class, MyHashtable, is defined that does nothing but keep track of the number of objects in a class. It also reports the size whenever rehash begins.

```java
import java.util.*;
import java.applet.*;
class MyHashtable extends Hashtable{
  // This is just used for instrumentation purposes.
  int ItemCount = 0;
  MyHashtable(){
    super();
  }
  MyHashtable(int initialLoad){
    super(initialLoad);
  }
  MyHashtable(int initialLoad, float loadFactor){
    super(initialLoad,loadFactor);
  }
  protected void rehash(){
    System.out.println("Rehashing at ItemCount =
    "+ItemCount); super.rehash();
  }
  public synchronized Object put(Object key,
                                      Object value){
    ItemCount++;
    super.put(key,value);
    return key;
  }
}
public class MyHashTest extends Applet{
  public void init(){
    MyHashtable h;
    String s;
    s= "Dummy string.";
    h = new MyHashtable();
    for (int i = 0;i<30000;i++){
      h.put(new Integer(i),s);
    }
    h = new MyHashtable(800,0.9f);
    for (int i = 0;i<30000;i++){
      h.put(new Integer(i),s);
    }
  }
}
```

This code prints out this response:

```
Rehashing at ItemCount = 76
Rehashing at ItemCount = 154
Rehashing at ItemCount = 308
Rehashing at ItemCount = 615
Rehashing at ItemCount = 1228
Rehashing at ItemCount = 2453
Rehashing at ItemCount = 4902
Rehashing at ItemCount = 9799
Rehashing at ItemCount = 19592
Rehashing at ItemCount = 721
Rehashing at ItemCount = 1442
Rehashing at ItemCount = 2885
Rehashing at ItemCount = 5770
Rehashing at ItemCount = 11538
Rehashing at ItemCount = 23073
```

Notice that the hash tables double in size each time they are rehashed. The second example initializes the size of the table to 800 objects and sets the threshold for rehashing at 0.9. This means that rehashing begins after 720 objects are in the hash table. You can write your own instrumentation functions to test some of the other features of hash tables like the access speed as a function of load.

You might also want to examine the results of running hashCode on your objects. If your hash table is exceedingly slow, this might be because the hashCode function is returning the same value again and again. You'll need to create a new version of hashCode that is better suited to your collection of objects.

Incidentally, the underlying algorithms for the hash table are not specified in the API documentation, so they may be changed or updated in the future. This may have a great effect if new versions of hashCode perform different than old versions.

Summary

Most C programmers will find that the greatest differences between C and Java lie in the area of data handling. LISP programmers, on the other hand, will feel quite comfortable. The lack of structures, the pointers that masquerade as objects, and the garbage collection are all potentially new features for C programmers. Still, I hope that many will consider them to be improvements that aid the programmer.

This chapter has also shown that:

- The basic types can be typecast between each other using hidden conversion routines. You can also access the conversion routines directly by calling static methods like `toString`.

- There is a set of classes for most of the basic types. To add confusion, these classes have the same names as the types, but different capitalization. `Float` is the object from this class, but `float` is the basic type. These objects take up more space because they come with the overhead of an object, but they can also be used wherever an object is called for. They're also called *wrapper* classes.

- Strings are implemented by a class, but there are many additional shortcuts built into the Java syntax. For instance, there is no need to enforce typecasting when concatentating a string with an integer.

- Arrays come in one dimension, but you can create arrays of arrays to build multidimensional arrays.

- Arrays must have set limits that are tested at both compile and run time.

- If you need to store a flexible collection of objects that is still kept in order, use the `Vector` class. This class will maintain a list that grows and shrinks as objects are added or deleted.

- Java offers a class of hash tables that you might want to use to build up databases.

Chapter 5

Class Structure

This chapter explains how to build your own Java classes so you can create complicated object-oriented hierarchies. You can also extend many of the basic elements in the Abstract Windowing Toolkit to build more complicated user interfaces.

The Java language is one of the most object-oriented languages that many programmers will encounter. The most popular object-oriented language in use today is C++, but this is just an extension of C. Java uses the object class as the basic foundation for programmers. In many ways it is quite similar to Smalltalk. If you want to write some software, you create a class, add some variables to the class, and then add some methods. A class definition is just a schematic diagram for constructing objects. It tells the Java interpreter which data elements to include and which methods can act upon the data.

This class structure has its advantages. In some cases, you might want to use Java to create a stand-alone program that does all of the work on its own. In most cases, however, you'll want to create a small program that travels across the Net, where it can inherit most of its behavior from software already locally supported at the browser. Java's strict object-oriented design forces you to create a class of objects in each case. If the code does it all, then the objects could be any type. If it is going to run remotely, then the objects will almost certainly come from a subclass of `Applet`. Java's object-oriented structure enforces a certain amount of symmetry.

Although the basic format of the `class` definition is straightforward, there are several important modifications that allow you to control behavior. The most important technique is allowing one class to be a subclass of another so it can inherit behavior from the top class. This can make programming much simpler and reduce the final size of the code.

Another important technique is controlling access to methods. You can use modification terms like `public`, `private`, and `final` to constrain access to methods and data. This allows you to write more secure code that is easier to modify over time. This feature is an important part of creating small objects that can run locally without changing or damaging the host system.

This chapter will show:

- How to create basic classes.

- How to access data in classes.

- How to arrange for inheritance between classes.

- How to control access to methods and data.

- How to typecast when necessary.

A Simple Class System

A good place to begin is with a simple program. Here's a fragment of some sort of inventory management system:

```
import java.applet.*;
  // Add all of the basic Java applet.
class InventoryItem{
  int MaxInStock = 0;
    // Maximum desirable stock levels.
  int ReorderLevel = 0;
    // When to reorder.
  int InStock = 0;
    // How many around.
```

```
    int OnOrder = 0;
      // How many should arrive.
}
public class Den1 extends Applet{
  InventoryItem beer, pretzels;
  public void init(){
    // Set up database.
    beer = new InventoryItem();
    beer.MaxInStock = 144;
    beer.ReorderLevel = 72;
    beer.InStock = 100;
    beer.OnOrder = 0;
    pretzels = new InventoryItem();
    pretzels.MaxInStock = 10000;
    pretzels.ReorderLevel = 5000;
    pretzels.InStock = 2000;
    pretzels.OnOrder = 0;
  }
}
```

The program creates two classes here, Den1 and InventoryItem. Den1 is a subclass of the standard Java class, Applet. It is included here so the software will run on browsers and applet runners. The other class, InventoryItem, is a simple bundle of four integers that records data about a particular item.

The mechanics of inheritance and subclassing are described on page 83.

Two objects, beer and pretzels, are created with the new command. The individual elements of each of these items are accessed with *dot notation*. The statement pretzels.Reorder.Level = 5000 stores the value 5000 in the second integer slot for the object pointed to by the pointer pretzels. This same dot notation is used to refer to methods created as part of the class.

The syntax of the class statement is simple:

Java is often said to have no pointers because of security problems. But object variables act as pointers. See page 71.

```
class Name {
  type1 var1;
  type2 var2;
  return_type method_name_1 ( type parameter){
  }
}
```

This is just a simple version. The class in the example, `Inventory Item`, fits this template perfectly. It has four variables of type `int`, but there are no methods. The class, `Den1`, has several extra keywords included in its line. There are several modifiers that can be included to change the behavior of the class structure, but they are covered later in this chapter.

In this case, the `return_type` is the type of the data that will be returned by the function. If this is set to `void`, then nothing will be sent back. If it contains an object name or a base type like `int`, the function must return that value. The compiler will check to make sure that there is a `return` statement that will send back the correct value. The compiler checks to make sure that all paths of the function will execute the `return` statement to make sure that the correct data is always passed back. It also ensures that there is a variable of the right type at the calling end to receive the data.

The `new` Statement

The `new` statement is used to create new objects. It was used in two places in the last example to create new objects from the class, `InventoryItem`. The `new` statement has three parts: the word "new," which indicates an object should be created, the name of the object class, and a set of parameters that might be passed into the creation method. The code that creates the object is known as a *constructor*, and it is a method that must have the same name as the class.

The code in the example does not define a constructor for the class `InventoryItem` so Java uses the generic constructor that inherits its behavior from the basic foundation of all classes, the class `Object`. This method grabs a section of memory (in this case 4 units of 32 bits), sets all of the variables to their initial value (in this case zero), and then returns a pointer to the new object.

A special type of variable known as a static variable holds one value for all objects created in a class. Static variables are described on page 73.

The first call to the constructor method `InventoryItem` returns a pointer for 4 bytes that is stored in the variable beer. The second call returns a pointer for 4 bytes that is stored in the variable `pretzels`. These 4-byte blocks are different.

Although there is a `new` statement, there is no corresponding Java command for destroying an object or releasing its memory. Many C and Pascal programmers may find this shocking, but programmers who've coded in LISP and Smalltalk will not be surprised. Java runs its own internal memory management routine known as a *garbage collector* that keeps track of which units of memory are in use and which are free.

Garbage collection is a simple process that is implemented in a variety of ways. The basic process scans the memory space and determines which objects are currently referenced by another part of the memory space. In this case, the objects for beer and pretzels would not be destroyed and their space reused because they are pointed to by the two variables beer and pretzels. These variables are part of the basic object from the class Den1, that is created when an applet begins running. When the applet stops running, its main object is destroyed and the two variables beer and pretzels are recovered. Now, nothing points at the two blocks of four integers and they too are free to be collected.

When you use objects, you must be careful to ensure that they are pointed to by a variable that keeps the information around as long as you need it. Here's a contrived example:

```java
import java.applet.*;
class Numb{
  int value;
  boolean IsPrime;
  void TestPrime(){
// Sets IsPrime correctly.
    if ((value % 2) == 0) {
      IsPrime = false;}
    else {
      IsPrime = true;
      for (int i=3; i<value; i+=2) {
        if ((value % i) == 0) {
          IsPrime = false;
          break;}
      }
    }
  }
}
public class NumberLab1 extends Applet{
  Numb x;
  public void init(){
```

```
      Numb y;
      x=new Numb();
      x.value = 121;
      y=new Numb();
      y.value = 17;
      x.TestPrime();
      y.TestPrime();
   }
}
```

*This is the first
example of a method
other than an init.
See page 74 for a
complete description
of how to create
methods correctly.*

The basic class Numb has two variables, the integer value and the boolean IsPrime. The first value contains a number and the second value is set to true if the value is prime by the method TestPrime.

There are two different objects created from the class Numb. The first, x, is defined as a variable for the class Den2. The second, y, is a local variable defined for the method init. The distinction between them is made clear in the "Methods" section of this chapter, but the key point here is that y is erased when the init method finishes executing. The x variable does not disappear. Both of these are pointers to a block of one integer and one boolean, but one will stick around while the other will become fair game for garbage collection.

This example is a simple program that does not begin to illustrate the complexity of applets and programming them. Still, it is important to recognize that the information pointed to by x will be available later, and the information pointed to by y will not. The next section offers a more elaborate example.

The finalize Keyword

The basic class for all objects also comes with a *destructor* method known as finalize. This is called when an object is removed from the system. If you need to optimize the destruction of an object, then you should override this function by defining your own. You might use this method to clear a distant cache or make sure that data is written to disk.

If you want to remove an object, you simply call its finalize method. This will remove its information from the system and leave the memory free for garbage collection.

Unpointers

Many experienced C and Pascal programmers are well versed in pointers. Learning how to create data structures and build networks of pointers that link them is an essential skill. Distinguishing between the pointer to a thing and the thing itself is one of the harder lessons for new programmers to master.

The hype for Java says that it has no pointers. This is largely because pointer arithmetic is very unsafe. If a rogue programmer can access any location in memory, then nothing is safe from view or modification. Java's designers decided to give programmers no access to pointers to solve this security problem.

The replacement for pointers is a variable that points to an object from a class. This *is* a pointer; you just can't manipulate it directly. This distinction is an important one. Here's a program that illustrates it:

```java
import java.applet.*;
  // Add all of the basic Java applet.
class InventoryItem{
  int MaxInStock = 0;
    // Maximum desirable stock levels.
  int ReorderLevel = 0;
    // When to reorder.
  int InStock = 0;
    // How many around.
  int OnOrder = 0;
    // How many should arrive.
}
public class Den2 extends Applet{
  InventoryItem beer;
  public void init(){
    // Set up database.
    InventoryItem pretzels;
    beer = new InventoryItem();
    beer.MaxInStock = 144;
    beer.ReorderLevel = 72;
    beer.InStock = 100;
    beer.OnOrder = 0;
    pretzels = new InventoryItem();
```

```
        pretzels.MaxInStock = 10000;
        pretzels.ReorderLevel = 5000;
        pretzels.InStock = 2000;
        pretzels.OnOrder = 0;
        System.out.println("First, beer.ReorderLevel =
                            "+beer.ReorderLevel);
        beer = pretzels;
        System.out.println("Now, beer.ReorderLevel =
                            "+beer.ReorderLevel);
        pretzels.ReorderLevel=7500;
        System.out.println("Finally, beer.ReorderLevel =
                            "+beer.ReorderLevel);
    }
}
```

The output looks like this:

```
First, beer.ReorderLevel =72
Now, beer.ReorderLevel =5000
Finally, beer.ReorderLevel =7500
```

In the code, two objects are created. Then the value of pretzels is assigned to beer. The value of beer.ReorderLevel jumps from 72 to 5000 after the assignment. The key lesson is that both beer and pretzels are *pointers* to two different collections of four integers. When the line beer=pretzels is executed, the pointer stored in pretzels is copied over to the pointer to beer. That is why the line pretzels.ReorderLevel =7500 changes the value of beer.Reorder Level as well.

This example can illustrate an important point about garbage collection. The process operates by looking for pointers to an object. When there are no pointers, then the data is free to be collected. In this case, the two pointers, beer and pretzels, are created in different places. The variable pretzels is a local variable. When the init finishes computation, that pointer will disappear. There will still be a pointer, though, to the four integers that were originally created and assigned to pretzels. The pointer beer will keep that data alive. The four integers created in the line, beer=new InventoryItem(); are free game for the garbage collector to recover.

This example doesn't illustrate the true extent of garbage collection because there are no other methods in the basic class Den2 that might be executing after init finishes. In other more robust programs, this will not be the case.

Static Variables

All of the variables assigned to classes described so far are called *instance variables*. This is because a new copy is created for each instance. There is another type known as a *static variable* that is the same for each object that is a member of the class.

Here's an example:

```
class Tire{
  static int diameter;
  Date installationDate;
  String manufacturer;
}
class Car{
  Tire leftFront = new Tire();
  Tire rightFront = new Tire();
  Tire leftRear= new Tire();
  Tire rightRear = new Tire();
  //...
}
```

The variable diameter has the modifier static before its definition. The Java compiler will set up one separate integer that will hold the diameter for all tires. This example was chosen because many cars will have four tires with the same diameter. The tires may be replaced at different times and come from different manufacturers, but the diameter will be the same. This can save memory and it can also be used in some cases to simplify a program.

Static variables have one extra feature that has the potential to be confusing. The value of diameter can be accessed in two different ways. Obviously, leftFront.diameter = 15 makes sense. But you can also execute Tire.diameter = 15. Both will have the same effect. This technique will not work with instance variables.

Methods

The procedures, subroutines, and functions in Java are known as *methods*. Each is a member of a class and each has access to all of the variables available to objects in that class, including all of the static and instance variables associated with a class as well as the variables that may have been defined in superclasses from which the current class inherits information. Each method can also define local variables to accomplish its job.

Superclassing and inheritance are described beginning on page 83.

   Each method can also define a set of *parameters* or *arguments* that are used to pass information into a method. A method definition might look like this:

```
class Car{
  Tire leftFront = new Tire();
  Tire rightFront = new Tire();
  Tire leftRear= new Tire();
  Tire rightRear = new Tire();
  //...
  void SwapTires(Tire a, Tire b){
    Tire temp;
    temp = a;
    a = b;
    b=temp;
  }
  public void RotateTires(){
    SwapTires(this.leftFront, this.rightRear);
    SwapTires(this.leftRear, this.rightFront);
  }
}
```

   The first line of the method contains the keyword void, which tells the compiler that the method will not return any information; the name of the method, SwapTires; and the list of parameters, a and b, which are both objects from the class Tire.

   As you may have noticed in other examples, the method is invoked with the same dot notation that is used to access the variables of a class. The second procedure, RotateTires, calls SwapTires twice. Somewhere else in the software, an object, say BobsCar, might be created from the class Car. If you wanted to rotate Bob's tires, you would invoke the method with the call `BobsCar.RotateTires()`. The parentheses are necessary.

When methods pass parameters, they pass objects by reference and basic types by value. That means that the two tires being passed into `SwapTires` are passed in as pointers to some data, not as the data itself. If you change the values of the data addressed by the pointers, then the changes will affect all other pointers addressing the same data. If you change the value of basic types, however, this change will not affect other instances of the variable.

Here's an example that illustrates how variables are passed into method calls:

```
import java.applet.*;
class StringObj{
  String contents;
  StringObj(String a){
    contents = a;
  }
}
public class ReferenceTest extends Applet{
  int left,right;
  String first,second;
  StringObj alpha,beta;
  void ChangeInts(int a,int b){
    a = 5;
    b = 6;
    System.out.println("Inside ChangeInt a="+a+" b="+ b);
  }
  void ChangeStrings(String a,String b){
    a = "Hi";
    b = "Ho";
    System.out.println("Inside ChangeStrings a=
                        "+a+" b="+ b);
  }
  void ChangeStringObj(StringObj a,StringObj b){
    a.contents = "Hi";
    b.contents = "Ho";
    System.out.println("Inside ChangeStrings a=
                        "+a.contents+" b="+
```

```
        b.contents);
      }
      public void init(){
        left = 10;
        right = 20;
        System.out.println("Inside init left="+left+"
                            right="+ right);
        ChangeInts(left,right);
        System.out.println("Inside init left=
                            "+left+"right="+ right);
        first = "Foo";
        second = "Bar";
        System.out.println("Inside init first=
                            "+first+" second="+ second);
        ChangeStrings(first,second);
        System.out.println("Inside init first=
                            "+first+" second="+ second);
        alpha = new StringObj("Foo");
        beta = new StringObj("Bar");
        System.out.println("Inside Init alpha=
                            "+alpha.contents+" beta="+
beta.contents);
        ChangeStringObj(alpha,beta);
        System.out.println("Inside Init alpha=
                            "+alpha.contents+" beta="+
beta.contents);
      }
    }
```

The output looks like this:

```
Inside init left=10 right=20
Inside ChangeInt a=5 b=6
Inside init left=10 right=20
Inside init first=Foo second=Bar
Inside ChangeStrings a=Hi b=Ho
Inside init first=Foo second=Bar
Inside Init alpha=Foo beta=Bar
Inside ChangeStrings a=Hi b=Ho
Inside Init alpha=Hi beta=Ho
```

In the first two cases, the integers and the strings are passed by value. A new copy is created inside of the method and changes do not propagate. In the third case, the two objects from class StringObj are passed by reference. Any changes made inside the method will affect the object itself and the changes can propagate.

You should be careful about this detail because it is different from the way that Pascal and C handle passing data. Both of them require you to explicitly determine whether you are passing data by reference or by value.

Overloading Methods

Java has one feature that may seem surprising at first to C, Pascal, LISP, and Fortran programmers. You can create several methods with the same name that take different arguments or parameters. The program code can contain multiple versions of the same method with different sets of parameters. In practice, Java will treat them all as separate methods that are not the same. It will use the types of the arguments to differentiate them. You can't have two methods with the same name and the same list of arguments.

This solution is a concession to the programmers who've grown used to defining procedures or functions that accept optional parameters. This is common in the world of C or LISP. The programmer has direct access to the calling stack and can call information from it. Naturally, this can be dangerous because a clever programmer can also use this technique to suck off more information from the stack.

Here's an example of how two methods can be defined with the same name:

```
class Car{
  Tire leftFront = new Tire();
  Tire rightFront = new Tire();
  Tire leftRear= new Tire();
  Tire rightRear = new Tire();
  //...
  void SwapTires(Tire a, Tire b){
    Tire temp;
    temp = a;
    a = b;
```

```
    b=temp;
  }
  public void RotateTires(){
    SwapTires(this.leftFront, this.rightRear);
    SwapTires(this.leftRear, this.rightFront);
  }
  public void RotateTires(Tire t1, Tire t2, Tire t3,
                          Tire t4){
    SwapTires(t1,t2);
    SwapTires(t2,t3);
    SwapTires(t3,t4);
  }
}
```

There are now two versions of RotateTires. If the compiler encounters a method call of the form RotateTires() then it will match
this with the first version that simply swaps the tires diagonally. It will
use the second version if it finds one call of the form:

```
RotateTires(this.leftFront, this.leftRear,
            this.rightRear,this.rightFront);
```

Overloading method names like this is a useful technique to keep
your methods straight.

Constructor Methods

Most of the classes we've seen defined in Java code to this point use
the generic Java *constructor* that is created with the basic object. This
simply sets up a block of data of the right size and stores the correct
initial values. The earlier examples of the car's tires show the call to
new Tire().

You can also define your own constructors to do any additional
work that might be necessary. For example:

```
class Tire{
  static int diameter;
  public Date installationDate;
  String manufacturer;
}
```

```
class Car{
  Tire leftFront ;
  Tire rightFront ;
  Tire leftRear;
  Tire rightRear ;
  //...
  public Car(){
    leftFront = new Tire();
    leftFront.installationDate = Date.todaysDate();
    rightFront = new Tire();
    rightFront .installationDate = Date.todaysDate();
    leftRear= new Tire();
    leftRear.installationDate = Date.todaysDate();
    rightRear = new Tire();
    rightRear .installationDate = Date.todaysDate();
  }
}
```

Note that the variable `installationDate` *is now a* `public` *variable. See page 89 for a description of the keyword's actions.*

In the earlier examples, the values of `leftFront` were filled by the `new` commands where the instance variables were defined at the top of the class. In this example, there are no `new` commands. The variables are filled inside the method `Car`. This constructor must have the same name as the class. It cannot define a return value as it is returning a new object of this class.

In this example, the constructor also sets the `installationDate` instance variables of each tire to a value returned from a hypothetical method `todaysDate`. This type of behavior is often specified inside a constructor.

Naturally, you can also overload the definition of `Car` or whatever the name of your class happens to be. All of the constructors up to this point have taken no parameters, but you don't need to follow that lead.

Class or Static Methods

The keyword `static` is used with variables in class definitions to indicate that a variable should be shared by all objects of the same class. The keyword is also used to modify the behavior of methods, but the purpose is generally something different. In the case of methods,

Static methods are

often used like units

in Pascal or separate

files in C.

the `static` keyword is used as a way to break your code into separate
files for easy access.

The methods that are designated `static` can be invoked with just
the class name and the name of the method. Strings are defined as a
class and they have several static methods like `valueOf`. If you want
to convert an integer into a string, you can invoke the static method
with the line x=`String.valueOf("5")`. Java will find the right method
for an integer and produce the integer 5 for the variable x. The `String`
class also contains a wide variety of other methods that are not static.
The function x.`equals("five")` will return `false` because x and the
string `"five"` are not the same. In this case, the method is invoked
with the standard format.

The standard Java class `String` describes a set of static methods
that can be used throughout the program. Other files or classes that
require it can simply include the class. You should try to use this
means of abstraction whenever possible because it is an effective way
to create reusable code.

Static methods can also be invoked at the time a class is created.
Here's an example:

```
class Numbers {
  static first,second,third,fourth;
  static {
    first = 2;
    second = first * first;
    third = second * second;
    fourth = third * third;
    System.out.println("Numbers Static Values Set");
  }
// ...
}
```

The code that does the squaring is executed when the class is first
loaded into the Java interpreter. Placing the `println` code here will
announce the completion. You might be surprised to discover that this
doesn't happen until another class creates a `new` object of the class
`Numbers` or until one of the methods is called. This saves memory and
effectively does the job of segment loaders.

The main **Static Method**

When Java starts up a new class, it looks for the main function that is called, just like C. This book has avoided using this feature in most of the examples because these examples are built as applets that inherit much of their behavior from the Abstract Windowing toolkit. Somewhere in the depths of Java, there is a method with the name main that the Java run-time mode calls to begin the execution of the applet. Eventually this code invokes the init method that is used in many of the examples here.

If you write Java code that is not going to run as an applet, you need to define your own main routine. Here's an example:

```java
class Square{
  int x;
  public static main(String arg[]){
    x = 2;
    x = x*x;
    System.out.println(x);
  }
}
```

The function main must be defined as both public and static. It must also accept the array of Strings known as arg. This is because the Java run-time environment that is used to fire up a naked Java class like this can take command-line arguments, just like C code running in a UNIX environment. These arguments appear in the array.

public functions can be accessed from outside the class. See page 89.

The code must be stored in a file with the name of the dominant class and the suffix .java, which in this case is Square.java. When it is compiled, the byte code ends up in the file Square.class. The run-time interpreter can pick out the main method from this file.

A Web browser like Netscape fires up Java code differently. When you add the tags for the applet, it goes to the source site and loads the class from that directory. Then it runs the applet code, which eventually calls the init routine of the applet.

More detailed information about the structure of an applet is given in Chapter 9.

The this **Keyword**

Just as there are times when a person must use the words "me" or "I," an object must have the freedom to refer to itself. Java includes the keyword this as a pointer to the current object. For instance, in the example of the class Car, you might write some code that referred to this.leftFront, the instance variable of the object that is currently being executed. The this keyword is necessary if you happen to be inside a method that has also defined a local variable or a parameter with the same name, leftFront. If there is no conflict or ambiguity, then the this is optional.

Defining your own constructors is described beginning on page 78.

The this keyword is especially useful when you are creating objects and linking them together. In the Car class, it is easy for any method defined as part of the class to refer to the four tires. But there is no way for the tires to refer to their owners. Here's an extended example that illustrates how to use the this keyword:

```
class Tire{
  static int diameter;
  Date installationDate;
  String manufacturer;
  Car installedOn;
  void setInstalledOn(Car s){
    this.installedOn = s;
  }
}
class Car{
  Tire leftFront ;
  Tire rightFront ;
  Tire leftRear;
  Tire rightRear ;
  //...
  public Car(){
    leftFront = new Tire();
    leftFront.setInstalledOn(this);
    rightFront = new Tire();
    rightFront .setInstalledOn(this);
    leftRear= new Tire();
    leftRear.setInstalledOn(this);
    rightRear = new Tire();
    rightRear .setInstalledOn(this);
  }
}
```

The new method in the `Tire` class takes one parameter, s, and assigns it to the current Tire object's instance variable `installedOn`. The `this` keyword in this method is optional because there is no ambiguity of which version of `installedOn` is to receive the data.

The second method in this example, `Car`, is a constructor. These special methods responsible for creating objects are defined beginning on page 78. In this case, after a new `Tire` is created, you can fill the Tire's pointer `installedOn` by running the command `setInstalledOn` and passing it the parameter `this`.

installedOn could also be a static variable if all tires will only be installed on one car.

Inheritance

One of the most powerful tools in object-oriented programming is the process of inheritance. This allows you to create a hierarchy of classes and distribute code to the most effective place. Graphical user interfaces are one of the best examples of how this technique can save plenty of code.

If you were creating a drawing program like Adobe Illustrator or MacDraw, you might create a class called `DrawObject` that would contain a number of different methods for manipulating triangles, squares, text, and lines. You might create one method that would indicate that an item was selected by drawing little boxes on the corners of the object. You could create another method that would let the user drag an item by changing the x and y coordinates.

The power of inheritance would come into play when you created *subclasses* that inherited behavior from their *superclass*. In Java, this is done when a new class is created, like this:

```
public class Triangle extends DrawObject {
//...
}
```

The keyword `extends` means that `Triangle` is a subclass of `DrawObject` and `DrawObject` is the superclass of `Triangle`. In this class, you would create methods for actually drawing a triangle. The code for dragging or drawing the selection boxes would be *inherited* from the superclass. This saves you the trouble of defining different dragging methods for all of the possible triangles, squares, and lines that might be part of a drawing program.

Here's a simple example of how you might create two classes in Java:

```
class Transportation{
  int MaxLoad;
  int PeopleCapacity;
}
class TankerTruck extends Transportation{
  int Gallons;
  TankerTruck(int size){
    PeopleCapacity = 2;
    Gallons=size;
    MaxLoad = 2 * 300 + 10 * Gallon;
  }
}
class Sedan extends Transportation{
  int StereoWattage;
  Sedan(int StereoSize, int doors) {
    if (doors = 2) {
      PeopleCapacity = 4;
    else
      PeopleCapacity = 6;
    MaxLoad = 300 * PeopleCapacity;
    StereoWattage = StereoSize;
  }
}
```

Both TankerTruck and Sedan are subclasses of Transportation. That means that they automatically come with the instance variables PeopleCapacity and MaxLoad. The two constructors for these classes have access to these values and set them accordingly.

Methods and Inheritance

Methods can also be inherited by subclasses. You can create one simple method that might hold for the basic objects and then create a more sophisticated or appropriate method that will cover the subclasses.

Here's another example from the Transportation class:

```
class Transportation{
  int MaxLoad;
  int PeopleCapacity;
  void Horn(){
    System.out.println("Honk.");
  }
}
class TankerTruck extends Transportation{
  int Gallons;
  TankerTruck(int size){
    //...
  }
  void Horn(){
    System.out.println("A ooo Ga.");
  }
}
class Sedan extends Transportation{
  int StereoWattage;
  Sedan(int StereoSize, int doors) {
    // ...
  }
}
```

If you create an object from the class Sedan and call it BobsCar, then BobsCar.Sedan will print out the word "Honk." It inherited that behavior from its superclass, Transportation. On the other hand, an object from the class TankerTruck will print out "A ooo Ga" if you happen to invoke its Horn method. The version of Horn defined in the TankerTruck class is said to *override* the version in Transportation.

The super Keyword

From time to time, you may find yourself wanting to use both the basic version of a function defined in the base class and also add some specialized details that may be essential to the action in a subclass. For instance, you might create some large data structure in the base class. You could duplicate this code in the subclass while adding the few details, but this would take up more disk and memory space, which is at a premium if the program will travel over the network to be executed.

The keyword super is the solution. The word tells the Java compiler to search in the superclass for the method. Here's an example:

```
class Transportation{
  int MaxLoad;
  int PeopleCapacity;
  void Horn(){
    System.out.println("Honk.");
  }
}
class Sedan extends Transportation{
  int StereoWattage;
  SparkPlug p1,p2,p3,p4,p5,p6;
  OilFilter o1;
  AirFilter a1;
  Sedan(int StereoSize, int doors) {
     // ...
  }
  void TuneUp(){
    p1 = new SparkPlug();
    p2 = new SparkPlug();
    p3 = new SparkPlug();
    p4 = new SparkPlug();
    p5 = new SparkPlug();
    p6 = new SparkPlug();
    o1 = new OilFilter();
    a1 = new AirFilter();
  // etc.
  }
}
class LowRider extends Sedan{
  AirShocks s1,s2,s3,s4;
  void TuneUp(){
    super.TuneUp();
    s1= new AirShocks();
    s2= new AirShocks();
```

```
    s3= new AirShocks();
    s4= new AirShocks();
  }
}
```

In this example, the class structure is extended another level. LowRider is a subclass of Sedan and it inherits much of its behavior from Sedan. In this hypothetical example, much of the work of tuning up a car is done in the Sedan.TuneUp routine. The plugs and filters are replaced there. The LowRider car, however, is a special instance of a sedan where the shocks and the suspension system have been modified to ride lower to the ground. A tuneup might also include new air shocks.

If an object from the LowRider class invokes the TuneUp method, the code from the superclass, Sedan.TuneUp, will be executed first. Then the shocks will be replaced.

Although this example is a bit hypothetical, it is a good illustration of when to use the super keyword. You don't need to use it to call the overridden method, but that is how it is used in most common cases.

Java is very environmentally conscious. The old SparkPlug, AirFilter *and* OilFilter *objects will be automatically collected with the garbage and recycled.*

Overriding Constructors

There are many times when you would want to override a constructor, but still use the keyword super to refer to the constructor of the previous method. The major problem with this is that the names become confusing. While it is quite possible to create two methods with the same name, TuneUp, in both Sedan and LowRider, it is not possible to do the same with constructors. The constructor for Sedan has the name Sedan and the constructor for LowRider has the name LowRider.

Java has a special way of using super with constructors:

```
class LowRider extends Sedan{
  AirShocks s1,s2,s3,s4;
  LowRider(){
    super();
    s1= new AirShocks();
    s2= new AirShocks();
    s3= new AirShocks();
    s4= new AirShocks();
```

```
  }
  void TuneUp(){
    super.TuneUp();
    s1= new AirShocks();
    s2= new AirShocks();
    s3= new AirShocks();
    s4= new AirShocks();
  }
}
```

In the constructor for the class LowRider, the super keyword is called with parameters but there is no method specified. The constructor for the superclass is implied. But what if the right phrase was super.sedan()? This would create an ambiguity because it might be necessary to actually create an object from the class Sedan when you're constructing a member from its subclass. Should the compiler create one new object or two?

The solution is to require you to use just the super keyword. The Java compiler also requires you to use the super keyword as the first line in the constructor.

Class Casting between Objects

Pascal programmers are used to converting data elements between different types by using a technique called *typecasting*. C programmers have been forced to do this more often now that the ANSI definitions of C and C++ force more use of types. Java enforces strong rules about casting between objects: the objects must be related through inheritance.

Here's an example that uses some of the definitions of Sedan and LowRider:

```
class AutoPark extends Applet{
  public void init(){
    Sedan blueCar;
    LowRider redCar;
    Sedan firstInLine;
    firstInLine = blueCar;
    firstInLine = (Sedan) redCar;
```

```
    }
}
```

In this example, blueCar is from the class Sedan so it can easily be installed in firstInLine. The object redCar, however, is from the class LowRider so it can't be inserted directly. It must be typecast into the right type with the word (Sedan) in parentheses in front of it.

Finding the True Class of an Object

The class name in parentheses used in typecasting is just a syntactic convenience. The object still contains all of the extra information bound into it from the class LowRider. The data has not been altered; it's still there. Examine this:

```
String myClass = firstInLine.getClass().getName();
```

It might seem like there is magic going on here, but it is simple. Classes themselves are objects. The base of all objects contains a method getClass that returns the pointer to this class. These "class" objects also have a method defined for them that returns a String with the name in it. This would return "LowRider" if the data for redCar was stored in firstInLine and "Sedan" if the data for blueCar was stored there.

There is also a boolean operator, instanceof, that can be used to test whether an object is an instance of a particular class. Here's an example:

```
if (firstInLine instanceof LowRider) {
  firstInLine.Hop(10);
}
```

This would call the hypothetical method Hop only if firstInLine is from the class LowRider.

Protection and Publicity

Many programming languages come with built-in syntactical structures that prevent you from calling all of the procedures. Pascal builds units that can hide some procedures in the local implementation. Many APIs come with hooks that only allow you call some routines. This is a way of providing more abstraction to make life easier for the programmer.

Java also provides similar mechanisms for the same reasons. But it also needs to provide some protection and security. Java would like to ensure that the incoming applet cannot write to the file system even if the Java system itself can do it. So some subroutines may be forbidden because they provide the opportunity for danger.

There are three modifiers that are placed on the first line of a method declaration, used to control the access to a method by other methods: public, private, and protected.

The first is public, which designates that a method should be made available to all requests from inside or outside the class. The public keyword can be applied to both classes and their variables. The compiler enforces discipline by requiring that public variables must be found inside public classes. Here's an example:

```java
public class Vote {
  public String winner;
  int[] count;
  public static int Bill=0;
  public static int Bob=1;
  public init(){
    count=0,0;
  }
  public recordVote(int forWhom){
    if (forWhom==Bill){
      count[Bill]++;
    } else if (forWhom==Bob){
      count[Bob]++;
    }
    if (count[Bob]>count[Bill]){
      winner="Bob";
    } else if (count[Bob]<count[Bill]){
      winner="Bill";
    } else {
      winner="Tie.";
    }
```

```
  }
}
```

This example shows how some of the information inside of the class Vote is declared public. In fact everything except array count is public. This means that any class that creates an object from the class Vote can access this data. You may not want the array count to be accessible to outside forces. This may be because you want to force all outside programmers to use the recordVote method in case the class is modified later or because you don't want them to have access to the basic data.

This last example has left the status of count ambiguous. If you want to ensure that no other class can handle the data, you should use the private keyword. This will block access to all other objects of any class, even if they are from a subclass. You might want to make the count array private to keep other objects from actually looking at the final count. Methods designated as private can't be called from outside.

You might find that the private keyword is too restrictive. There is an intermediate-level word, protected, that allows other objects in the same package to use it. If you combine the two keywords, private and protected, then you can restrict access to only subclasses. Here's an example:

The keyword package *allows several classes to be bundled together into a large layer of abstraction. It is described on page 100.*

```
class Foo {
  private protected int Count;
  protected IncrementCount(a){
    Count=Count+a;
  }
}
public class Fu extends Foo {
   public AddAndPrint(a){
    Count = Count+a;
    System.out.println(Count);
  }
}
class Bar {
  public OtherAdd(a){
    IncrementCount(a);
  }
}
```

In this example, the variable Count is controlled by both the private and the protected keywords. This means that only objects that are the same class or a subclass of it have access to it. This means that the routine AddAndPrint can access the variable directly because Fu is a subclass of Foo. Also, a subclass can override any method of its superclass that is marked protected, but it can't override a method marked private.

Any object from the class Bar, on the other hand, must use the accessor method, IncrementCount, to change the value. That method is simply protected, so it is accessible because Bar is from the same package.

Neither the private nor the protected keyword can be used to modify a class designation.

The final Keyword

You can also add the modifier final to a method or a variable. If this is included, it removes the possibility of subclassing that method or variable. The effect of this is different on methods and variables. The variable is essentially turned into a constant because it can't be changed by any subclass.

The method, on the other hand, continues to behave in the same way, but it can't be replaced by a local version in a subclass. This effect can be used in two ways. The first is to provide some security. You might want to allow someone to create a subclass of your object type to inherit all of the behavior without being able to insert their own version of the behavior. Imagine some code like this:

```
public class SemiSecret{
  public final void WriteDataToFile(String data){
    // Writes the data to some file.
  }
  private final void SecretInternalMethod(){
    // This shouldn't be accessed from outside.
    WriteDataToFile("My Secret");
  }
}
public class MyClass extends SemiSecret{
  public void WriteDataToFile(String data){
```

```
    SendDataOutInternet(data);
    super(data);
  }
}
```

This code will *not* work because the routine WriteDataToFile is designated as final. That means that the subclass MyClass can't replace WriteDataToFile. This is a good thing, because it would allow the subclass to insert a tap routine, SendDataOutInternet, that would send information out the Internet. This information would be called whenever an object from the MyClass class would trigger the routine SecretInternalMethod. Although SecretInternalMethod is private, it can still be called by some other method inside of SemiSecret. The final keyword prevents someone from inserting their own version of a method to replace the standard one.

The second, and perhaps more important use, of the keyword final is to help the compiler save time. If a method is designated final, then the compiler knows that no new version may be substituted at run time by a subclass. There is no need to wait for a dynamic evaluation to look for the right function. It's right here. The compiler can in-line the function and save the laborious process of finding the right method at run time. This can be a significant timesaver if you write many small methods. If there are only a few lines of code in a method, then the process of switching contexts by calling a new method can be more time-intensive than the small amount of computation in the method.

The moral is: Use the final keyword with methods as often as you can.

Summary

This chapter has shown how to create a hierarchy of objects that can be used to efficiently keep track of data and the work that needs to be done to it. The Java inheritance structure is a very straightforward and clean implementation of object-oriented ideas, and this makes it relatively easy to learn.

Here's what's been covered in this chapter:

- How to use classes to create a hierarchy for data and the methods that operate upon it.

- How methods and data override versions in superclasses.

- How to cast objects into different types.

- How to check from which class an object comes.

- How to create and destroy objects.

- How to compare objects.

Chapter 6

Interfaces and Packages

You can use interfaces to allow a class to inherit be-
havior from multiple classes. Packages are used to keep
large collections of classes straight.

One of the fundamental lessons a programmer learns is to keep breaking apart programs into smaller, manageable chunks. The class hierarchy built by the `class` construct described in Chapter 5 is a good
beginning that can serve many small and medium-sized programs.
Larger projects, however, require even more structure.

Interfaces and packages are two other solutions offered by Java.
Interfaces allow you to enforce consistency across multiple objects.
They're Java's solution to multiple inheritance. *Packages* are tools for
naming a large group of classes. All of the basic classes used in Java,
like `String`, for instance, can be found in the package `java.lang`.
The compiler will automatically include them. If you create your own
packages, you'll have to import them by name, but you'll only need
to import one package.

Abstract Methods

Before introducing interfaces, you should understand how to use the
`abstract` keyword. This keyword is used to delay defining the code

for a particular method. It works like the Pascal keyword `forward` or the C prototype. If you define a method with the `abstract` keyword, you're merely reserving a place for the method. You must define it in some subclass of the method. Here's what a definition of several abstract methods might look like:

```
public abstract class Road {
   abstract void DrawRoad();
   abstract int FindMedian(int[] x);
// ...Other fully formed methods.
}
public class Superhighway extends Road {
   void DrawRoad(){
     //...
   }
   int FindMedian(int[] x){
     //...
   }
}
```

In the class Road, both of these examples end with a semicolon and offer no code. The definitions for `DrawRoad` or `FindMedian` will come later from some other subclass of Road. There are some consequences. Java will not let you create an object from the class Road because all of the methods aren't available. You can't just type `Road Route66=new Road()`. You must create a subclass and this subclass must provide code for all of the `abstract` methods in its inheritance hierarchy.

You'll want to use `abstract` methods if you can't provide a global definition for a method that will work with all objects from that class. Or you just might want to avoid writing some placeholding function that will never be called. In either case, you can create variables with the type of this abstract class, but you can't fill them with a `new` constructor. You'll need to use the constructor for the subclass with a full definition.

That is, you can create a variable, x, of type Road, but you can't simply assign x=new Road(). Instead, you can create an object from class Superhighway and assign it to x. If you call x.drawRoad(), you can be assured that there will be a fully formed definition.

Interfaces

An *interface* is just a slightly different version of a class that acts like the abstract mechanism. It contains a list of variables and a list of the methods that can change the variables. However, the guts of the methods are missing. The interface is just a hollow shell that describes what variables and methods will be available. It's just a design document, not the code itself.

These prototypes for functions shouldn't be unfamilar to C and Pascal programmers. Some of the newer versions of C provide ways for programmers to specify the names and parameters of the functions. Pascal requires programmers who split up code into units to place a list of the procedures and their parameters in a section labeled interface. The Pascal and C approaches are provided to make compiling and linking faster and more efficient. In Java, however, interface is used to implement *multiple inheritance.*

The idea behind multiple inheritance is to have a class inherit behavior from more than one superclass. For example, the class of Bartender might inherit some of its behavior from the class of Psychiatrist and from the class of Servant. But just as humans can get in trouble when they serve two masters, classes that inherit behavior from multiple superclasses can get unwieldy. They're often called *fragile*.

Interfaces are a solution to many of the problems programmers have experienced with multiple inheritance because interfaces don't offer the same powerful features as full-fledged multiple inheritance. When a class *implements* an interface, it provides complete code for every method specified in the interface. But it doesn't inherit any behavior or code from this interface because there isn't any code to inherit. The interface is like a law that binds the class to provide these methods.

The main reason you would use an interface is because you want to pretend it is a class when shuffling around objects. Here's a simple example with pets:

There is no superclass to an interface unless it is explicitly defined. That is, the basic methods from the base class Object are not included.

```
interface Noisy {
  void makeNoise();
}
class Pet {
```

```
    String name;
    int Birthdate;
      // In days since 1/1/1980.
    int LastDateFed;
      // In days since 1/1/1980
    int FeedingInterval;
    int myX,myY,myZ;
      // Location.
    void Move(int x, int y, int z){
      // Code to move location
      myX+=x; myY+=Y; myZ+=Z;
    }
}
class Dog extends Pet implements Noisy {
  void makeNoise(){
    System.out.println("Bark.");
  }
}
class Cat extends Pet implements Noisy {
  void makeNoise(){
    System.out.println("Meow.");
  }
}
class Fish extends Pet {
  void Move(int x, int y, int z){
    // Assume water level is at z=0. So myZ<=0 to live.
    myX+=x; myY+=Y; myZ+=Z;
    if (myZ>0) {myZ =0;}
  }
}
```

A number of the more common Java classes are actually interfaces. The basis for threads, Runnable, is an interface so you can make objects deep in your hierarchy into threads. Threads are covered in Chapter 7.

   This code created one interface, Noisy, a base class called Pet, and three subclasses: Fish, Cat, and Dog. The three subclasses inherit behavior from Pet. So if they don't contain a version of Move, they will simply use the basic version provided by Pet. The class Fish contains a slightly modified version that makes sure the Fish stays under z=0—an admittedly lame approximation of reality.

   Two of the three subclasses also implement the interface Noisy. This means that they must provide a method called makeNoise that takes no parameters and returns nothing. If this isn't there, then the compiler will flag the omission with an error.

Now, it is quite possible to execute code with variables of type `Noisy`. This variable could contain either a `Dog` or a `Cat`. If you defined x to be type `Noisy`, then you could execute `x.makeNoise()` and know that there would be an implementation of `makeNoise` available to run.

Variables

Variables can be defined in interfaces as well, but they aren't as "variable." They are, by definition, `final` and `static`. That is, they're constants even though the Java lexicon calls them `final static` variables. If you define a variable in the interface, then all classes that implement the interface will have access to these values.

Interfaces and the `extends` Keyword

The keyword `extends` also works with interfaces in a number of ways. You can, for instance, use `extends` to make one interface act like a subclass of another. For instance:

```
interface MathFacts{
  double pi=3.141592;
  double e=2.718;
}
interface ChemistryFacts extends MathFacts {
  double AvogadrosNum=6.023e23;
}
```

If you were to implement the interface `ChemistryFacts`, you would get definitions for all three variables pi, e, and `AvogadrosNum`. In this example, only variables are used to define constants in the interface. This is a common usage. Many programmers like to place all of their global constants in one location where they can be easily found and manipulated. You can easily add abstract method definitions as well and the behavior would also be the same.

The extends keyword will also work with classes that implement interfaces. If one class implements an interface, then the information will also be carried along to the subclasses. For instance:

```
class ChemBasics implements ChemistryFacts{
  // some basic code for converting units
  double PoundsToKilograms(double pounds){
    //...
  }
  // ...
}
class FullereneSynthesisSimulation extends ChemBasics {
  // more code
  // pi and e are defined here.
}
```

In this example, the variables from MathFacts were inherited by FullereneSynthesisSimulation from its superclass ChemBasics.

Other Interface Facts

A class can implement many different interfaces. You would do this with this format:

```
public class Foo extends Bar implements Moo, Boo, Hoo {
  // ...
}
```

You can use the keyword public to define a variable or method in an interface, but it does nothing. All methods and variables are automatically public. You cannot use the private or protected keywords to modify how they behave.

In summary, interfaces are a nice way to use multiple inheritance without encountering the confusion that can occur when there are many chains of interitance. If a method is not defined, it can only come from one chain of descendants. If variables don't come from this chain, then they're constants.

Packages

All of the examples in this book are very short programs that can easily fit in one file. If they rely upon outside classes, they usually use either the basic classes like String that are fundamental parts of the language, or they rely on large-scale inheritance from a class like `Applet`. So far, there has been no explicit way provided to organize your work into several files and reuse certain classes in several programs. The package is this solution.

One of the basic packages that comes with Java is `java.lang`. It includes the definitions for classes like `String` and `Integer`. When you compile a Java program, the structure of these classes is automatically imported. All other packages must be imported using an explicit `import` command. For instance, you may have noticed that many of the complete examples in the book come with the first line `import java.awt.*`. This tells the compiler to load the class, variable, and method definitions from all packages that begin with `java.awt`. These happen to be the classes for the Abstract Windowing Toolkit (AWT). These include classes like `Button.class` or `Canvas.class`.

The Java designers have created this in a big hierarchy that is mimicked by the directory structure. For instance, the class `Button.class` is found in the directory `awt` which in turn is in the directory `java`. This is usually found in `classes` directory where the compiler can locate it. The line `import net.*` would tell the compiler to load the definitions from the class files found in the directory `net`, which would probably be in the `classes` directory.

Information on the AWT can be found in Chapter 11.

Some have proposed making this hierarchy universal or at least as universal as the Internet. Each machine with an IP address would have its own `classes` directory that would contain all of its locally defined classes. The domain name of the computer would be flipped around and appended to the front of the hierarchy. So the line `import gov.whitehouse.socks.java.awt.*` would tell the compiler to go to the machine `socks.whitehouse.gov` and load the definitions in the directory `java.awt`. This is a neat idea because it will turn the Internet into a vast collection of programs.

Here's a list of the Java packages from the Java 1.0 distribution that you might want to import. More packages might be included in future distributions.

Naturally, there are some problems with such a global solution. What if one machine is off-line? Can you have a backup? What if there is a machine with the name `java.socks.whitehouse.gov`? Where does the domain name end and the Java stuff begin?

`java.lang` The basic classes for the wrappers like `Integer` and essential classes like `Array` or `String`. This is imported by the compiler automatically.

`java.applet` The classes for creating applets designed to be run by browsers like HotJava or Netscape. Almost all of the examples in this book import this class because they're set up to run as applets, not stand-alone code.

`java.io` The code for handling files, streams, and other input and output. These are often not allowed by the applet classes.

Descriptions of hash tables can be found on page 58 and vectors are described on page 56.
`java.util` The basic extra data structures like `Hashtable` or `Vector`.

`java.awt` Most of the classes from the Abstract Windowing Toolkit. You use this with the applet classes.

`java.awt.image` The image-loading and manipulation classes. Java includes many of these because they anticipate that the language will often be used to provide animation.

`java.awt.peer` These allow you to link up with native code.

`java.net` This is code for hooking up directly with the network to implement protocols like HTTP.

`sun.applet` This is a different package than for the applets that will run on browsers.

`sun.audio` Classes for loading sound files and playing them.

`sun.awt` Another version of the AWT. It includes `motif` files for motif-like windows.

`sun.misc`

`sun.net` A more complete set of network protocols. They include, for instance, FTP and NNTP protocols. Applets don't include this to keep things secure.

`sun.tools` A very complete set of tools that you can use to debug code or play with the guts of the language.

The packages from the `java` hierarchy are intended to be used on local browsers. The packages from the `sun` hierarchy might not be available in many cases. They include more powerful tools that aren't secure. You would use them if you were using Java as a system programming language.

Creating Your Own Packages

You're most likely going to want to create your own packages. This is very simple to do. All you need is to put the keyword package at the top of a file and put a name after it. The class definitions can follow. Here's an example:

```
package Ships;
public class Floating{
  //...
}
public class Barge extends Floating {
  // ...
}
public class Scull extends Floating {
  //...
}
public class Battleship extends Floating {
  //...
}
```

If you were to compile this code, you would end up with four files: Floating.class, Barge.class, Scull.class, and Battleship.class. If you wanted to import all of them, you would type import Ships.*.

The most important fact to remember about Java and packages is that the code is *dynamically linked*. That means that the compiler will load the information about a package being imported during the compilation. If anything is amiss or out of line, the compiler will raise an objection. Otherwise, it will produce final code that contains only dynamic links to the package.

What happens if you change the code in the package? Imagine that you created a class Titanic that imported the package Ships so it could extend Floating. After you compiled Titanic.java, the product Titanic.class would contain links to Floating.class, but it would *not* contain the code from Floating.class. If you went back and changed or modified Floating.class, then all of the calls would access these new methods. Things could easily break if Floating was changed.

This is the tradeoff of using dynamically linked languages. If new code was added to the class Floating without changing any of the methods that were originally called by the class `Titanic`, then nothing would happen. In fact, if you improved some of the old methods in `Floating` or fixed a bug, then these changes would be automatically included. This is often considered a feature. You just have to be aware that it can lead to a run-time failure.

Summary

Packages and interfaces are simple tools that are essential parts of a modern, full-sized programming language. They allow you to manage large projects by breaking up programs into smaller sections. Interfaces provide much of the flexibility of multiple inheritance without the confusion that can occur where there are many copies of methods floating around.

Here are the fundamental lessons of the chapter:

- Abstract methods allow you to specify an interface and require all descendant classes to implement it.

- Abstract methods save you the trouble of creating dummy methods at the top of the class hierarchy. This discipline is important.

- Interfaces are just collections of abstract methods.

- Each class can only inherit behavior from its one superclass, but it can implement many interfaces. This creates a clear chain of command.

- Packages place classes into groups so they can be imported with single statements.

- Classes in packages are grouped into subdirectories. This hierarchy is also part of the naming convention of packages.

Chapter 7

Threads

If you want to do several things at once, you can create multiple threads that will handle the tasks. This is a great idea if you want to do plenty of calculation at the same time that you're trying to access a distant Web site. If you're using only one thread and you try to access the Web site, the rest of the program will be held up waiting. Multi-threading adds efficiency.

Java is a *multi-threaded* language. That means that there may be several methods executing at once. You'll want to use this feature whenever you need to do several slow or intermittent tasks at once. Gathering information from the Internet is an ideal application for threads because you never know when the information is going to arrive. The Net can often delay data by several seconds. A multi-threaded applet can process something else while it is waiting for the information to arrive.

When you create a thread, you must specify how it will start, what it will do, and how it will stop. The easiest way to do this is to create a subclass of Thread. This is the base class for all threads and it offers several basic methods: start, stop, run, suspend, and resume. The first two, start and stop, are called when a thread begins and when it is ended. The method run defines just what the thread is supposed to do when it is started. The other two methods, suspend and resume, are used when the operating system might need to pause threads.

Once a thread is created and its `start` method is invoked, it will
run on its own until the run method terminates or something else calls
the `stop` method. If you create several threads and start them all, then
your code will be doing multiple things at once.

The depth of the multitasking illusion is different with different
operating systems. In some cases, there is no multitasking built into
the operating system, so a thread will only yield to another thread
if it explicitly makes the decision itself. In other cases, the illusion of
doing several things at once is faked by the operating system. You
just start up the threads and each of them seems to be executed in
parallel. In reality, the CPU is switching between threads quickly and
automatically. This makes it seem as if all threads are going at once. In
some extreme cases, there will be multiple CPUs and different threads
will be executed by different processors. This can often be slower if
there is substantial communication between threads.

Here's a quick example that shows how threads can work:

```
import java.applet.*;
class CountThread extends Thread {
  public String name="No Name";
  int count=0;
  public void run(){
  for (int i=0; i<5; i++){
    count++;
    System.out.println("Here in thread "+name+"
                       the count is:" + count);
    }
  }
}
public class ThreadTest1 extends Applet {
  CountThread t1,t2;
  public void init(){
    t1=new CountThread();
    t1.name = "Uno";
    t2 = new CountThread();
    t2.name = "Dos";
    t1.start();
    t2.start();
  }
}
```

The code creates two threads, t1 and t2, and starts them running. Each of them executes a simple loop that spits out its name and some local data. Here's what the output looks like:

```
Here in thread Uno the count is:1
Here in thread Dos the count is:1
Here in thread Uno the count is:2
Here in thread Dos the count is:2
Here in thread Uno the count is:3
Here in thread Dos the count is:3
Here in thread Uno the count is:4
Here in thread Dos the count is:4
Here in thread Uno the count is:5
Here in thread Dos the count is:5
```

The data from this example was generated on the Macintosh version of the Sun JDK 1.0. The threading is handled automatically by the operating system (MacOS 7.5.2) and the output of both threads is interleaved.

If your operating system doesn't offer multi-threading support or if you want to create applets that might run in that situation, you will want to use the method yield. If this is executed by a thread, it will immediately pause the current thread and give up control to the next one. You may also use this function in fully multi-threaded environments if you want to try to time when a method gives up control.

Operating systems without multi-threading will first spit out all of the data from thread t1 and then follow with the output for thread t2.

Pausing Threads with sleep

A related method is known as sleep. There are two versions. The first takes one parameter that specifies the number of milliseconds to sleep. Executing sleep(2000) will turn off that particular thread for two seconds. The second version takes two parameters. The first is the amount of rest time in milliseconds as before. The second parameter specifies an additional number of nanoseconds. So sleep(2,3) waits two milliseconds and 3 nanoseconds.

Here's an example using this command:

```
import java.applet.*;
class CountThread extends Thread {
  public String Sound="No Name";
```

```
  int count=0;
  int sleepAmount;
  public void run(){
    for (int i=0; i<5; i++){
      count++;
      System.out.println(count+":   "+Sound);
      try{this.sleep(sleepAmount);}
      catch (InterruptedException ForgetIt) {};
    }
  }
}
public class ThreadTest2 extends Applet {
  CountThread t1,t2,t3;
  public void init(){
    t1=new CountThread();
    t1.Sound = "Beep";
    t1.sleepAmount=5;
    t2 = new CountThread();
    t2.Sound = "Bop";
    t2.sleepAmount=19;
    t3=new CountThread();
    t3.Sound="Orp";
    t3.sleepAmount=220;
    t1.start();
    t2.start();
    t3.start();
  }
}
```

And here's the result:

```
1:   Beep
1:   Bop
1:   Orp
2:   Beep
2:   Bop
3:   Beep
3:   Bop
4:   Beep
2:   Orp
```

```
4:    Bop
5:    Beep
5:    Bop
3:    Orp
4:    Orp
5:    Orp
```

The slowest thread, the one that outputs `Orp`, ends up finishing last. Notice, however, that both `Beep` and `Bop` are just interleaved even though one process waits 5 milliseconds and the other waits 19. This is because the amount of sleep here is negligible. In both cases, more than 19 milliseconds have gone by before a thread gets its chance to execute again. If the machine were faster or the system load were lighter, then `Beep` would have finished significantly sooner than `Bop`.

The `sleep` command is encased in a `try` block to catch the possible exception `InterruptedException`. This exception will come to the thread if it is interrupted in the process of waiting. This exception is not a `RuntimeException` so you cannot ignore it. Plus, `run` is overriding a function from the class `Thread` so it can't be redefined to `throw` `InterruptedException`. You must catch it here.

Exceptions are described in detail in Chapter 8.

Stopping Threads

Most threads die whenever their `run` method stops executing. Each of the `run` methods defined in the versions of `CountThread` defined so far die on their own accord. They contain finite `for` loops.

There are many occasions, however, where you might want a thread to last indefinitely. The thread might be processing incoming data and reporting it on the screen whenever it arrives. A stock ticker or a news broadcast are two examples that someone might want to build. These require an infinite loop in the `run` routine. In these cases, stopping a thread is a job that is often necessary. To do this, you simply execute the `stop` method for a particular thread.

You must make an effort to stop your own threads and clean up after yourself. Although Java's garbage collection will recover memory that is no longer referenced, it is not so clever about threads. In fact, you'll need to be as careful with threads as you might have been with memory if you were programming in another language like C.

Here's an example of an infinite loop:

```java
import java.applet.*;
class AdvertisingThread extends Thread {
  public String Name="No Name";
  int count=0;
  int sleepAmount;
  public void run(){
    while (true){
      count++;
      System.out.println("No!"+ Name+" is the best.");
      try{this.sleep(sleepAmount);}
      catch (InterruptedException ForgetIt) {
        System.out.println("            Interrupted!");
      };
    }
  }
}
public class DieThread extends Applet {
  AdvertisingThread t1,t2;
  public void init(){
    t1=new AdvertisingThread();
    t1.Name = "Sudz R Uz";
    t1.sleepAmount=5;
    t2 = new AdvertisingThread();
    t2.Name = "Kleen Masheen";
    t2.sleepAmount=200;
    t1.start();
    t2.start();
  }
  public void destroy(){
    t1.stop();
    t2.stop();
  }
}
```

The full uses of the applet methods init *and* destroy *are described in Chapter 9.*

The threads from the class AdvertisingThread will repeat their message forever until they are stopped. This is done explicitly in the routine destroy. This is a routine that is called whenever an applet is killed. This is usually done when your browser removes an applet from its cache. Or if you're using an Applet Viewer, it will happen when the window is closed.

What happens if you don't execute `t1.stop()`? Won't Java's garbage collector simply notice that a thread has no references anymore? Not necessarily. Threads have a life of their own and they can haunt you if you don't kill them off. Stopping threads is especially necessary if you use the `Runnable` class described soon.

Occasionally, you might want to do something when the `stop` method is called. Imagine, for instance, that you wanted to use some of the background time to try to factor a large number. You might start up a thread in the background and have it continually try different factors. If it found the answer, it would report it immediately. But if it was stopped, the routine would merely report how far it got.

Unfortunately, this `stop` method is marked `final` in the definition of the class `Thread`. That means you can't substitute your own version for `stop` to close files, write final information, or report on progress. The solution is to watch for an exception with the name `ThreadDeath`. This is a `RuntimeException` that is thrown whenever something kills a thread. Here's what the code might look like:

`final` *methods can't be overridden in the subclass. See page 92.*

```
try{
  t1.start();
  while (test) {
  // Some code that could execute t1.stop().
  }
} catch (ThreadDeath e) {
  // do the clean up work.
  throw e
}
```

The cleanup work will only be executed when t1 dies. You must rethrow the exception so the thread will see its final end.

Threads will also end if some error is thrown and there is no `catch` waiting for it within the thread. For instance, you could divide by zero inadvertently. The thread will die and report this in an error box. Here's a bad example:

You can also use the `join` *command to wait for the death of a thread. See page 127.*

```
import java.applet.*;
class SuicideThread extends Thread {
  public String Name="No Name";
  int count=0;
  int sleepAmount;
  public void run(){
```

```
    while (true){
      count++;
      System.out.println(Name+":  "+count+" Value"+
                         (10/(6-count)));
      try{this.sleep(sleepAmount);}
      catch (InterruptedException ForgetIt) {
        System.out.println("          Interrupted!");};
    }
  }
}
public class DieThread2 extends Applet {
  SuicideThread t1,t2;
  public void init(){
    t1=new SuicideThread();
    t1.Name = "Bob";
    t1.sleepAmount=5;
    t2 = new SuicideThread();
    t2.Name = "John";
    t2.sleepAmount=200;
    t1.start();
    t2.start();
  }
  public void destroy(){
    t1.stop();
    t2.stop();
  }
}
```

Here's what is printed out before the crash:

```
Bob:   1 Value2
John:  1 Value2
Bob:   2 Value2
Bob:   3 Value3
Bob:   4 Value5
John:  2 Value2
Bob:   5 Value10
John:  3 Value3
John:  4 Value5
John:  5 Value10
```

And here is what the hapless user would see:

```
java.lang.ArithmeticException: / by zero
  at SuicideThread.run(DieThread2.java)
java.lang.ArithmeticException: / by zero
  at SuicideThread.run(DieThread2.java)
```

Notice that John continued to run after Bob died. One thread died, but the other kept on living. This can be a good feature if you're relying upon a fault-tolerant environment to contain your errors. But it can also introduce strange errors. Imagine that Bob was really a thread responsible for watching an engine on a plane and ringing a loud bell if the engine failed. If that thread failed because of some divide-by-zero function, then no one would even notice that the thread was dead. The rest of the threads would continue to function as if nothing had happened. This is why you should strive to keep everything in good repair by catching exceptions and anticipating problems like this.

The Runnable **Class**

Another technique for creating a thread is to have a certain class implement the class Runnable. Most of the functionality for a thread is hidden in this class. Thread is just a subclass of Object that implements Runnable. You can do the same thing with your own class if you choose.

The interface for Runnable is simple. It just contains the method run. You must provide a definition for this. It does not contain any information, however, about the other methods described above. There is no provision for start or stop. You must provide them yourself.

Another confusing part of using the Runnable interface is that you must start up a different thread that runs the object. One constructor for the class Thread takes an object from the Runnable class as a parameter. It will substitute the run function in this class as its own in much the same way that some birds will raise the young of another if the egg happens to land in their nest.

Here's an example:

```
import java.applet.*;
class CountThread implements Runnable {
  public String Sound="No Name";
```

```
    int count=0;
    int sleepAmount;
    public void run(){
      for (int i=0; i<9; i++){
        count++;
        System.out.println(count+":   "+Sound);
        try{Thread.sleep(sleepAmount);}
        catch (InterruptedException ForgetIt) {
          System.out.println("           Interrupted!");};
      }
    }
}
public class ThreadTest3 extends Applet {
  CountThread t1,t2;
  public void init(){
    t1=new CountThread();
    t1.Sound = "Beep";
    t1.sleepAmount=5;
    t2 = new CountThread();
    t2.Sound = "Bop";
    t2.sleepAmount=200;
    new Thread(t1).start();
    new Thread(t2).start();
  }
}
```

The output should be familiar:

```
1:  Beep
1:  Bop
2:  Beep
3:  Beep
4:  Beep
2:  Bop
5:  Beep
6:  Beep
3:  Bop
7:  Beep
8:  Beep
9:  Beep
```

```
4:   Bop
5:   Bop
6:   Bop
7:   Bop
8:   Bop
9:   Bop
```

Although the structure of this class ThreadTest3 is very similar to the structure of ThreadTest2 or ThreadTest1, there are important differences in the syntax. First, notice that the new objects from the new version of CountThread can't be started on their own. A new thread needs to be started and passed the objects t1 or t2 to run as their own.

In this case, there is no reference kept to the new threads. They're not stored anywhere so you can't issue a stop command later. This doesn't mean that they're going to be killed in a garbage collection run. In fact, threads can live for a long time past their creator. This example, for instance, uses an init method from an Applet class as its main function. When the applet is killed, the threads can still live on. I tried to kill these threads by killing the applet and they kept popping back to life. The stdout window would keep appearing.

You might also have noticed that this version of CountThread uses the command Thread.sleep instead of this.sleep to start the pause. It turns out that sleep is a static method that is applied to whichever thread is currently running. It is *not* a regular method. This allows you to use it when you implement Runnable instead of creating a subclass of Thread.

Deadlocking Threads

One of the most famous examples in computer science system theory is the story of the dining philosophers. The story goes that five philosophers are eating dinner at a round table at a Chinese restaurant. For some strange reason, the restaurant has only placed one chopstick to the right of each philosopher. That is to say, there are five chopsticks and five philosophers arranged in a circle around the table, alternating philosopher, chopstick, philosopher, chopstick.

In order to eat, the philosophers must place hygienic considerations aside and cooperate by sharing chopsticks. A philosopher can eat if the chopstick to the left and the chopstick to the right are free. They grab both, eat for a bit and then release them. The example is used in many system design classes to show adequate distribution of resources among competing processes.

It turns out that the job can be difficult. Here's an example of some code that just doesn't work:

```java
import java.applet.*;
class Chopstick{
  boolean Free;
    //Set to be true if it is available.
  Chopstick(){
    Free = true;
  }
  public boolean Grab(){
    if (Free) {
      Free = false;
      return true;}
    else {
      return false;
    }
  }
  public void Release(){Free = true;
  }
}
class Philosopher extends Thread {
  Chopstick left,right;
  String Name;
  boolean gotLeft = false;
  boolean gotRight = false;
  Philosopher(Chopstick l, Chopstick r){
    super();
    left = l;
    right = r;
  }
  public void run(){
    Long amount;
    //this.sleep(Math.random()*10000);
      // Wait a random amount.
    while (true) {
```

```
      if (left.Grab()) {
        gotLeft = true;
        yield();
      };
      if (gotLeft && right.Grab()) {
          gotRight = true;
          System.out.println(Name+ " is eating!");
          try {this.sleep((int)(Math.random()*20000));}
          catch (InterruptedException e) {};
          left.Release();
          right.Release();
          gotLeft = false;
          gotRight = false;
          System.out.println(Name+ " has stopped
                              eating.");
          try {this.sleep((int)(Math.random()*20000));}
          catch (InterruptedException e) {};
            // Wait for more food.
        }
      else {
        System.out.println(Name + " can't get both
                            chopsticks.");
      }
    }
  }
}
public class Dining extends Applet {
  Chopstick c1,c2,c3,c4,c5;
  Philosopher p1,p2,p3,p4,p5;
  public void init(){
    c1 = new Chopstick();
    c2 = new Chopstick();
    c3 = new Chopstick();
    c4 = new Chopstick();
    c5 = new Chopstick();
    p1 = new Philosopher(c1,c2);
    p1.Name = "Socrates";
    p2 = new Philosopher(c2,c3);
    p2.Name = "Kurt Cobain";
    p3 = new Philosopher(c3,c4);
```

```
    p3.Name = "Jim Morrison";
    p4 = new Philosopher(c4,c5);
    p4.Name = "Emanuel Kant";
    p5 = new Philosopher(c5,c1);
    p5.Name = "Jeremy Bentham";
    p1.start();
    p2.start();
    p3.start();
    p4.start();
    p5.start();
  }
  public void destroy(){
    p1.stop();
    p2.stop();
    p3.stop();
    p4.stop();
    p5.stop();
  }
}
```

In this case, no one can eat. Each philosopher quickly tries to grab the chopstick to their left. By the time they get a chance to go for the chopstick on their right, their neighbor has it. This is known as a *deadlock*.

In this example, the yield command ensures that each of the five threads will deadlock each time because whenever it is encountered, the thread passes control on to the next available thread. If the yield command is not there, several of the philosophers might successfully grab their right chopstick before their neighbor gets it. The distribution of cycles between the multiple threads can often be somewhat random when system chores get in the way. This would ruin the example for teaching purposes.

The example is important because it is quite possible that deadlocks can only occur in strange situations. For instance, the five philosophers here might only deadlock one out of a million times without the yield commands in place. But that one chance will happen eventually. If you are going to write Java code that uses multiple threads, you may find that it locks up occasionally. It is often because of a problem like this.

Here's a solution for the run routine that looks better:

```
public void run(){
    Long amount;
    while (true) {
      if (left.Free && right.Free){
          ignore = left.Grab();
          ignore = right.Grab();
           System.out.println(Name+ " is eating!");
          try {this.sleep((int)(Math.random()*20000));}
          catch (InterruptedException e) {};
          left.Release();
          right.Release();
           System.out.println(Name+ " has stopped
                          eating.");
          try {this.sleep((int)(Math.random()*20000));}
          catch (InterruptedException e) {};
             // Wait for more food.
      }
      else {
        System.out.println(Name + " can't get both
                        chopsticks.");
      }
    }
  }
```

In this example, each philosopher tests to see if both the `left` and `right` chopstick are free. If they are, then it immediately Grabs both. This may seem like a better solution, but it could still deadlock. Imagine the chance occurrence where each thread starts running and gets three lines before it is preempted by the scheduler. That is, each of the five philosopher threads are paused between when they grab the left chopstick and when they go for the right. This is much less likely than the case above, but it could still happen. These possiblities, however small, must be anticipated because many crucial computer systems execute code like this billions if not trillions of times. Any weird case will happen eventually. Cutting down the steps between when both chopsticks are grabbed may help matters, but it won't get rid of the problem entirely. The `synchronized` modifier is the only solution.

The synchronized Keyword

The synchronized keyword is used to tell the Java system to run a method from beginning to end without allowing another method to be processed at the same time. You would use it to prevent some of the problems like the ones that confront the dining philosophers. You might, for instance, create a synchronized method that would check both chopsticks and grab them if they're both available. Java would run this code without letting another method get any time to grab at the chopsticks. This would prevent the deadlock.

Here's a new version of the run method from the Philosopher class that uses a synchronized method called GrabSticks:

```
public synchronized boolean GrabSticks(){
  // Goes after both sticks. Returns true if successful.
  boolean answer = false;
  if (left.Grab()){
    gotLeft = true;
    if (right.Grab()) {
      gotRight = true;
      answer = true;
    } else {
      left.Release();
      gotLeft = false;
    };
  };
  return answer;
}
public void run(){
  Long amount;
  while (true) {
    if (GrabSticks()){
        System.out.println(Name+ " is eating!");
        try this.sleep((int)(Math.random()*20000));
        catch (InterruptedException e) ;
        left.Release();
        right.Release();
        gotLeft = false;
        gotRight = false;
        System.out.println(Name+ " has stopped
```

```
                              eating.");
        try {this.sleep((int)(Math.random()*20000));}
        catch (InterruptedException e) {};
          // Wait for more food.
      }
    else {
      System.out.println(Name + " can't get both
                         chopsticks.");
    }
  }
}
```

The success of this system can be seen in the output. The five philosophers effectively share the chopsticks without deadlocking and each of them gets a chance to eat.

The GrabSticks routine is short and does not do any other extraneous work. This is a good idea because all other threads are stopped while this method executes. The shorter it can be, the better. If you need to do a substantial amount of work that must be synchronized, you will probably be in better shape if you can break it into short routines. This will ensure that all threads will get some time.

Endless loops in synchronized *routines can crash the entire program. Avoid them.*

synchronized **Blocks of Code**

The synchronized keyword is not limited to methods. In fact, you can create a block of code that grabs complete control of some variable while it executes. This approach can be more graceful than designating an entire method as synchronized. To do this, you simply type the keyword synchronized, place the protected variable after it in parentheses, and follow that with a block of code delineated with curly brackets. If any other method tries to access that particular variable while that block of code is executing, the other method will be stopped until the block is finished.

Here's another version of the run method from the Birder class as an example. The program simulates a database and shows how data can be corrupted when two threads try to access it. The synchronized keyword here is intended to prevent incorrect data from being reported.

```
import java.applet.*;
class Bird {
  long totalWeight;
    // Total number of grams of all samples found.
  long samplesFound;
    // How many are found.
  String name;
  Bird(String n){
    name = n;
    totalWeight = 0;
    samplesFound = 0;
  }
}
class Birder extends Thread{
  Bird SearchList[] = new Bird[3];
    // Scan these.
  Birder( Bird a,Bird b, Bird c){
    super();
    SearchList[0]=a;
    SearchList[1]=b;
    SearchList[2]=c;
  }
  public void run(){
    int weight;
    int numb;
    float average;
    while (true){
      // Search for a random bird. Perhaps by looking
      // through a database.
      // Fake it through random numbers.
      numb=(int)(3 * Math.random());
      weight = (int)(20 * Math.random());
      synchronized(SearchList[numb]){
        SearchList[numb].samplesFound++;
        SearchList[numb].totalWeight+=weight;
        average=SearchList[numb].totalWeight
          /SearchList[numb].samplesFound;
        System.out.println("The Average for"
          +SearchList[numb].name+ " is "+average);
      }
```

```
    }
  }
}
public class BirdBrain extends Applet{
  Bird b1,b2,b3,b4,b5;
  Birder q1,q2,q3,q4,q5;
  public void init(){
    b1 = new Bird("Oriole");
    b2 = new Bird("Bobwhite");
    b3 = new Bird("Sparrow");
    b4 = new Bird("Eagle");
    b5 = new Bird("Falcon");
    q1=new Birder(b1,b2,b5);
    q2=new Birder(b4,b2,b3);
    q3=new Birder(b1,b5,b3);
    q4=new Birder(b1,b4,b5);
    q5=new Birder(b4,b2,b3);
    q1.start();
    q2.start();
    q3.start();
    q4.start();
    q5.start();
  }
  public void destroy(){
    q1.stop();
    q2.stop();
    q3.stop();
    q4.stop();
    q5.stop();
  }
}
```

This example simulates using several threads to search for data. You might write a database like this if you were trying to do a study of multiple databases that could only be accessed over the Net. Imagine, for instance, that five ornithologists keep logs of birds they've observed in some network-accessible form. You want to compute the average weights of these different birds by combining the results from all five logs. Naturally, polling these remote databases over the network can be quite slow so you decide to use threads to do the work. Instead of actually implementing this, a random number generator simulates the process of locating a bird and its weight.

These multiple threads won't cause a deadlock like the case of the dining philosophers, but weird errors can creep into the results if the program ignores the possibility that two threads will access the same bird at the same time. In this particular case, there is no danger that the final results will be corrupted. The run method will only add the new weight into the total and increment the total number of samples. If two run methods try to change the same Bird, it doesn't really matter in what order these additions occur. The end result is still the same because addition is commutative.

But the computation of average is important. Imagine this sequence of commands:

```
q1 increments b1.samplesFound
q1 increments b1.totalWeight
q2 increments b1.samplesFound
q1 computes average and prints it out
q2 increments b1.totalWeight
q2 computes average and prints it out
```

This sequence would be possible without the synchronized keyword protecting the Bird. The first value of average reported would be wrong because q2 would have incremented samplesFound without adding in the additional weight.

You could have used a synchronized *method to solve this as well.*

The synchronized keyword prevents any other method from altering SearchList[numb] while another method is operating in these blocks. You'll want to use this keyword in similar situations when you have multiple threads manipulating data. This example is somewhat innocuous. The final data is not corrupted. Only the updates can be corrupted. This is often not the case. It should be easy to imagine cases where two different threads can produce dangerous combinations of data if their work is interleaved.

Threads and Priorities

If you write programs that use many threads, there are going to be instances when you want to control the amount of time given to each thread. You can do this yourself using the yield command, but you can't rely upon Java to support any complicated scheme for parceling out time. In fact, the current versions of the language only offer half a solution that is not very precise about how it works. You can set the *priority* of a thread, but you can't be certain how different implementations of Java will treat this priority.

The priority of a thread is a number that ranges between 1 and 10. Each thread also has three variables: MIN_PRIORITY, NORM_PRIORITY, and MAX_PRIORITY. They set the smallest allowed priority, the normal priority, and the largest allowed priority for a particular thread. You can adjust these, but they must remain consistent, that is, MIN_PRIORITY $\leq$ NORM_PRIORITY $\leq$ MAX_PRIORITY.

You can change the priority of a thread with the command setPriority. This call must pass it an integer that satisfies the constraints of the minimum and maximum priorities. If you fail, this will throw an IllegalArgumentException. Another command, getPriority, will return the priority of a thread.

In general, higher priority threads get precedence over the lower priority threads until a yield or a sleep command is called. A better description cannot be generated until more Java implementations are well known and available.

Juggling Threads

In each of the previous examples, threads have been used to control multiple processes that might work at the same time. Both the Philosopher and the Birder operated independently of each other. The synchronized keyword was used to make sure they didn't step on each other's toes.

Threads can also interact directly. They can send messages to each other by calling each other's methods. They can interrupt another when one is sleeping. If one thread is dying, another can wait for this to happen. These techniques can give you the power to control very complicated processes, but they can also introduce even more headaches.

The sleep and interrupt Commands

The simplest technique is to use the sleep command to pause a thread while waiting for another thread to interrupt this sleep. The sleep command throws the InterruptedException whenever such an interrupt occurs. If you catch this exception, you can do the work that needed to wait for the interruption. This is a good way to juggle different tasks.

The `join` Command

There are cases when you want one thread to wait for another to finish running. The `join` method will do this. If you call `t.join()`, execution will pause until `t` finally dies. You can pass in either one or two parameters in much the same way as the function `sleep`. The commands look like this:

```
public final synchronized void join(long millis)
    throws InterruptedException
public final synchronized void join(long millis, int nanos)
    throws InterruptedException
public final void join() throws InterruptedException
```

Each of these functions will throw an `InterruptedException` if something interrupts during the waiting.

Daemon Threads

The UNIX world is filled with Daemons. The term is used to refer to background system processes.

Some threads are only used for background processing; these are called *Daemon* threads. Java offers a method for the class of `Thread` known as `setDaemon`. This takes a boolean value. If you pass it `true`, then the thread is marked as a Daemon.

This makes a difference when an applet or an application is about to terminate. This happens when all of the non-Daemon threads are completed. This saves you the trouble of keeping track of these extra threads you might spawn to handle background work.

The routine `isDaemon` returns a boolean identifying the status of a `Thread`. Also, if you try to change the Daemon status of a thread while it is active, you will get an `IllegalThreadStateException`.

Groups of Threads

If you create many different threads, you might find yourself getting somewhat confused. Java also offers a class called `ThreadGroup` that can be used to keep the threads straight. These ThreadGroups can contain either Threads or other ThreadGroups piled in hierarchies.

The standard Thread constructor will assign a new Thread to the currently operating ThreadGroup. When Java code starts up, the base ThreadGroup is set to be main. Applets can create more ThreadGroups from time to time. If you're not going to create many threads, you can simply leave your threads in this group.

If you want a Thread to belong to a particular ThreadGroup, then you must specify this when it is constructed. There are versions of the Thread constructor that take a ThreadGroup as a parameter. Once this is set, it can't be changed.

The threads in a group can be suspended and resumed as a group using the commands suspend and resume. If you want to permanently stop all threads in a group, then stop will accomplish this. The destroy command should only be used as a last resort because it simply trashes all of the information about all of the threads in a group. This may be necessary if the stop command doesn't do the job. You can also poll and adjust the maximum priority for all of the threads in the group with the commands getMaxPriority and setMaxPriority.

One handy feature of a ThreadGroup is the ability to define a method known as uncaughtException. If you remember, a thread will die if it generates an Exception that isn't caught. If this happens, the method uncaughtException will be invoked with the thread and the exception passed as parameters. You can use this to clean up from a random error, but it may be unwise to use this as a patch for a bad piece of code.

You should be aware that the API documentation warns that setMaxPriority *will not affect threads in the group that might already have a higher priority. It only affects newly created threads.*

If you need to manipulate all of the threads in a group, you can get an array filled with them by executing the command enumerate. There are two different versions of this method. One simply takes an array of Thread as a parameter and fills it up. You must make sure that the array is large enough to hold all of the threads. The activeCount command will provide an *estimate* of this size. The API clearly states that this is an estimate—a term that should be frightening to programmers. The second version takes a boolean parameter that controls the recursion of the process. If multiple ThreadGroups are in a hierarchy, then this boolean can be used to start or stop recursion.

There are also two additional versions of enumerate that are used to fill an array of ThreadGroup. One takes just the array. The other takes an additional boolean that controls the recursion. activeGroupCount is used to get an estimate of the number of ThreadGroups in a ThreadGroup.

Finally, there are two commands to help you orient yourself when scanning through these groups of threads. getParent will return the parent of a group. The method parentOf takes another ThreadGroup and returns true if one ThreadGroup is "equal to or is the parent of" another ThreadGroup.

Thread Constructors

There are a number of different constructors for the Thread class. Here they are:

```
public Thread()
public Thread(Runnable target)
public Thread(ThreadGroup group,
              Runnable target)
public Thread(String name)
public Thread(ThreadGroup group,
              String name)
public Thread(Runnable target,
              String name)
public Thread(ThreadGroup group,
              Runnable target,
              String name)
```

Summary

Many Java programmers will never need to master multi-threaded applications that might deadlock. Most applets will be small, self-contained objects that don't do much except display some cool information. One or two threads will probably handle all of the work that needs to be done. Even in these situations, it is important to recognize the fundamental lessons about how multi-threaded systems can create sneaky bugs when they grab for the same resources. Programmers who want to build complicated systems that run many different threads must be sure to watch for these problems.

Here are the basic lessons from this chapter:

- A thread is an object with methods for starting, stopping and running.

- When a thread starts, it executes its run method until this method finishes. Then the thread ends.

- Threads can be started and stopped by code running in other threads—within the security limits.

- Thread groups are used to manage large groups of threads as well as to enforce security features. Threads cannot access threads in their parent group.

- The synchronized keyword is used to prevent two threads from interfering. You use it when you've got global data that might be affected. You can also use it to prevent deadlocks.

- Programmers using threads must be wary of deadlocks. They can occur when threads try to grab for the same resources.

Chapter 8

Exceptions

This chapter describes Java's error-handling mechanism, which is contained in a class called exceptions. *For instance, you might define an exception called* My MissingFileException *and whenever a file-opening routine can't find the file, it will "throw" this exception. You can also define another part of the program to "catch" it. This allows you to handle errors and unwind the program gracefully to fix them.*

Many computer programs generate errors from time to time. When the programs were simple data processing tools that took input and returned some form of text output, it was relatively easy to handle errors. You simply printed an error message. The invention of graphical user interfaces, however, made this simple strategy difficult and unwieldy. You might divide by zero in one corner of the code, but to open a dialog box announcing the error, you must move to another part of the code.

This problem is even greater if you're programming with an object-oriented toolkit. If you're extending a popular or commonly defined collection of objects, then you need to fit into the existing hierarchy. You can't simply create dialog boxes or change data structures in any old place. This is one reason why exceptions are used in Java and other toolkits.

Exceptions are just a mixture of error names and a toteboard that
is used to keep track of where to go when an error is found. In Java,
they're a class of objects and some methods used to manipulate them.
Two commands, try and catch, tell Java to record a particular type
of error on the toteboard with a place to go when it is found. Another
command, throw, announces that an error of a particular type was
found. Java checks the toteboard and finds the right place to jump to
immediately.

Here's a simple example of how try and catch work:

```
int z;
try {
  s =  "5agi42";
  z =  Integer.parseInt(s,10);
  System.out.println("I won't get printed.");
} catch (Exception e){
  System.out.println("An exception was thrown here.");
}
```

When this code is executed, the code for the Integer constructor
will try to create an integer out of the string "5agi42" and it will fail.
So it *throws* an exception, in this case the exception with the name
NumberFormatException. The catch command will immediately begin executing. "An exception was thrown here." will be printed,
not "I won't get printed."

The exception code can unwind exceptions over a deep nest of
calls. Here's an example:

```
import java.applet.*;
import java.lang.*;
public class ExceptionTest1 extends Applet{
void CauseTrouble(){
  int z;
  String s="Hoo";
  z = Integer.parseInt(s,10);
}
void LookForTrouble(){
  CauseTrouble();
  System.out.println("No trouble found in
                     LookForTrouble.");
}
```

```
public void init(){
  try {
    LookForTrouble();
    System.out.println("No trouble found here.");
  } catch (Exception e) {
    System.out.println("Found some trouble here.");
  }
    LookForTrouble();
      // This call generates an error.
}
}
```

The output for this is one line from the exception handling catch routine:

```
Found some trouble here.
```

That was generated by the first call to LookForTrouble made inside of the try brackets. When that execution was unwound by the error, the place to go to was erased. The second call, however, was made with no protection so it generated an error that was sent out of the standard error channel. Here's what the output looks like:

```
java.lang.NumberFormatException: Hoo
  at java.lang.Integer.parseInt(Integer.java:141)
  at ExceptionTest1.CauseTrouble(ExceptionTest1.java)
  at ExceptionTest1.LookForTrouble(ExceptionTest1.java)
  at ExceptionTest1.init(ExceptionTest1.java)
  at sun.applet.AppletPanel.run(AppletPanel.java:243)
  at java.lang.Thread.run(Thread.java:289)
```

The code returns the entire calling chain with the information that will allow you to pinpoint the problem. You could solve this one by adding an additional pair of try and catch routines to grab the error. *Note:* This solution can be dangerous if you use it as an all-purpose error-solver. If errors are caused by fundamental problems with the architecture of the program, you will only make it worse by trying to patch errors with a try and catch pair. These routines could start catching errors at odd times and in odd places.

Exception handling can create more bugs than it solves if you use it capriciously.

The catch routines can be much more specific. This allows you to tailor to the needs of the code. The syntax is structured something like a list of if-then-else clauses. The first exception to match is chosen. Here's an example:

```
try{
  LookForTrouble();
} catch (ArithmeticException e) {
  System.out.println("There was problem with the
                      arithmetic.");
} catch (NumberFormatException e) {
  System.out.println("The number wasn't formatted
                      correctly.");
} catch (Exception e) {
  System.out.println("Exception caught at last possible
                      moment.");
}
```

In this example, there are three layers of catch statements looking for errors. The first grabs all exceptions from the class Arithmetic Exception, the second one snags the ones from the class NumberFormat Exception, and the third pulls down all exceptions from the base class, Exception. If the same version of LookForTrouble is used again, then a NumberFormatException will be generated and grabbed by the second catch statement. The output will be "The number wasn't formatted correctly."

There is one additional part to the catch line. If you want to define a block of code to execute after all of the exception handling is finished, you use a finally clause as the last part of a catch chain. This code is always executed. You might use it, for instance, to close a file that was opened in the try block. If the file is there, then no exception will be generated and the file must be closed. If the file isn't there or some exception was generated when the data turned out to be the wrong type, it would still be necessary to close the file. Here's a quick example:

```
try{
  LookForTrouble();
} catch (ArithmeticException e) {
  System.out.println("There was problem with the
                      arithmetic.");
} catch (NumberFormatException e) {
```

```
    System.out.println("The number wasn't formatted
                        correctly.");
} catch (Exception e) {
    System.out.println("Exception caught at last possible
                        moment.");
} finally {
    System.out.println("I'm always printed."}
```

Throwing Your Own Exceptions

The try and catch keywords are used to handle exceptions, and the examples in the first part of the chapter were generated by Java's internal classes. You will want to include try clauses around many parts of your code that call these internal mechanisms. But you may often find yourself in a position to generate your own exceptions. These might be some of the basic exceptions defined for Java or they might be special subclasses of Exception that you create for your own purposes.

Here's an example of LookForTrouble:

```
void LookForTrouble() throws NumberFormatException{
  String s = "Trouble";
  int z = 0;
  if (s.equals("Trouble")){
    throw new NumberFormatException();
  } else {
    z = Integer.parseInt(s,10);
  }
}
```

It should be obvious from this example that NumberFormatException and the throw command are calling the constructor to create a new object. This object can also include any amount of data that might be necessary to help you debug the program or recover from the problem.

Also note that the definition line for LookForTrouble includes the text throws NumberFormatException. That tells the compiler to watch for this type of exception when leaving the method. This will allow it to optimize the solution of problems if they occur.

Here's an example of your own type of exception:

```
class PetesException extends Exception{
  String time;
    //Holds the time of the exception.
  Obj ProblemObject;
    // What went wrong?
}
```

You might throw such an exception with code like this:

```
PetesException t = new PetesException();
t.time = "Right now!";
t.ProblemObject = pt;
throw t;
```

When it is finally caught, this information will travel with the exception, like this:

```
try {
  // ...
} catch (PetesException e) {
  System.out.println("Error happened at:"+e.time);
}
```

The throws keyword

The throws keyword can be a bit tricky. Not all exceptions are alike. There are three major exception classes: Error, Exception, and RuntimeException. Each is used in a different context. The Error class contains a set of exceptions that are generated during the compilation and linking of the program. For instance, one of these is known as ClassCircularityError and emerges when two classes are found that extend each other. Most Errors can't be handled by most programmers of Java so you can ignore them in most cases.

The difference between the class Exception and its subclass RuntimeException is more subtle. Both are used throughout many different programs, but they designate different types of exceptions. Some regular Exceptions include NoSuchMethodException and IllegalAccessException. These are pretty serious language-level problems. The class of RuntimeException, on the other hand, contains more prosaic versions that may often occur through no fault of the programmer. Some of these include NullPointerException, IndexOutOfBoundsException, or ArithmeticException. You may find that you're checking for these on a fairly regular basis.

The major difference between Exception and RuntimeException is that you must explicitly create the control flow for members of Exception by using the keyword throws. If a method is going to generate a certain method without handling it, then you must indicate this in the keyword. Members of RuntimeException, on the other hand, are more common, so they have been exempted from this requirement.

The self-defined exception, PetesException, is a subclass of Exception. That means that it must either be explicitly caught by a method or the method must indicate that it throws the exception. Here's an example:

```
import java.applet.*;
import java.lang.*;
class PetesException extends Exception{
  String time;
    //Holds the time of the exception.
  Object ProblemObject;
    // What went wrong?
}
public class ExceptionTest2 extends Applet{
void CauseTrouble() throws PetesException{
  int z;
  String s="Hoo";
  PetesException t = new PetesException();
  t.time = "Right now!";
  t.ProblemObject = null; // For now.
  throw t;
}
void LookForTrouble() throws PetesException{
  CauseTrouble();
  System.out.println("No trouble found in
                    LookForTrouble.");
}
public void init(){
```

```
   try {
     LookForTrouble();
     System.out.println("No trouble found here.");
   } catch (PetesException e) {
     System.out.println("Trouble found at time: "+e.time);
   } catch (Exception e) {
     System.out.println("Found some trouble here.");
   }
     // LookForTrouble(); // Can't compile with this here.
}
}
```

Both CauseTrouble and LookForTrouble have the words throws
PetesException in the first line of their definition. The compiler warns
of errors if they're not there. The method init, on the other hand, does
not need this label in its first line because it catches the exception (in
this case twice). The second call to LookForTrouble would not compile
unless this tag line is added.

The compiler is forcing you to explicitly deal with your errors and
provide a solid, predetermined chain from their creation to the place
where they're finally resolved. This feature should prevent exceptions
from flying all about the program.

Of course, you should immediately realize that you can get around
the problem in two ways. The first is to make your exception a subclass
of RuntimeException. That means it inherits all of its behavior from
this class including its ability to work without the word throws. You
may be forced to do this if you want to toss an error across a large,
strange class hierarchy dictated by someone else.

For instance, you could not merely create a class like this:

```
class MyInteger extends Integer {
  public String toString() throws PetesException
                                  CauseTrouble();
    return "None of your business.";
  }
// ...
}
```

This class would fail to compile. The definition of toString is
found in the superclass, Integer, and it can't be made more complicated in a subclass. You might create some object from class MyInteger

and pass it to some method that is looking for an object from `Integer`. This is entirely legal. But if that method tries to invoke `toString`, it might inadvertently create a `PetesException` that it wasn't expecting. Suddenly, exceptions are flying everywhere.

Another solution is to bracket a problematic method call with a blank `try` and `catch` pair:

```
try{
  CauseTrouble();
} catch (Exception e) {
// do nothing
}
```

This is also dangerous to do and you should avoid it unless you're sure that you simply want to ignore a particular type of exception.

Rethrowing Exceptions

Once you catch an exception, you can rethrow it. You might want to do this if the exception needs to be dealt with further up the chain. Here's an example:

```
public void CheckTime () throws PetesException{
  try {
    LookForTrouble();
  } catch (PetesException e) {
    if (e.time.equal("Right Now!"))
      throw e;
    else {
      // Do nothing as it is an old exception.
    }
  }
}
```

This `catch` statement will have a crack at the exception generated by `CauseTrouble` and it will throw it on if it happens to come with the time string set to `Right Now!`. Otherwise the exception will die at this location. The method must officially throw `PetesException` because it is rethrowing it.

Major Run-time Errors

Here are some of the major run-time errors defined by Java and some
suggestions for when to worry about them. None of them must be
explicitly trapped by including the throws keyword in the definition
of a method.

ArithmeticException A divide-by-zero error is the most common
    type of this exception.

ArrayStoreException If you try to store an object of the wrong type
    to an array, this exception will arise. This may not be caught by
    the compiler because it is possible for you to store objects in more
    generically typed variables. For instance, this should generate an
    error:

```
void Test (){
   Integer i;
   Float[] f = new Float[5];
   Object k;
   i = new Integer(3);
   k = (Object) i;
   f[1] = k;
}
```

ClassCastException When you try to cast an object into the wrong
    class, you'll get this exception. This arises at run time because
    you're allowed to cast objects into their superclass and then cast
    them back. Here's an example that goes awry:

```
void Test (){
   Integer i;
   Float j;
   Number n;
   i = new Integer(3);
   j = new Float(3.3f);
   n = i;
   System.out.println(n.toString());
   i = n;
   n= j;
```

```
    System.out.println(n.toString());
    i = n; //ERROR HERE.
}
```

In the first instance, you could recast n into i because the object was from the class `Integer`. In the second case, you couldn't because it came from `Float`.

`EmptyStackException` When a stack is empty, this is raised. Used with the `Stack` class.

Stacks are described on page 230.

`IllegalArgumentException` Methods that don't like the data in their arguments will throw these exceptions. For instance, `setPriority`, a method used to set the priority of a thread, will return this exception if you pass it a value between the minimum and maximum allowable priority. This changes at run time.

`IllegalThreadStateException` If you do something wrong with a thread, then this emerges. For instance, executing a thread's `start` method twice will trigger this one. Also calling `countStackFrames` while a thread is still running will set this off. A thread must be stopped.

`NumberFormatException` This is caused whenever you ask one of the numerical objects to try to parse some data. For instance, it is raised if you try to execute the static method `Integer.parseInt` (`"a93KK"`).

`IllegalMonitorStateException` Monitors are used to stop conflicts on synchronized variables. Problems with these states generate this error.

`IndexOutOfBoundsException` If an index is out of bounds, you'll have to deal with this. This is just a superclass for the next two exceptions.

`ArrayIndexOutOfBoundsException` If an array index is out of bounds, you'll have to deal with this.

`StringIndexOutOfBoundsException` If a string index is out of bounds, you'll have to deal with this.

NegativeArraySizeException If you try to create an array using a variable that sets its size and this variable happens to be negative, then catch this one.

NullPointerException If you don't initialize some object pointers, you'll be stuck with this exception.

SecurityException This is a generic warning of a security problem. You'll find it invoked in the classes SecurityManager, Thread, and ThreadGroup. Most of the exceptions will occur in calls to methods in SecurityManager. This class is used to load other classes and you can subclass it if you want to add additional security features.

Plain Exceptions

You must use a throws command to explicitly chart the course of these exceptions.

AWTException   The AWT is the Abstract Windowing Toolkit bundled with Java 1.0 and built into the latest versions of Netscape. If anything goes wrong in this setup, you can get one of these exceptions.

ClassNotFoundException   The code in classes Class and ClassLoader will try to locate classes. If they can't be found, here's what you get.

CloneNotSupportedException   Some objects can't be cloned.

IOException   This is a superclass for the next classes.

EOFException   You can use this to test for the end of a file.

FileNotFoundException   You'll see this when a file isn't available.

InterruptedIOException   Threads can sometimes be interrupted in the middle of working on the input or output. This exception is then generated.

MalformedURLException   You can create your own URLs and ask a browser to do something with them. This emerges if you've put in a bad URL.

`ProtocolException`   Some of the Java toolkits include code for handling TCP, IP, FTP, and HTTP. If something goes wrong, this comes along.

`SocketException`   This indicates problems with a socket.

`UTFDataFormatException`   You used the wrong format for data.

`UnknownHostException`   The TCP/IP processes can't locate a particular host. Your DNS server might be down.

`UnknownServiceException`   A socket doesn't offer this service.

`IllegalAccessException`   You're not allowed to do what you're trying to do.

`InstantiationException`   Something has gone wrong in the process of creating or using a class from `java.lang.class`.

`InterruptedException`   When threads are interrupted, they raise this exception.

`NoSuchMethodException`   You tried to call a method that wasn't available.

Summary

Exceptions are a powerful and graceful way to handle problems that occur. Object-oriented programming encourages you to create thousands of tiny methods that occasionally subclass each other. This mesh, however, turns into a mess if you want to break out of one method because of a problem. The exception mechanism forces you to draw explicit paths when they're necessary and ensures that troubles get fixed.

Here are some of the most important lessons from this chapter:

- Exceptions are a way to unwind execution across multiple methods. They're like a cross-method `break` command.

- Exceptions are a class. If you want to create your own, you only need to `extend` the class.

- An exception is created with a `new` command and then thrown with a `throw` command.

- Exceptions are "caught" with the `catch` command, which is paired with the `try` command. A block of code is marked by the `try` command. If an exception is raised in the process of executing this code, it should be caught by the `catch` commands that follow.

- Some exceptions require you to explicitly mark the path of recovery by marking what exceptions are thrown by a method in the first line of the method's definition. This can prevent arbitrary exceptions floating around the system.

- If you need to avoid using the `throws` keyword in the definition of a function, you should create an exception that is a subclass of `RuntimeException`. The compiler does not enforce the rule for these.

Chapter 9

Applets on Web Pages

If you want to send your applet to a Web browser, you need to embed it in an HTML document. For the most part, the Web browser treats applets like images and typsets them as rectangular regions. This chapter explains how to place applets on Web pages.

Most people interested in Java today want to use it to add cool software to their Web pages. Java is a full-featured development tool, but most of the excitement in the software world is about Java's little applications that can travel over the Internet and do neat things for the distant user. These programs must necessarily be small because the Internet is still a slow medium, and they must not have any potential to do harm because one virus could do serious remote damage.

The solution is the Java *applet*. This is a class that provides many of the basic features a program needs to operate. It can start itself, draw things on the screen, provide many widgets for the user to input information, and then shut itself down. All of this is built into the basic class. If you want to write your own code to run on a distant browser, you can just create a subclass of `Applet` and inherit all of this power.

This approach solves both size and security problems. First, you only need to ship along the code to do your special tasks. The mundane chores are inherited from the `Applet` class and every browser will maintain this locally. This limits the size of the code that travels on the network. Second, the structure of an applet does not give the incoming code any of the features it needs to wreak havoc. The Applet class doesn't have an "erase file" feature, so the incoming code can't do that.

This chapter will describe how to build a Web page with a Java applet, how to construct a variety of simple applets, and also how to take advantage of the features that the Applet class offers.

Adding an Applet to a WWW Page

Many of the examples in this book are applets. I chose to use this format because I think it is the most common way that people will use Java in its early years. In the future, Java may become the most common programming language for all system work, but for now, the Web will drive its use.

Adding an applet to a Web page is as simple as placing two HTML tags. It is similar to adding an image. You're just creating a box and the Web browser will do the job of fitting the text, images, and applets into place. Here's an example:

The <APPLET> tag
doesn't have to be
capitalized. In fact,
you can use
<applet>. Unlike
Java, HTML is not
case sensitive.

```
<HTML>
<HEAD><TITLE>Applets Away</TITLE></HEAD>
<BODY>
<br>
<H3>Here's an Applet</H3>
<APPLET CODE="Spots.class" WIDTH=300 HEIGHT=200>
If you can read this message, then your browser can't
    support Java applets.
</APPLET>
</BODY>
```

Attributes are just
parameters that are
passed inside of the
<APPLET> tag. There
are other parameters
that can be passed in
the text in between the
opening and closing
tags.

The two tags <APPLET> and </APPLET> mark the place where an applet should be. The command also takes *attributes* that guide the position of this applet. The most important one is the attribute for CODE, which gives the name of the Java class that will be loaded and run. In this example, the browser will look for the file Spots.class in the same directory on the Web server as the current HTML page.

This file must be the Java byte code produced by the Java compiler. The browser will load this locally and check it out to make sure that it does not contain any hidden viruses that might cause trouble. It does this by looking for errant memory references and problems like array references that fall off the ends of an array. The file must also be the byte code for a class that is a subclass of the Java class Applet. This class is shipped with all compilers and their browsers.

The other major parameters for the <APPLET> tag are as follows:

HEIGHT=*n* The height of the applet's box will be *n* pixels.

VSPACE=*n* This adds *n* pixels of padding to the top and the bottom of the applet box. It effectively makes it bigger.

WIDTH=*n* The applet's box will be *n* pixels wide.

HSPACE=*n* An extra *n* pixels of padding are allocated to both the left and the right of an applet box.

CODEBASE=*directory* The CODE tag specifies the name of the class, but this attribute specifies the directory. Use this if you don't end up storing the class in the same directory as the Web page that uses it.

The one remaining major attribute is ALIGN. This controls how the applet is aligned in its box. All HTML browsers set the type to fit the size of the current browser. An applet is just another box that can float on the page like an image. If you've used the <IMG> tag with HTML, then you'll understand this. It works in the same way.

Here are the options you can use with the ALIGN attribute:

ALIGN=LEFT The applet is on the left and the text flows down the right of it until it reaches the end of the applet or the first occurrence of a <CLEAR> tag. The <CLEAR> tag specifies when to stop wrapping text around an applet's box.

ALIGN=RIGHT The applet is on the right and the text flows down the left of it until it reaches the end of the applet or the first occurrence of a <CLEAR> tag.

ALIGN=BASELINE or ALIGN=BOTTOM The applet is incorporated into a line of text and the bottom of the applet is aligned with the bottom of the line of text.

ALIGN=MIDDLE The applet is incorporated into a line of text and the middle of the applet is placed at the baseline of the text.

`ALIGN=TEXTTOP` The applet is aligned with the top of the text in the line, which might not be the highest item.

`ALIGN=TOP` The highest item in the line is found and the top of the applet is set to be aligned with the top of this item.[1]

`ALIGN=ABSMIDDLE` The largest item in the entire line is found, even if it is not adjacent to the applet, and the middle of the applet is set to the middle of this largest item.

`ALIGN=ABSBOTTOM` The lowest of the items in the line is found and the applet is aligned with it.

Here's an example of some HTML code that overuses some of these `ALIGN` tags. The image from this is shown in Figure 9.1:

```
<HTML>
<HEAD><TITLE>Alignment Fun </TITLE></HEAD>
<BODY>
Here is the
<applet code=Star width=25 height=25 align=texttop>
Missing Applet</applet>
TEXTTOP applet. And here is the BASELINE
<applet code=Star width=25 height=25
align=BASELINE></applet>
Here is the MIDDLE
<applet code=Star width=25 height=25
align=MIDDLE></applet>
Here is the TOP
<applet code=Star width=25 height=25 align=TOP></applet>
Here is the ABSBOTTOM
<applet code=Star width=25 height=25
align=ABSBOTTOM></applet>
<BR><BR>
<applet code=Star width=25 height=25 align=LEFT></applet>
This is the text that should flow around
the applet off to the left. It should
just pour like cheesecake batter into a mold.
```

---

[1] Consistency would demand that this be labeled `ABSTOP`?

```
But let me say that again. It should pour
like salt into a salt shaker cementing its
reign upon the table and the
blood pressure of the hypertensive.
</BODY>
</HTML>
```

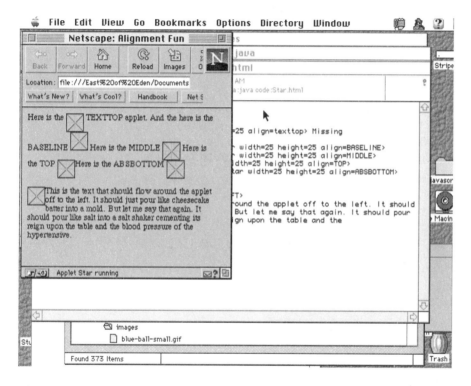

Figure 9.1. Several ALIGN tags are used to place the Java applet Star in and around text. The browser treats the applet as a box and aligns the text in the same way that it handles an image.

This introductory section just treats an applet as a box. We'll discuss this more later in the chapter, but the Star.java file is printed here in case you're curious. Notice how short the file is. The Star class inherits all of its behavior except its painting ability from the Applet class. Only the painting code would need to travel on the network.

```
import java.applet.*;
import java.awt.*;
public class Star extends Applet {
  public void paint(Graphics g){
    g.setColor(Color.red);
    g.drawLine(0,0,25,25);
    g.setColor(Color.blue);
    g.drawLine(25,0,0,25);
    g.setColor(Color.green);
    g.drawLine(12,0,12,25);
    g.drawLine(0,12,25,12);
    g.setColor(Color.black);
    g.drawLine(0,0,0,24);
    g.drawLine(0,24,24,24);
    g.drawLine(24,24,24,0);
    g.drawLine(24,0,0,0);
      // x=25 and y=25 are clipped off!
  }
}
```

Creating Applets

The last section used a tiny applet known as Star, which was, in reality, an object from the Star class. The code in the Star.java file simply defined what the object would do if its paint routine was called. The rest of the behavior was inherited from the major class Applet.

Remember that Applet with a capital "A" is a class while applet with a lowercase "a" is a package. This distinction comes from Sun. You don't need to be as subtle when you write your own code.

The Applet class comes with eleven major routines that you can replace by overriding them. They are:

init() This routine will be called when the applet is first loaded into the browser. If you need to load images, find parameters, or create some data structures, this is where you should do the work. Many of the simple examples in the book demonstrate the behavior of the language using the init routine as a surrogate for the main routine. Now you can understand its real place in Java.

start() start is not the same thing as init. It gets called every time a page is displayed. This isn't the same thing as when the applet is loaded. Many browser users might leave a page and then return.

This routine will be called whenever the page is displayed. You should coordinate the actions of any `start` routine with a `stop` routine.

`stop()` When a browser leaves a page, it calls the `stop` method of each applet on the page. You might want to suspend the CPU-hogging threads here because they won't be stopped. If the threads are probing the Net or doing crucial tasks, you can leave them running. Make sure that the threads are started in a `start` routine so they'll start up again if the page is revisited.

`destroy()` This routine is the last thing that an applet gets to do during its life. If you override this method, you'll be able to shut down threads and finish up any other tasks. Java cleans up memory automatically so you won't have to free it up, but you must remember to stop all the threads permanently. They will keep running and running and running.

`paint(Graphics g)` The g is an item from the `Graphics` class. You can pass this to a variety of drawing routines and they'll draw the right thing in the applet's box in the browser. Note that the browser will clip the drawing to the box defined by the `WIDTH` and the `HEIGHT` attributes in the `<APPLET>` tag.

`mouseDown(Event evt, int x,int y)` This routine is invoked whenever the browser finds a mouse click beginning in the applet's box. You should arrange to respond to mouse clicks here. This should be coordinated with the `mouseUp` event to ensure good user-interface design principles. Return `true` if you've handled the event and it can be forgotten.

`mouseUp(Event evt, int x,int y)` When a mouse button is released in an applet, this routine is invoked. Good user-interface design dictates that you let users back out of a mouse click by releasing it over a benign area. You should try to imitate this by responding to both the `mouseDown` and the `mouseUp` routines. Return `true` if you've handled the event and it can be forgotten.

`mouseDrag(Event evt, int x, int y)` When a mouse moves when the button is down, then this routine is called. You can use it to drag things. You should move the objects in tow and then call `repaint`. Return `true` if you've handled the event and it can be forgotten.

An applet will end when all non-Daemon threads are stopped. You can also designate background threads as Daemon threads and they'll be stopped automatically when the main, non-Daemon threads end. See page 126.

Note that the mouse routines here are actually part of the `Component` class. The `Applet` class is a descendant of this class.

mouseMove(Event evt, int x, int y) If the mouse moves when
    the button is up, this routine is executed. This is rarely used. Return
    true if you've handled the event and it can be forgotten.

mouseEnter(Event evt, int x, int y) When a mouse enters a
    component, this routine is invoked. You might want to change the
    shape of the mouse or display some help information to indicate
    what a particular component does. Return true if you've handled
    the event and it can be forgotten.

*Components are
discussed on page 174.*

mouseExit(Event evt, int x, int y) This routine is invoked when
    the mouse leaves a component. It is a complement to the mouseEnter
    routine. Return true if you've handled the event and it can be for-
    gotten.

If you want to create your own applet, you should override at least
one of these routines. The Star applet just described overrides the
paint method to fill a box with a few lines. Many of the applets from
the early part of the book just override the init routine. You have a
fair amount of flexibility in how you approach the design.

Here is an example of a simple BoxFun applet that will draw some
boxes on the screen. It has routines for starting, stopping, painting,
and watching the mouse. All of the other details are handled by the
Applet class.

```
import java.applet.*; //Basic applet routines.
import java.awt.*;
class TheBox{
  static int lastNum=0;
  int num;
  int x,y; //Where it is.
  Color c;
  void paint(Graphics g){
    g.setColor(c);
    g.fillRect(x,y,20,20);
    g.drawString(Integer.toString(num),x,y);
  }
   TheBox(int blah,int blah2){
    this.x=blah;this.y=blah2;
    num=lastNum++;
```

```
      if (lastNum>10){
        lastNum = 0;
      }
      int choice=(int)(Math.random()*5);
      switch (choice) {
        case 0:
          c=Color.red;
          break;
        case 1:
          c=Color.blue;
          break;
        case 2:
          c=Color.green;
          break;
        case 3:
          c=Color.yellow;
          break;
        default:
          c=Color.white;
          break;
      }
    }
}
public class BoxFun extends Applet {
  TheBox[] Boxes = new TheBox[10];
  int LastBox = 0;
  String message="";
  public void init(){
    message="Applet Init'ed.";
    for (int i=0;i<10;i++) Boxes[i]=null;
  }
  public void start(){
    message="Applet started.";
    repaint();
  }
  public boolean mouseEnter(Event evt, int x, int y){
    message="Mouse entered ("+x+","+y+")";
    repaint();
    return true;
```

```
  }
  public boolean mouseExit(Event evt, int x, int y){
    message="Mouse exited ("+x+","+y+")";
    repaint();
    return true;
  }
  public boolean mouseUp(Event evt,int x, int y){
    Boxes[LastBox++]=new TheBox(x,y);
    if (LastBox>=10) LastBox = 0;
    repaint();
    return true;
  }
  public void paint(Graphics g){
    for (int i=0;i<10;i++){
      if (Boxes[i]!=null)
        Boxes[i].paint(g);
    }
    g.drawString(message,10,10);
  }
}
```

The BoxFun class has one important method, paint. This defines
how the program will present its information in the window it gets.
The methods like mouseUp actually create the boxes. Calling repaint
forces the applet code to call the paint method again. Figure 9.2 shows
the result of running the program with an Applet Viewer.

The term attribute
comes from SGML,
which is the
foundation for
HTML. The first
name between the
"<" and ">"
symbols is the tag
name. The rest of the
information is
attributes.
Technically, much of
the information in the
<PARAM> tag is also
an attribute to that
tag.

Parameters and Applets

The <APPLET> tag can take *attributes* that are embedded inside the
tag. These include data tags for controlling the alignment and size of
the applet's box. You can also pass *parameters* to the applet with the
<PARAM> tag. Attributes from the <APPLET> tag are used by the browser
to control how and where it displays the applet, but parameters are
used to pass information to the applet. The browser doesn't look at
parameters. It just passes them through.

Parameters are a good way to reuse the same code over and over.
You might create an animation applet and then use it on many different

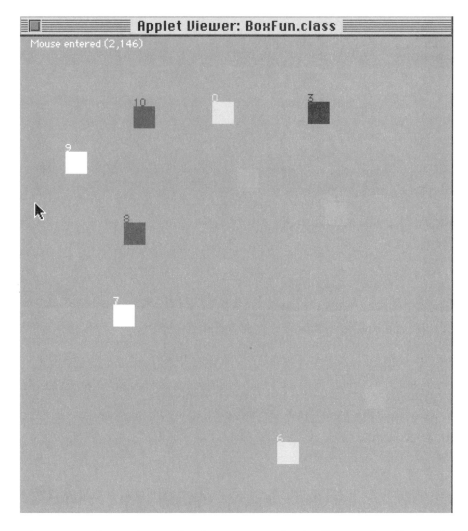

Figure 9.2. This is the result of starting up the BoxFun applet. The applet responds to mouse clicks by drawing a box.

pages by passing in the names of the GIF files that make up the frames of the applet. This would save you the trouble of compiling different versions for each page.

There are two parts to the parameter mechanism. The first is the <PARAM> tag that is placed in the HTML file. Here are some examples of the tags you might use:

```
<PARAM NAME=who VALUE="Fred">
<PARAM NAME=age VALUE="32">
<PARAM NAME=Planet VALUE="EARTH">
```

This code will pass three strings, "Fred","32", and "EARTH". Inside your applet, you can get these values with code like this:

```
int age;
String who;
String Planet;
who=getParameter("who");
if (who == null) {
  who = "Nobody";
}
String ageString = getParameter("age");
if (ageString == null){
  age = 0;
} else {
  age = Integer.parseInt(ageString);
}
Planet=getParameter("Planet");
if (Planet==null){
  Planet="X";
}
```

The routine getParameter will recover the strings by name. This must match exactly. If you want to convert the strings to a different type, then you must call a routine like parseInt. If the parameter is not in the HTML, the getParameter routine will return a null and it is your responsibility to test for this. In this code, I added dummy values to prevent any later problems that might raise a NullPointerException. Debugging errors like this can be a pain.

Other Applet Methods

There are a number of other methods that you might want to use with an applet. Here's a list of some of the more important ones:

URL getCodeBase() This routine will return a URL pointing to the location where the applet's code came from. You can use this to load images, text, or other information without hard-coding locations into the applet. If you move the applet to another machine, then using this routine saves you the trouble of changing the code.

`URL getDocumentBase()` This returns the URL of the HTML document that invoked the applet. You can use it in the same way that you might use `getCodeBase`.

`void resize(int width, int height)` If you need to change the size of the applet, this will change the box size to the new `width` and `height`. If the applet is part of a layout on a complicated browser screen, this can really rearrange the screen.

`void showStatus(String message)` This will display a string in the status section of the browser, which is often along the bottom section of the window. You might use this to offer help methods when the mouse drifts over a component.

`Image getImage(URL s)` This is the preferred way to load an image. The most important thing to realize about this method is that it does not wait around for the image to be loaded. It spawns a thread that goes out searching for the image data from the Net and returns control right away. If you later try to draw the image, you will only get the data that has already arrived.

This technique is a great approach to imitate. You should try to spawn your own threads to handle time-consuming tasks so the user interface will continue to be served.

`Image getImage(URL s, String name)` This will also load an image, but it will search for the image `name` and only use the URL as a base.

`AudioClip getAudioClip(URL s)` This works like `getImage`, but it loads a sound file that you can later play.

`AudioClip getAudioClip(URL s, String name)` This works like `getAudioClip`, but it uses `name` to specify the file and it only uses URL as the base location.

`void play(URL s)` This loads and plays an audio clip. If it can't find it or the load fails, you won't hear a thing. In some early versions of Java Applet Viewers, you still won't hear a thing because the audio part hadn't been implemented yet.

`void play(URL s, String name)` This works like `play`, but it uses `name` to specify the file and it only uses URL as the base location.

`AppletContext getAppletContext()` An `AppletContext` is essentially an object that contains a list of all of the applets that are currently running in one location. If there are several applets on one page, then this context would contain pointers to all of them. You can use this routine to access the other applets. This is the basis for inter-applet communication.

Components, Containers, Panels, and Applets

The Java toolkit includes a number of types of objects in a hierarchy. Applets are only the lowest of the subclasses. A `Component` is the foundational class for the objects that are displayed on the screen. Components are objects that respond to keys, mouse clicks, or other events. They can draw themselves and control their own fonts and background colors. The basic parts of the Abstract Windowing Toolkit (AWT), such as slide bars or scrolling displays, are subclasses of the class `Component`.

A `Container` is a component that can hold a bunch of components. You might use it to hold a bunch of controls or other objects that react to events. One of the more important methods in this class is `layout`, which places the components on the screen.

A `Panel` is a container with the ability to get information from a `Peer`, that is, to respond to outside messages that might not be events. You may use this functionality if you want applets to coordinate their behavior on the screen. Finally, an `Applet` is a panel with the methods for starting, stopping, initializing, and destroying itself.

At first glance, this hierarchy might not make sense. If applets are the basic unit a Java programmer would create to run on a browser, why would someone want to make them such a distant subclass of the basic component? Or for that matter, why would someone want to make a basic `Container` that gathers together some components a subclass of the `Component` class itself? The answer is to create a hierarchy of components and containers that can be deeply nested. A `Container` can hold a bunch of `Components` as well as several `Containers`. The `Container` class is a subclass of `Component` so it counts as a `Component`. An `Applet` is also a `Component`.

Summary

This chapter has described how to build a basic applet using some simple drawing routines and subclassing the essential methods.

Chapter 10

Graphics in Java

This chapter will show you how to draw shapes and forms on the screen. You will want to use this if you tap into the power of the Abstract Windowing Toolkit.

Applets communicate with the user through graphics and tools. Aside from sound, drawing things on the screen is the only method for communicating with the user. The Java graphics package is a fairly straightforward drawing system that should be familiar to anyone who has written programs for microcomputers. Java's graphics routines are quite similar in flavor to Apple's QuickDraw or Microsoft's Windows toolkit, but they are not as extensive.

If you haven't worked in either of these arenas, the Java graphics routines should still be fairly simple to learn. Java offers you the ability to change color and draw lines, rectangles, and ellipses. The only major difference between Java and other graphics routines is that Java's origin, (0,0) in the coordinate system, is in the upper lefthand corner. The x axis increases horizontally left to right as might be expected, but the y axis increases from top to bottom. This approach is standard on many computers but it doesn't match the graphs drawn in math class where the y axis increases from bottom to top.

The Abstract Windowing Toolkit is described in Chapter 11.

java.awt.Graphics

As before, the case of the first letter is important. Graphics is a class. awt is the package.

The Java graphics package includes a number of different drawing routines that are built around the class Graphics. In many cases, the paint routine from your applet will be given an object from the Graphics class. If you want to draw in it, you simply execute some methods from the class. Occasionally you will want to create your own Graphics objects, but this will usually be in cases where you want high performance to create a good impression during animation.

drawLine

If you want to draw a line, this routine accepts four arguments: the (x,y) coordinates of the start and the (x,y) coordinates of the end. Here's a routine that will draw lines on the screen:

```
import java.awt.Graphics;
import java.applet.*;
public class g1 extends Applet {
  public void paint(Graphics g){
    for (int i=0;i<100;i+=10){
      g.drawLine(i,i,i+10,i);
    }
  }
}
```

You can see the result in Figure 10.1.

drawRect **and** fillRect

Rectangles can be drawn, filled, rounded, and given a faux-3D look with the Java toolkit. Here are the routines:

```
  g.drawRect(left,top,width,height);
    // Draw a rectangle with upper left corner at
    // (left,top) and bottom right corner at
    // (left+width,top+height).
  g.fillRect(left,top,width,height);
    // Draw a rectangle as with drawRect, but fill it with
    // the line drawing color.
```

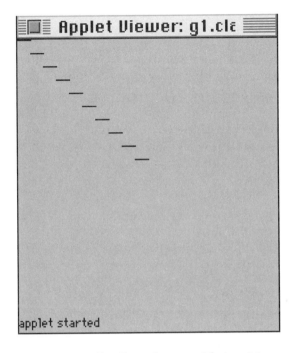

Figure 10.1. Ten lines drawn with drawLine.

```
g.drawRoundRect(left,top,width,height, horizontal-radius,
                vertical-radius);
g.fillRoundRect(left,top,width,height, horizontal-radius,
                vertical-radius);
  // Draw or fill a rectangle with rounded corners.
  // The size of the rounding is determined by
  // horizontal-radius and vertical-radius.
g.draw3DRect(left,top,width,height,polarity);
  // Draw a rectangle as usual, but add shading to give
  // it the appearance of three-dimensionality. If
  // polarity is set to be true then it appears as if
  // the rectangle bursts from the screen. If it is
  // false, then it will look indented.
```

These rectangle-drawing routines string together line-drawing routines, fill routines, and arc-drawing routines. The corners of rounded rectangles are created by taking an ellipse, cutting it into quarters, bursting it, and adding lines for the flat section. That is, each of the corners is just a quarter of an ellipse and its proportions are determined by the horizontal and vertical radii.

Here's a rectangle-drawing applet:

```java
import java.awt.Graphics;
import java.applet.*;
public class g2 extends Applet {
  public void paint(Graphics g){
    for (int i=0;i<140;i+=20){
      g.drawRect(i,5,15,45);
    }
    for (int i=0;i<140;i+=20){
      g.fillRect(i,55,15,45);
    }
    for (int i=0;i<140;i+=20){
      g.drawRoundRect(i,100,20,45,10,15);
    }
    for (int i=0;i<100;i+=20){
      g.draw3DRect(i,150,15,35,true);
    }
  }
}
```

The results can be seen in Figure 10.2.

drawPolygon and fillPolygon

Note that the class Polygon is not part of the class Graphics so you need to import it separately. In this example, the entire java.awt package is imported.

You can create polygons on the screen by building up an array of the x coordinates and also an array of y coordinates. These define the corners of the polygon. The polygon is not connected by drawPolygon unless you add the final point into the array. fillPolygon will implicitly close the boundary so it can fill it.

There is also a class Polygon that can be used to create polygons for drawing. You can either create a blank polygon with the routine Polygon() and add points to it with the method addPoint(x,y), or you can feed the constructor two arrays of points.

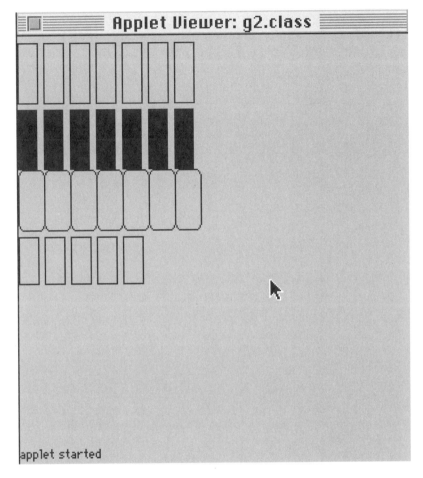

Figure 10.2. Some rectangles drawn with the Graphics methods. Note that the results from draw3DRect (bottom row) aren't very prominent. Different color combinations can increase the results, but it is still not great.

Here's an example:

```
import java.awt.*;
import java.applet.*;
public class g3 extends Applet {
    int[] X = new int[100];
    int[] Y = new int[100];
```

```
    int count;
    Polygon p;
  void makePoly(int offX,int offY){
    X[0]=offX+14;
    X[1]=offX+38;
    X[2]=offX+22;
    X[3]=offX+19;
    X[4]=offX+2;
    Y[0]=offY+2;
    Y[1]=offY+22;
    Y[2]=offY+23;
    Y[3]=offY+39;
    Y[4]=offY+12;
    count = 4;
  }
  public void paint(Graphics g){
    makePoly(10,10);
    g.drawPolygon(X,Y,count);
    makePoly(10,100);
    g.fillPolygon(X,Y,count);
    p= new Polygon();
    p.addPoint(100,120);
    p.addPoint(140,142);
    p.addPoint(130,162);
    p.addPoint(142,122);
    p.addPoint(90,92);
    g.fillPolygon(p);
  }
}
```

The output can be seen in Figure 10.3.

drawOval **and** drawArc

You can draw ellipses and parts of ellipses using the routines drawOval and drawArc. They can be filled in with the corresponding methods fillOval and fillArc. The parameters for drawOval and fillOval are actually the coordinates for the smallest rectangle that encloses the oval. That is, you feed in the left, the top, the width, and the height parameters.

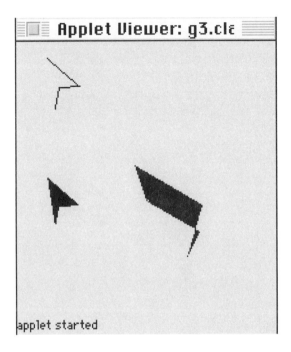

Figure 10.3. Three polygons drawn in an applet.

The `drawArc` routine takes two additional parameters that indicate the start and length of the arc when measured in degrees. Zero degrees is at high noon and the values increase clockwise. So ninety degrees is at the right side of the circle.

Here's an example:

Some documentation differs on the way that the `drawArc` draws its arcs. This data is based upon the MacJDK version from Sun.

```
import java.awt.Graphics;
import java.applet.*;
public class g4 extends Applet {
  public void paint(Graphics g){
    for (int i=0;i<140;i+=20){
      g.drawOval(i,5,15,45);
    }
    for (int i=0;i<140;i+=20){
      g.fillOval(i,55,15,45);
    }
```

```
    for (int i=0;i<140;i+=20){
      g.drawArc(i,100,20,45,i+10,i+100);
    }
    for (int i=0;i<140;i+=20){
      g.fillArc(i,150,20,45,i+10,i+100);
    }
  }
}
```

The results can be seen in Figure 10.4.

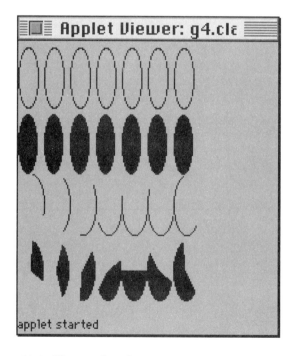

Figure 10.4. The results of the paint routine from class g4.

drawString

If you want to draw text on the screen, you'll need to create a Font object first. This class specifies the names of the fonts, the font style, and the size. Then you can draw the data on the screen. Here's a simple example:

```
Font k= new Font("TimesRoman", Font.PLAIN, 24);
g.setFont(k);
g.drawString("Hi!");
```

The first line uses the constructor for the class Font to build up the font object that is passed to the Graphics object in the second line. The first parameter to the constructor is the name of the font. There are five "universal" fonts that are available in all browsers: Courier, Dialog, Helvetica, Symbol, and TimesRoman. You can also get a list of fonts by executing the method getFontList() from the class java.awt.Toolkit.

There are two different stylistic effects that can be mixed and matched: Font.BOLD and Font.ITALIC. These constants are defined in the class Font, but they're actually integers. You can add them together to mix them. The command k=new Font("Courier", Font.ITALIC + Font.BOLD , 12) will generate a bold and italic font.

The Java drawString routine is not very powerful. If you feed it carriage returns or line feeds embedded in the string, it will ignore them. For that reason, you'll often need to calculate your own layout information for drawing strings upon the screen. There is a class FontMetrics that is returned by the Graphics method getFontMetrics. The FontMetrics object has several methods that spit out the ascent, descent, leading, and the overall height of a character. The *ascent* is the height of a capital letter. The *descent* is the distance below the baseline that a letter like "g" will drop. The *leading* is the recommended amount of space to put between lines. Finally, the *height* is the overall height of a line of characters that includes capital letters and descenders, that is, the height from the bottom of a "y" to the top of a capital "M."

This code shows some of the more interesting methods in the FontMetrics class:

```
public int getLeading()
  // Returns the suggested line spacing or leading.
  public int getAscent()
  // Returns the distance between the baseline and
  // the top.
public int getDescent()
  // Returns the distance between the baseline and
  // the bottom of a letter like lowercase g.
```

```
public int getHeight()
  //Returns the sum:  leading + ascent + descent.
public int charWidth(int ch)
  // Given a character ch, find the width.
public int stringWidth(String str)
  // The width of a string. I.e. the sum of its
  // character widths.
public int charsWidth(char data[],
                      int off,
                      int len)
  // Sum up the length of the characters in the array.
  // Start with character ''off'' and go through
  // ''len'' characters.
public int[] getWidths()
  // Returns the widths of the 256 basic characters.
```

Some of the extra functions for calculating widths can be quite helpful if you're creating a word processor or doing plenty of active formatting on the screen.

Here's an example:

```
import java.awt.*;
import java.applet.*;
public class g5 extends Applet {
  public void paint(Graphics g){
    int w=200;
    int h=150;
    g.drawRect(10,10,w,h);
    Font f=new Font("Courier", Font.PLAIN,18);
    g.setFont(f);
    FontMetrics fm=g.getFontMetrics();
    g.drawString("Courier", 11,10+fm.getHeight());
    f=new Font("TimesRoman",Font.ITALIC,12);
    g.setFont(f);
    fm=g.getFontMetrics();
    g.drawString("TimesRoman", w-fm.stringWidth
         ("TimesRoman"),10+fm.getHeight());
    f=new Font("Symbol",Font.PLAIN,18);
    g.setFont(f);
    fm=g.getFontMetrics();
```

```
    g.drawString("Symbol",10,h);
    f=new Font("Dialog",Font.PLAIN,18);
    g.setFont(f);
    fm=g.getFontMetrics();
    g.drawString("Dialog",w-fm.stringWidth("Dialog"),h);
  }
}
```

The results of this example can be seen in Figure 10.5. You will notice that the drawing of the strings begins on the baseline.

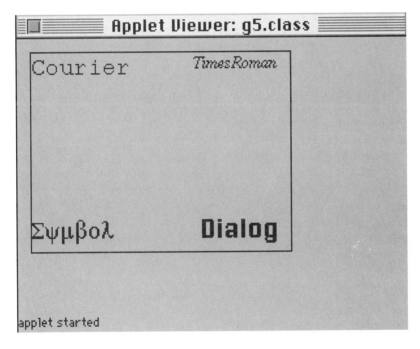

Figure 10.5. The results of the paint routine from class g5.

Colors

Of course Java offers the programmer the ability to choose color using a basic model that is common to most machines. Each color is made up of a combination of red, green, and blue (RGB). The strength of each component is specified by a byte that can take values between 0 and 255. (255,255,255) is white, (255,0,0) is pure red, (0,255,0) is pure green, and (0,0,255) is pure blue. Naturally, (0,0,0) is black.

This model is far from perfect because the individual graphics environments are so different. Some people continue to use gray-scale monitors or laptop displays. Computers that only show 256 colors are quite common. Many monitors are not calibrated, so one person's red could be much closer to another person's magenta. The local Java environment will do its best to display any particular color, but you cannot be assured of standardization.

A color is just an object from the class Color. The class comes with several static constants that can be used if you need them. Here's a table of color values:

Object Name	Red	Green	Blue	Object Name	Red	Green	Blue
Color.cyan	0	255	255	Color.blue	0	0	255
Color.black	0	0	0	Color.green	0	255	0
Color.gray	128	128	128	Color.lightgray	192	192	192
Color.darkgray	64	64	64	Color.white	0	0	0
Color.red	255	0	0	Color.yellow	255	255	0
Color.magenta	255	0	255	Color.cyan	0	255	255
Color.pink	255	175	175	Color.orange	255	200	0

The Color class comes with three constructors. The most commonly used one will probably be the one that takes three integers between 0 and 255 that specify the red, green, and blue intensities respectively:

```
Color lineColor=new Color(140,23,190);
```

Another version will accept three floating-point numbers between 0.0 and 1.0. They will be remapped to bytes between 0 and 255. A third version takes just one 32-bit integer. The red value is stuck in bits 16 through 23, the green value in bits 8 through 15, and the blue value in bits 0 through 7. You might call it like this:

```
Color lineColor = new Color(1423424);
```

The function getHSBColor is technically not a constructor because it doesn't have the name Color, but it does create a color object using the hue, saturation, and brightness (HSB) model. These are specified by three float parameters between 0.0 and 1.0. You can convert between the two models with the functions HSBtoRGB and RGBtoHSB.

The Color class comes with some basic methods for manipulating the colors. You can extract the individual elements with the three routines getBlue, getRed, and getGreen. If you want all values combined into one integer, you use getRGB.

There are two functions, brighter and darker, that will return a different version of the same color that is either brighter or darker.

An example of using the darker method can be seen on page 212.

Using Colors

The Graphics class uses the objects from the Color class to decide how to paint objects in the window. If you want to use code like drawOval or drawRect and have the result come out in a certain color, you just use the command setColor with the current Graphics object like this:

```
g.setColor(Color.red);
```

This color can also be retrieved with the getColor method if you need to cache it or modify it.

The background of the applet is normally gray. If you need to change it, you can use setBackground. This method is part of the definition of the Component, which is a superclass of the Applet. You can't execute this with the Graphics package. Naturally, there is also a getBackground method. The setForeground method affects all objects in the applet and makes them draw in this color.

Color Models

The Java AWT also offers another set of objects for manipulating colors. This is the ColorModel object and its subclasses IndexColorModel and DirectColorModel. You might use these classes to create images with a smaller number of bits per pixel.

For instance, if you only wanted to use eight colors in an image, then you would specify an index color model with three bits per pixel. The code would supply the alpha, red, green, and blue values for each item in the table.

A direct color model, on the other hand, would allow you to pack three bits of alpha value, two bits of red intensity, five bits of green intensity, and three bits of blue intensity into 13 bits of a pixel. The flexibility is at your service.

Summary

This chapter has explained how to use the basic routines to draw in the browser's window. These are the basic building blocks for graphical programs that present information to the user in informative ways. The most important lessons from the chapter are:

- The Graphics object is for drawing.

- You can create another Graphics object if you want to double-buffer the output.

- You can draw all of the standard shapes (line, rectangle, ellipse) with one of Java's built-in routines.

- Java comes with several built-in fonts. You can draw text at any place in an applet window using one of them.

- Colors can be created with either the RGB or HSB model.

Chapter 11

The Abstract Windowing Toolkit

This chapter explains how to access the power of the Java Abstract Windowing Toolkit (AWT) to create graphical user interfaces with a minimal number of statements.

Java's Abstract Windowing Toolkit (AWT) provides a number of different tools that can be used to create devices like scrolling lists or pull-down menus for the user. These types of interfaces should be familiar to anyone who has used computer GUIs, but there are some interesting differences between traditional GUIs and the HTML/Web interface.

The greatest difference is the level of abstraction. Most programming systems require that the programmer dictate exactly where the tool components will appear on the screen. This is natural in a setting where you have control over the window, but it is different from the spirit of HTML. The text distributed for WWW browsers is deliberately only semi-formatted. Only the paragraph breaks and the major components of the text are marked by tags. The browser does the final layout and fits the text into the size available locally.

The Java AWT offers the programmer the same amount of flexibility. You can create the interface components and let Java arrange them on the screen with a built-in "layout" function. Some users may find this disconcerting because they want absolute control over the placement of items. Others may enjoy letting automatic code handle that responsibility.

In Chapter 10 you saw how to draw and color with some basic geometric forms. These are useful features by themselves, but most programmers are now accustomed to building user interfaces using a basic toolkit. All of the major operating systems offer collections of widgets like checkboxes and scrollbars that can be strung together to create a user interface. The Java Abstract Windowing Toolkit is no exception.

There are several differences, however, between the Java AWT and the tools offered by many of the other systems. The Java AWT contains another level of abstraction that allows you to ignore layout details. Many programmers who work with standard toolkits simply place the widgets in locations on the screen. If windows change size, they reposition the widgets explicitly themselves. Some of the better class libraries like the Think Class Libraries also have layout functions that can handle some of this for you. The Java AWT is like this. It will lay out the widgets on the screen if you want it to do so.

There are some advantages to letting the AWT handle layout for you. Java code that will travel across the Net does not have much control over the browser that will run it. It might be running on a small screen or on a large one; it might get stuck in a small window or a large one. HTML, the markup language for text, leaves the layout up to the local machine. If you allow the Java AWT to do the layout, it will try to make the best of the local screen. If there is plenty of space, it will grab it. If the window is small, everything will be shrunk accordingly.

But there are also disadvantages. You may not like the range offered by the AWT layout function. You might not approve of how it makes decisions for extremely small or extremely large screens. You can override the layout commands by explicitly locating the components yourself.

Despite these aesthetic arguments, most users will find that the Java AWT is an excellent toolkit for creating basic user interfaces to run on different machines throughout the Internet.

The Component Hierarchy

Java provides a number of different classes that arrange the different user interface widgets into a fairly deep hierarchy. Each class offers a different collection of features, but they work together as a whole.

At the base of this collection of tools is the Component class. This class provides all of the basic code for drawing on the screen and handling events from the keyboard or the mouse. All of the objects in the AWT are descended from Component.

There are four classes that fall immediately below Component in the hierarchy. The Canvas class will display images, the TextComponent will format text for you, and the Button class will provide simple interface buttons. The last of the four subclasses, Container, will bundle together several objects from the Component class and lay them out on the screen in an intelligent fashion.

Of the three basic Component subclasses, only TextComponent has an additional descendent, known as TextField. It is used to input information.

The objects from the Component *class will be refered to as "components," without a special font.*

The Container class, however, has many important subclasses. The two immediate ones are Panel and Window. The Panel class provides a slightly more powerful communication capability between panels. The Applet class is itself a subclass of the Panel class. This means that it is also a component and it can be manipulated as a component.

The Window class has two subclasses: Frame and Dialog. The Frame class is used to a create a frame inside the browser while the Dialog class will create a separate dialog box that will pop up on the screen. You can also create your own windows that appear with their own menu bars. This can be something of a security problem if people believe that the window is controlled by their own machine. If the Java applet creates a window and asks for a password, the Java applet can grab the password and send it home. People used to be able to trust the software running on their own machines. Now, even that may be suspect.

The components will act as the basic building blocks for the user interface. You'll create a bunch of them and group them together into panels. These panels themselves are components so you can nest objects easily and create strange hierarchies. You're only limited by the complexity of the information on the screen, not the structure of the AWT. Obviously, deeply nested collections of components, frames, and panels are bound to cause confusion.

Creating Components

You create a component as you do any other object. Then you add it to a panel or a container that is responsible for displaying it. The standard applet is also a panel, so you will often be adding the component to this panel. Here's an example:

```
Label l = new Label("Hi!!!");
add(l);
```

The component here, a label, is created with the text Hi!!! and added to the basic object running this code. You would probably place this code inside the init method of an applet so the add method would insert the label into the applet's basic panel.

The various layout functions are described later in this chapter.

The Panel class comes with a basic layout function. This will place the components in the panel in some fashion. The default is FlowLayout, which works much like text. The components are added left to right until there is no more horizontal space. Then the next row is begun.

The method locate *will take an x and y coordinate and find the component located there.*

You may want to position a component on your own. The move method will move a component to a particular (x,y) position and leave it there. If you need to ask a component where it is, you can execute location and it will return the information in a Point object.

The component's basic code from the class will also handle events like mouse clicks or key clicks. You can modify the behavior of a component by subclassing the component and replacing either the action or the handleEvent method that would normally handle these events.

A full description of events and actions can be found beginning on page 206.

The next several sections describe the basic components; the layout functions for placing them on the screen will follow. Finally, methods for having them react to events will finish up the chapter.

Basic AWT Components

Button

Many objects react to the methods getLabel *and* setLabel, *but they often use the information internally. The* Button *uses it to control the message.*

The button is one of the most commonly used components. If you create one, you can override the action method to react to someone pushing it. The basic constructor, Button, takes a string as the one parameter. This is the label for the button. You can access it with the method getLabel and change it with the method setLabel.

Here's some code that shows a basic applet that will resize itself when a button is pushed. You can see four copies of this applet being run by the JDK Applet Viewer in Figure 11.1. Each one corresponds to a size after one of the four buttons is pushed. If these applets were run in a browser, the HTML formatting would arrange and rearrange the boxes after the size changed. In the Mac version of the Applet Viewer, they simply exist as separate windows and the figure shows them that way.

```java
import java.awt.*;
import java.applet.*;
public class buttontest extends Applet {
  Button b1,b2,b3,b4;
  public void init(){
    b1=new Button("Wide");
    add(b1);
    b2=new Button("Tall");
    add(b2);
    b3=new Button("Small");
    add(b3);
    b4=new Button("Big");
    add(b4);
  }
  public boolean action(Event e, Object a){
    if (e.target instanceof Button) {
      if (a.equals("Wide"))
        resize(400,100);
      else if (a.equals("Tall"))
        resize(50,400);
      else if (a.equals("Small"))
        resize(100,100);
      else if (a.equals("Big"))
        resize(400,400);
    }
    return true; // Lie even if there is an error.
  }
}
```

The four buttons are easy to create in the init method. The action event of an applet handles basic events like calls to components. If a component is activated, such as the case of a button when it is clicked upon, then action will be invoked. The event in this case includes the

The section describing actions in detail can be found beginning on page 206.

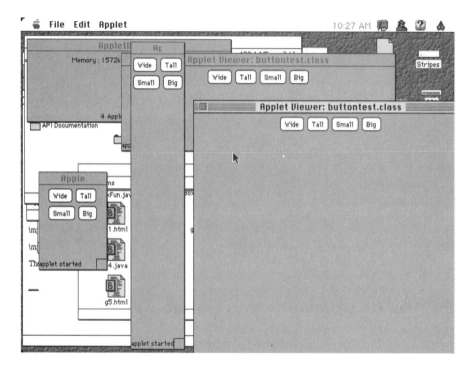

Figure 11.1. Here are four different versions of the buttontest applet running in four different windows. A different button has been pressed in each applet, creating the sizes on the screen.

target of the event, a button object. The name or label of the object is held in the parameter of the event. The resize method can be used to change the size of any component, but here it is used to resize the applet itself.

Checkboxes and Radio Buttons

Checkboxes are little boxes that act as toggle switches between on and off, or more precisely, between true and false. Radio buttons are groups of checkboxes, only one of which can be true at a particular time. Some user interfaces like the Macintosh distinguish between checkboxes and radio buttons and give them distinct looks. The Java

AWT blends the two together into one class, but displays them slightly differently.

The basic constructor is Checkbox(String s) and it takes a string that will be displayed to the right of the box as a label. As usual, you can access and change this label with the commands getLabel and setLabel. If you want to turn a checkbox on or off, simply execute setState(Boolean state). If state is true, then the checkbox is selected and displayed inset with light shading on the lower and right sides. If state is false, then the checkbox is officially unselected and the displayed on some systems as if it's raised from the panel, that is, the light shading is on the left and the top.

The other major constructor takes three arguments:

```
Checkbox(String s, CheckboxGroup g, Boolean initialState);
```

The string sets the label and the initialState determines whether the checkbox is selected or unselected. The CheckboxGroup is a small class of objects that is used to group together checkboxes so they act like radio buttons. You might create a group like this:

```
CheckboxGroup talk = new CheckboxGroup();
add(new Checkbox("To-may-toe",talk,false));
add(new Checkbox("To-mah-toh",talk,true));
```

This code will only allow one of the two buttons to be selected at a time. These buttons will also be displayed on other systems as raised or inset diamonds or lozenges as opposed to the tiny squares used for checkboxes. You use the setCurrent method to choose which radio button is in play.

The following code generates a few checkboxes and puts them on the screen. Figure 11.2 shows the applet running on the MacJDK Applet Viewer. Notice that the standard Macintosh checkbox is used for *both* the radio buttons and the stand-alone checkboxes. Individual systems may display this differently.

If you pass null for the CheckboxGroup into the constructor, you'll get a checkbox, not a radio button.

```
import java.awt.*;
import java.applet.*;
public class checkboxtest extends Applet {
  Checkbox c1,c2,c3,c4,c5,c6;
  CheckboxGroup g;
```

```
public void init(){
  g=new CheckboxGroup();
  c1=new Checkbox("To-may-toe",g,false);
  add(c1);
  c2=new Checkbox("To-mah-toh",g,false);
  add(c2);
  g.setCurrent(c1);
  c3=new Checkbox("Free Checkbox");
  add(c3);
  c4=new Checkbox("Also Free Checkbox", null, false);
  add(c4);
}
}
```

A full description of events and actions can be found beginning on page 206.

You can see that this code does not provide any action if the checkboxes are flipped. You can do this in the same way that you watch for events that hit buttons.

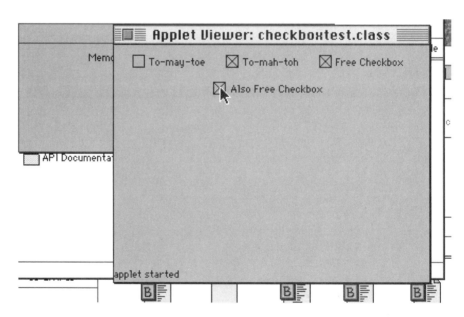

Figure 11.2. Here are four different checkboxes displayed in flow layout. The first two are grouped together. Clicking on one will reverse the other. The other two can change on their own.

Pull-down Menus

The Choice class of components produces a pull-down menu that allows you to choose among a variety of choices. The constructor, Choice(), takes no parameters. If you want to add new items to the list of choices, you execute addItem(String s).

Here's some sample code:

See page 185 to see how to use the action *routine with* a Choice *component.*
Every time a new choice is made, action *is invoked.*

```java
import java.awt.*;
import java.applet.*;
public class choicetest extends Applet {
  int count = 1;
  Button b1,b2,b3,b4;
  Choice c;
  public void init(){
    b1=new Button("One");
    add(b1);
    b2=new Button("Two");
    add(b2);
    b3=new Button("Three");
    add(b3);
    b4=new Button("Four");
    add(b4);
    c = new Choice();
    c.addItem("Un");
    c.addItem("Deux");
    c.addItem("Trois");
    c.addItem("Quatre");
    add(c);
  }
  public boolean action(Event e, Object a){
    if (e.target instanceof Button) {
      if (a.equals("One"))
        c.select(0);
      else if (a.equals("Two"))
        c.select(1);
      else if (a.equals("Three"))
        c.select("Trois");
      else if (a.equals("Four"))
        c.select("Quatre");
    }
```

```
    return true; // Lie even if there is an error.
  }
}
```

This code produces four buttons and a choice menu (Figure 11.3). There is a link between the buttons and the choice menu, but not in the other direction. If you click on a button, it will change the selection in the menu. Notice that there are two different types of parameters that you can pass the `select` method. The first type takes an integer and it selects the item on the pull-down menu using the integer as an index. In this case, the first item added was "Un," so the numbers are off by one. The second version of `select` accepts a string. This will scan the items of the choice menu and select the one with a matching label.

You can also choose items from a selection using the List *component described starting on page 189.*

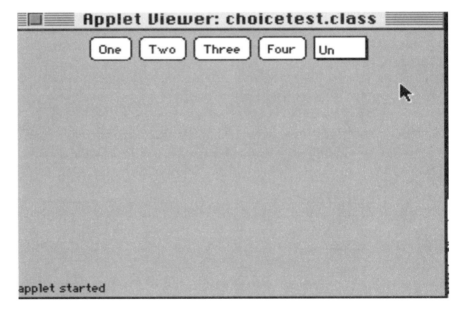

Figure 11.3. Here are the four buttons and a pull-down menu. The menu simply shows the current selection.

Labels and Text Fields

If you want to add text to a system built with AWT, you can do it in two simple ways. The Label class will print some text with three types of justification. If you want the text to be editable, then you can use the component `TextField`. The location can be set manually with the move command or it will be set automatically by the layout function. Here's code that will produce some text:

```
add(new Label("I'm automatically aligned on the left."));
add(new Label("I'm also left-aligned.", Label.LEFT));
add(new Label("I'm centered.", Label.CENTER));
add(new Label("I'm pushed to the right.",Label.RIGHT));
```

You can simply draw the text with a drawString command as well, but that code is not a component inside the AWT and comes with none of the attendant feature (or hassles). See Chapter 10 for information on drawstring.

You may find that the alignment commands can be confusing if you rely upon the layout function to set the boxes around the label components. If you leave the sizing of the component up to the AWT, then you cannot be sure how the alignment will work out.

There are four commands that you might find useful. `getText` will produce the text being displayed and `setText` will let you change it. You should use these commands if you change text. Creating and destroying components is slow because it puts more demand upon the garbage collector and the layout manager. You can also modify the alignment of text with `getAlignment` and `setAlignment`.

If you want to create editable text, then you need to use the `TextField` command. It will only offer a single line of editable text. If you need more, turn to the `TextArea` command. There are four different constructors that work like this:

```
import java.applet.*;
import java.awt.*;
public class TextFieldTest extends Applet {
  TextField t1;
  public void init(){
    add(new TextField(12));
      // 12 Characters is the minimum size.
    add(new TextField("I'm a start up message."));
      // No minimum size.
    add(new TextField("I'm also a start up.",28));
      // Both size and startup message.
    add(new TextField());
      // A blank constructor.
  }
}
```

The results of using these four different constructors can be seen in Figure 11.4. You'll notice that the fields flow directly together in this figure because the layout manager is FlowLayout. In this case, it often makes sense to alternate between regular Label components and TextField components because the layout manager will keep them next to each other.

The final constructor shows what happens if you pass in no parameters. You get a blank input field that is not immediately usable. You must change the dimensions of the component using a method prescribed for that superclass.

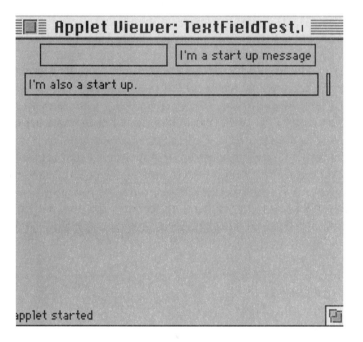

Figure 11.4. Here are four TextField components created in a window.

The TextField component comes with several other important methods. You can grab the number of columns with getColumns, but there is no corresponding setColumns listed in the Java 1.0 API. If you want to get the text out of the TextField, then execute getText. To change it, run setText.

You can manipulate what is selected inside the TextField with a number of different functions. getSelectionStart and getSelection End will return the positions of the selection's beginning and end in the text. getSelectedText will return the selection itself. If you want to change the positions of the selection, then select takes two integers for the start and the end while selectAll selects everything.

You can also manipulate the behavior of the TextField by controlling the character that is echoed to the screen when a user types. This is often done when you're asking for a password. The setEchoCharacter method takes a character and ensures that it will appear on screen instead of the typed character. getEchoCharacter will tell you what that character is. There is also a boolean function, echoCharIsSet, that returns true if the echo character is replacing something.[1]

Finally, setEditable takes a boolean parameter and turns a TextField on and off. You can test the current value with the method isEditable.

You may or may not want to interfere with the events of the TextField components. They will respond to key clicks and mouse clicks on their own. In most cases, it makes good sense for the user interface to wait until a button is pressed before the information is pulled out of a TextField. But if you need to intercede, the keyDown and corresponding keyUp commands are good beginnings.

The TextField component also generates a call to the action routine whenever a Return key is pressed. But it does not do anything if a mouse click or a Tab key changes the focus on a form. Here's an example that uses the action method to change the user interface selections. It is an extension of the version given earlier in the chapter.

Note that TextField is a subclass of TextComponent that offers the basic editing features. TextField offers extra routines to deal with echo characters and preferred sizes.

```
import java.awt.*;
import java.applet.*;
public class TextFieldTest2 extends Applet {
  int count = 1;
  Button b1,b2,b3,b4;
  Choice c;
  TextField t1;
  public void init(){
    b1=new Button("One");
    add(b1);
    b2=new Button("Two");
    add(b2);
```

---

[1]The setEchoCharacter command seems to crash the first beta of the MacJDK used to prepare this book, but it should be fixed in any version you use. It is not clear how you could turn off the echoing if you desired.

```
      b3=new Button("Three");
      add(b3);
      b4=new Button("Four");
      add(b4);
      c = new Choice();
      c.addItem("Un");
      c.addItem("Deux");
      c.addItem("Trois");
      c.addItem("Quatre");
      add(c);
      t1=new TextField("Ein",20);
      add(t1);
    }
    public boolean action(Event e, Object a){
      if (e.target instanceof Button) {
        if (a.equals("One"))
          c.select(0);
        else if (a.equals("Two"))
          c.select(1);
        else if (a.equals("Three"))
          c.select("Trois");
        else if (a.equals("Four"))
          c.select("Quatre");
      } else if (e.target instanceof Choice) {
        if (a.equals("Un"))
          t1.setText("Ein");
        else if (a.equals("Deux"))
          t1.setText("Zwei");
        else if (a.equals("Trois"))
          t1.setText("Drei");
        else if (a.equals("Quatre"))
          t1.setText("Vier");
      } else if (e.target instanceof TextField) {
        if (a.equals("Ein"))
          c.select(0);
        else if (a.equals("Zwei"))
          c.select(1);
        else if (a.equals("Drei"))
          c.select(2);
```

```
      else if (a.equals("Vier"))
        c.select(3);
    }
    return true; // Lie even if there is an error.
  }
}
```

In this case, the `action` routine responds to three different types of events by testing to see what class generated the event. The parameter passed to `action` by hitting the Return key is the text inside the `TextField`. You can see the result in Figure 11.5.

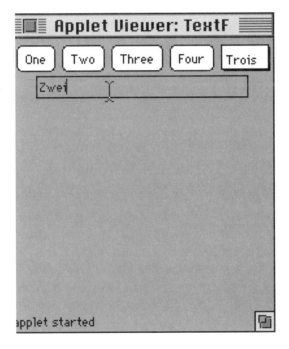

Figure 11.5. Here is a mixture of `Buttons`, a `Choice` component, and a `TextField` that interact through the `action` method.

Text Areas

If you need more than a line of text, then you should use `TextArea` instead of a `Label` or a `TextField` component. These components come with scrollbars and can be easily formatted to take up multiple lines. The basic constructor for a `TextArea` takes an initial string, a height, and a length. There are also three other constructors that will build a `TextArea` if either the initial string, the dimensions, or both are missing. If you don't specify the dimensions with a constructor, then you must change them separately with either the `resize` or `reshape` methods.

When the applet is running, you can modify the text with several commands. `insertText` accepts a string and an offset and then inserts that string into the `TextArea`. `appendText` adds a string to the end. If you want to replace one section of text, `replaceText` will take a string, a start offset, and an ending offset. It will delete all of the text between the start and the end and then insert the string in its place. There is no `deleteText` specified in the 1.0 API for the AWT, so you can use `replaceText` with an empty string.

The `TextArea` is also a subclass of `TextComponent` just like `TextField`. That means all of the functionality in the `TextComponent` class applies to `TextArea` components. You can use `select`, `selectAll`, `getSelectionStart`, `getSelectionEnd`, `getSelectedText`, `getText`, and `setText` in the same way.

The `TextArea` components come with scrollbars, but the API is not clear about how you can either access them or change their behavior.

Here's an example of how a `TextArea` class can be used. This example is somewhat more complicated because it uses a different layout manager. `GridLayout` will arrange the items in a square. In this case, the command `new GridLayout(2,2,3,3)` means "create a two-by-two grid of the components and leave three pixels between both the horizontal and vertical boundaries."

```
import java.awt.*;
import java.applet.*;
public class TextAreaTest extends Applet {
  TextArea t1,t2,t3,t4;
  public void init(){
    setLayout(new GridLayout(2,2,3,3));
    String s= "Here is line 1. It should be pretty long and
      wrap around. \n Here is line two. \n And line 3.";
    t1=new TextArea(s,10,20);
    t1.minimumSize(10,20);
```

```
      t1.preferredSize(15,45);
      add(t1);
      t2=new TextArea(s,5,30);
      t2.minimumSize(5,30);
      t2.preferredSize(15,40);
      add(t2);
      t3=new TextArea(s, 7,20);
      t3.minimumSize(7,20);
      t3.preferredSize(15,45);
      add(t3);
      t4=new TextArea(s,12,25);
      t4.minimumSize(10,20);
      t4.preferredSize(15,45);
      add(t4);
  }
}
```

Figure 11.6 shows two different versions of the same applet. Notice how the dimensions of the TextArea components were adjusted directly by the layout manager. This is one reason why you might want to use a constructor for TextArea that doesn't specify the initial size. In other layout forms, the size is kept unchanged.

You'll also notice that the minimumSize and preferredSize methods have no effect on the final product. Also, the figure does not show a horizontal scrollbar. The text is merely wrapped. This may be an artifact of the Macintosh OS, and programmers who use Java's AWT should be aware that the implementation may not be as constant as you may want. There are deeper issues about whether a cross-platform program should provide perfectly identical views or views that blend in correctly with the rules that govern the local OS. These issues have never been resolved and they probably never will be. You should be aware that someone porting Java to a new machine may have different views than you and you could be surprised by little details.

Lists

If you want a scrolling list of items like you find in many file-selection dialog boxes, the List class offers you a component that will handle

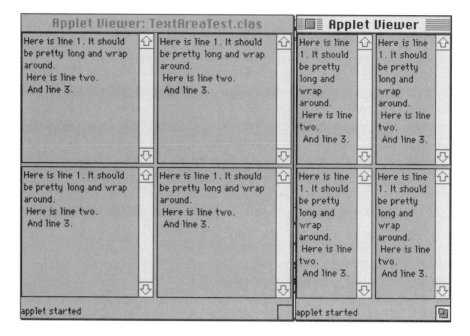

Figure 11.6. Here are four `TextArea` components arranged in a two-by-two grid by the `GridLayout` command. There are two versions of the applet running in two different windows to show how it is resized. The `minimumSize` and `preferredSize` methods have no effect.

this chore. You can build a list of items and let a user select multiple items.

There are two basic constructors. The first takes no arguments and produces a list whose dimensions are controlled by the layout manager. The second accepts an integer that specifies the number of visible lines and a boolean that controls whether the list allows multiple selection. Passing the constructor a `true` allows the user to select many different lines.

If you want to change the ability of a list to accept multiple selections, you can use the method `setMultipleSelections` that takes a boolean value as a parameter. `allowsMultipleSelections` returns the current setting.

The `addItem` command will insert items into the list. If you just pass `addItem` a string, it will place this item at the end of the list. If you also pass in an integer for the second parameter, it will add the new item after the existing item with that index. There are two versions of delItem. One takes a single parameter and deletes that item. (The first one is numbered 0.) The other takes a beginning and an end point. The method clear deletes them all. You can also change an item with the replaceItem method by passing a new string and the index.

The items in the list are either selected or deselected. You can access the data about what is selected or not in many different ways. The simplest method is to test a particular item with the method isSelected. Pass in the index and this method returns a boolean. You can also get an array of integers that contains the indices of all of the selected items. getSelectedIndexes returns the array. You should test for its size to prevent run-time errors. This information is also available as a string. getSelectedItem will return one item and getSelectedItems will return all of them. If none are selected, then null comes back.

You can change the selection of particular items with the select and deselect commands. And makeVisible will make a particular index scroll into view.

Here's some code that creates a list, adds and deletes a few items, and then interacts with a Choice component.

```java
import java.awt.*;
import java.applet.*;
public class ListTest extends Applet {
  List l;
  Choice c;
  public void init(){
    l=new List(10,true);
      // Ten lines with multiple selection allowed.
    l.addItem("alpha");
    l.addItem("bee");
    l.addItem("gamma");
    l.addItem("dee");
    l.delItem(1);
      // Delete "bee".
      // Remember the first element is zero.
    l.addItem("beta",1);
    l.replaceItem("delta",3);
    add(l);
    c = new Choice();
```

```
      c.addItem("Un");
      c.addItem("Deux");
      c.addItem("Trois");
      c.addItem("Quatre");
      add(c);
      l.select(2);
    }
    public void ToggleItem(int i){
      // Changes the state of a list item.
      System.out.println("Toggling Item:"+i);
      if (l.isSelected(i)){
        System.out.println("Deselecting.");
        l.deselect(i);
      } else {
        System.out.println("Selecting.");
        l.select(i);
      }
    }
    public boolean action(Event e, Object a){
      System.out.println((String)a);
      if (e.target instanceof List) {
        if (a.equals("alpha"))
          c.select(0);
        else if (a.equals("beta"))
          c.select(1);
        else if (a.equals("gamma"))
          c.select(2);
        else if (a.equals("delta"))
          c.select(3);
      }
      else if (e.target instanceof Choice) {
        if (a.equals("Un"))
          ToggleItem(0);
        else if (a.equals("Deux"))
          ToggleItem(1);
        else if (a.equals("Trois"))
          ToggleItem(2);
        else if (a.equals("Quatre"))
          ToggleItem(3);
      }
```

```
    return true; //Lie if an error.
  }
}
```

The code in the init routine just demonstrates how lists can be built up and changed. The ToggleItem is just something that will flip the state of a list item. The action method shows how to handle the actions that are generated by the List component. The second parameter comes with a string with the label of a particular item. You can interpret it how you want. The only problem is that the action is only generated when there is a double click. [2]

It is unclear to me why a double click generates an action and a single click doesn't. If you want to grab changes in a selection, you must watch for events of type LIST_SELECT and LIST_DESELECT and catch them by subclassing handleEvent.

Figure 11.7 shows how it looks.

A full description of handleEvent *can be found beginning on page 206.*

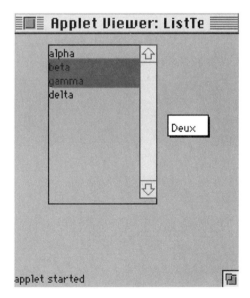

Figure 11.7. This applet contains a List component and a Choice component that are linked by the action method.

---

[2]The MacJDK implementation had several errors in the repainting of the List when I constructed this example.

Blank Canvas

One of the simplest subclasses of the Component class is the Canvas. This is basically a blank component with a paint method. If you want to draw your own information on the screen or create a particular type of indicator, then this is a good place to start.

The class only comes with a constructor method, addNotify, that is used to create a peer and a paint method. This next example shows how to build your own pie chart indicator by subclassing the Canvas class. The code PieDisplay class will accept both a maximum value and a current value. At any time, it will display the value as a percentage of the maximum by shading a circle using the drawArc method.

If you want to draw on the screen with the AWT, then you should create a canvas, as in the following code. Subclassing the applet's paint method is asking for trouble because you interfere with the redrawing of the control components. You can see the results of this code in Figure 11.8.

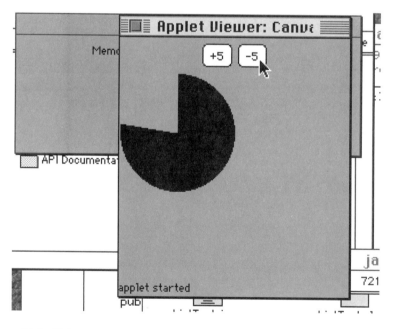

Figure 11.8. This PieDisplay class will draw a pie chart on the screen and modify it based upon the values sent to it.

```java
import java.awt.*;
import java.applet.*;
class PieDisplay extends Canvas{
  int Maximum;
    // The maximum value of the chart.
  int Value=0;
    // What is the value of the display.
  public PieDisplay(int v,int m){
    super();
    Maximum=m;
    Value=v;
  }
  public void setValue(int v){
    Value = v;
  }
  public int getValue(){
    return Value;
  }
  public void changeValue(int amount){
    int newValue = Value + amount;
    if (newValue>Maximum) {
      Value = Maximum;
    } else if (newValue<0){
      Value = 0;
    } else {
      Value = newValue;
    }
  }
  public void paint(Graphics g){
    double frac=360.0*((double)Value/(double)Maximum);
    g.fillArc(1,1,100,100,0,(int)frac);
  }
}
public class CanvasTest extends Applet {
  Button plus,minus;
  PieDisplay p;
  public void init(){
    plus = new Button("+5");
    minus = new Button("-5");
```

```
    p = new PieDisplay(100,200);
    p.resize(200,200);
    add(plus);add(minus); add(p);
  }
  public boolean action(Event e, Object a){
    if (e.target instanceof Button) {
      if (a.equals("+5"))
        p.changeValue(5);
      else if (a.equals("-5"))
        p.changeValue(-5);
      p.repaint();
      }
    return true;
  }
}
```

Scrollbars

Scrollbars are popular methods for inputting values because they provide simple ways to constrain the user's choices. It is quite easy to create a scrollbar that runs between 1 and 11 or 0 and 200. Numerical input boxes are clumsy by comparison.

The Scrollbar *class is a subclass of* Component, *the basic AWT class.*

The AWT offers scrollbars like all of the other major GUI APIs. These components behave in exactly the same way as scrollbars on the Macintosh or Microsoft Windows. The major constructor for the Scrollbar class takes five ints for parameters. They are as follows:

1. An int that specifies the orientation. The two acceptable values are Scrollbar.HORIZONTAL and Scrollbar.VERTICAL, which mean exactly what you think.

2. A value specifying the position of the slider upon creation.

3. The amount to increment or decrement when changing an entire "page." If you click on the slider, you can set the value to any increment. But if you click in the scrollbar, it will either increment or decrement the value by the "page" value.

4. The minimum value for the scrollbar.

5. The maximum value for the scrollbar.

You can also feed the `Scrollbar` constructor no parameters if you want to create an empty scrollbar that will be modified later. You can change the position of the slider with the commands `getValue` and `setValue`. The line increment is the amount that is added or subtracted when the arrows are clicked. This is normally 1. You can access the value with `getLineIncrement` and change it with `setLineIncrement`. Similarly, the amount of increment in a "page" is accessed with `getPageIncrement` and changed with `setPageIncrement`.

You can also use `getMaximum` or `getMinimum`, but if you want change these values, you must use `setValues`. This method accepts four `int` values which are the current value of the scrollbar, the page size, the minimum, and the maximum.

The `Scrollbar` class does not generate any calls to `action` when a user manipulates it. If you want your program to react to the scrollbars, you need to write your own version of `handleEvent`. This is a more general-level routine for controlling the interaction.

This simple example creates a simple "calculator" for computing the square or the square root of a number. The horizontal scrollbar ranges between 1 and 10 while the vertical bar ranges between 1 and 100. The vertical bar is always pegged to be the square of the horizontal bar. If either is manipulated, the `handleEvent` reacts and adjusts the other bar so that the right answer is preserved. The numerical values are displayed in the center.

This version uses the `BorderLayout` manager to arrange the components around the outside of the applet. This is a common choice when you're using the scrollbars. As you can see in Figure 11.9, the labels do not work well on the boundaries, but the scrollbars fit naturally.

For more information on `BorderLayout`, *please turn to page 205.*

```java
import java.awt.*;
import java.applet.*;
public class Sliderule extends Applet {
  Label m1,l1,l2;
  Scrollbar s1,s2;
  public void init(){
    setLayout(new BorderLayout());
    l1=new Label("x:",Label.RIGHT);
    s1= new Scrollbar(Scrollbar.HORIZONTAL,1,2,1,10);
    m1=new Label("1");
    l2=new Label("x squared:",Label.RIGHT);
```

```
    s2= new Scrollbar(Scrollbar.VERTICAL,1,10,1,100);
    add("North",l1);
    add("West",s2);add("South",s1);add("East",l2);add
      ("Center",m1);
  }
  public boolean handleEvent(Event evt) {
    if (evt.target instanceof Scrollbar) {
      if (s1.equals(evt.target)) {
        int v =s1.getValue();
        int vv=v*v;
        m1.setText(String.valueOf(v)+"  "+ String.valueOf
                    (vv));
        s2.setValue(vv);
      } else {
        int vv=s2.getValue();
        int v=(int)Math.sqrt(vv);
        m1.setText(String.valueOf(v)+"  "+ String.valueOf
                    (vv));
        s1.setValue(v);
      }
    }
    return true;
  }
}
```

Figure 11.9 shows the window with these scrollbars intact. You should also note that there are a number of events about the scrollbar that have predefined values. The code in this version of `handleEvent` simply reacted whenever the scrollbar was hit. You can also filter events by looking at the `id` field. Here are some static variables (constants) that may inhabit this field:

These events are static
variables in the Event
class.

SCROLL_PAGE_UP This is used if the click occurs in the bar, but outside the arrows or the slider. Either the bottom or the right is the UP half of the bar.

SCROLL_PAGE_DOWN This is used if the click occurs in the bar, but outside the arrows or the slider. Either the top or the left is the DOWN half of the bar.

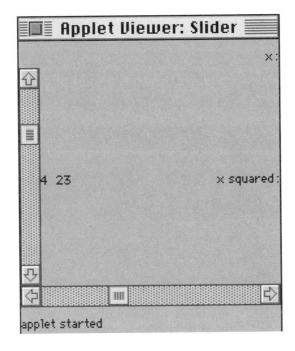

Figure 11.9. Here are two `Scrollbar` components placed in the "West" and "South" positions of a `BorderLayout`.

SCROLL_LINE_UP A click in the bottom or right arrow produces this event.

SCROLL_LINE_DOWN A click in the top or left arrow produces this event.

SCROLL_ABSOLUTE Action in the slider generates this event.

Panels

The `Panel` class is one of the most useful components, but it doesn't display anything at all. It merely aggregates several other components in one bigger box and lays out the components inside this panel. You might want to use this to create nested layers of components that are correctly laid out by the layout manager. These components are important tools if you intend to give the layout manager the power to arrange your widgets to fit into the local browser's window.

The Panel class is a subclass of the Container class. Most of the functionality that you'll use is actually built into the Container class. The only major advance is the addition of the addNotify method that is used to send messages to peers.

You add components to a panel in the same way that you add components to your applet. This shouldn't be surprising because the Applet class is a subclass of the Panel class. This next block of code creates two panels and arranges for both panels to be set up by the GridLayout manager. Four buttons are added to one and two labels are added to the other.

```java
import java.awt.*;
import java.applet.*;
public class PanelTest extends Applet {
  Panel p1,p2;
  Button b1,b2,b3,b4;
  Label l1,l2;
  int v1 = 100;
  int v2 = 100;
  public void init(){
    p1=new Panel();
    p1.setLayout(new GridLayout(2,2,3,3));
    p2=new Panel();
    p2.setLayout(new GridLayout(1,2,4,4));
    b1 = new Button("+5");
    b2 = new Button("+10");
    b3 = new Button("-5");
    b4 = new Button("-10");
    p1.add(b1);p1.add(b2);p1.add(b3);p1.add(b4);
    l1 = new Label("100");
    l2 = new Label("100");
    p2.add(l1);p2.add(l2);
    add(p1);
    add(p2);
  }
  public boolean action(Event e, Object a){
    if (e.target instanceof Button) {
      if (a.equals("+5")) {
        v1 = v1+5;
        v2 = v2-5;
```

```
      }
      else if (a.equals("-5")){
        v1 = v1-5;
        v2 = v2+5;
      }
      else if (a.equals("-10")){
        v1 = v1-10;
        v2 = v2+10;
      }
      else if (a.equals("+10")){
        v1 = v1+10;
        v2 = v2-10;
      }
      l1.setText(String.valueOf(v1));
      l2.setText(String.valueOf(v2));
      }
    return true;
  }
}
```

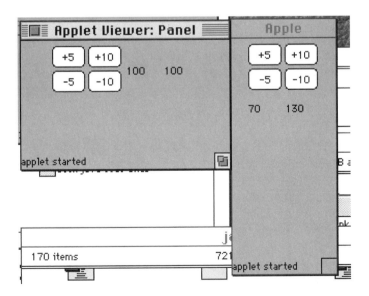

Figure 11.10. Here are two versions of the PanelTest applet. There are two panels that are arranged by the FlowLayout manager. The items inside each panel are arranged by a GridLayout manager.

Figure 11.10 shows two different version of the same applet running in two different windows. The inside of each panel is arranged by the `GridLayout` manager so the buttons and the labels fall into a nice grid. The panels, however, are governed by the applet's layout manager, which is the default `FlowLayout`. That means the components are added left to right, top to bottom, like English text flowing across a page. So the wide window displays p2 to the right of p1 but the tall page displays p2 below p1.

You can create any number of arbitrary layout schemes using nested panels. Obviously, nesting them too much may make things too complex for the user. Also, you may find that some objects are obscured if the window is small. If the area allocated to a panel is small, it may clip off some of the objects inside of it.

Layout Managers

The code in the previous section has used layout managers to place components in an applet. The AWT includes this functionality because the size of the box that will hold an applet is often unclear. It might be large or small because of the size of the HTML browser and the screen that is displaying it. The AWT designers hoped to include some semi-intelligent functions that would arrange the components in a box so they can look aesthetically pleasing in most cases.

The `FlowLayout` Manager

The basic layout manager is the `FlowLayout`, the default layout manager for any new panel. It will display the components like English words are displayed on lines on a word processor. Components are added to a line until the length is too long to fit, then a new line begins. You can change the intercomponent spacing and arrange for the lines to be either centered (`FlowLayout.CENTER`), left-justified (`FlowLayout.LEFT`) or right-justified (`FlowLayout.RIGHT`). The default is centered.

If you want to change the layout manager for an applet or a panel, you would type:

```
setLayout(new FlowLayout(FlowLayout.RIGHT),5,10);
```

The constructor for FlowLayout takes one parameter that defines the justification. The two integers that are passed to setLayout will control the horizontal and vertical spacing. The 5 means add five pixels between each component on a line.

Here's some code that illustrates how the FlowLayout manager can cause trouble:

```
import java.awt.*;
import java.applet.*;
public class FlowLayoutTest extends Applet {
  public void init(){
    setLayout(new FlowLayout(FlowLayout.LEFT));
    add(new Label("Name:"));
    add(new TextField(" type Cereal Name here",20));
    add(new Label("Rank:"));
    add(new TextField(" type your ranking here",30));
    add(new Label("Cereal Number:"));
    add(new TextField(" enter UPC Code",10));
  }
}
```

Figure 11.11 shows two different windows running the same applet. Notice how the line breaks can screw up the alignment of the

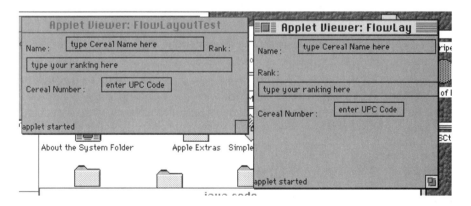

Figure 11.11. Here are two versions of the FlowLayoutTest applet. There are two panels that are arranged by the FlowLayout manager. Notice how the line breaks can be problematic if the size of the applet changes.

fields and the labels. The solution for problems like this is to either use panels and/or GridLayout managers. The FlowLayout manager is best for arranging panels.

The GridLayout **Manager**

The GridLayout manager places items on the corner of a grid and then grows or shrinks them until they fit. Here's the same code from before modified to use the GridLayout manager.

```
import java.awt.*;
import java.applet.*;
public class GridLayoutTest extends Applet {
  public void init(){
    setLayout(new GridLayout(3,2));
    add(new Label("Name:"));
    add(new TextField(" type Cereal Name here",20));
    add(new Label("Rank:"));
    add(new TextField(" type your ranking here",30));
    add(new Label("Cereal Number:"));
    add(new TextField(" enter UPC Code",10));
  }
}
```

The constructor for the GridLayout class takes either two or four parameters. The two in this example specify the number of rows and columns in the grid. If you add two extra parameters, they control the extra pixels added between components. Figure 11.12 shows two windows defined this way.

The GridLayout class will divide the length by the number of columns and the height by the number of rows and allocate a grid unit to each component. Sometimes, the component will grow to grab the entire rectangle.

See how TextArea *will react to the* GridLayout *manager on page 187.*

There is also a more complicated version known as the GridBag Layout. You can control many different facets of the way that items are displayed inside their rectangles on the grid by fiddling with the GridBagConstraints class. This level of detail is beyond the scope of this book. Please check out the API definition files, which include a long example.

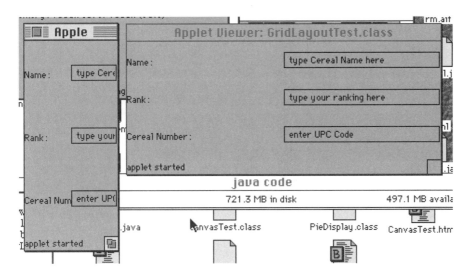

Figure 11.12. Here are two versions of the GridLayoutTest applet. Extra space can be a problem if the applet changes radically in size.

The BorderLayout **Manager**

The BorderLayout manager is quite useful when you're using scroll-bars or other thin items that must be placed around the outside of a box. The add method behaves differently when there is a BorderLayout method ruling the screen. You must specify the location of the component instead of simply adding them in order. There are five different locations that are recognized: North, East, South, West, and Center. Each of them is passed as a string to the add method, like this example:

```java
import java.awt.*;
import java.applet.*;
public class BorderLayoutTest extends Applet {
  Button b;
  Scrollbar s1,s2,s3,s4;
  public void init(){
    setLayout(new BorderLayout());
    s1= new Scrollbar(Scrollbar.HORIZONTAL,1,2,1,10);
    s2= new Scrollbar(Scrollbar.VERTICAL,1,10,1,100);
    s3= new Scrollbar(Scrollbar.HORIZONTAL,1,2,1,10);
    s4= new Scrollbar(Scrollbar.VERTICAL,1,10,1,100);
```

```
    b=new Button("Press me");
    add("North",s3);
    add("West",s2);add("South",s1);add("East",s4);
    add("Center",b);
  }
}
```

Figure 11.13 shows two different versions of the BorderLayoutTest applet. The scrollbars adhere to the outside borders and grow and shrink with the size of the window. The rest of the window is allocated to the center component. In this case a Button object is used to show how some components are ruled by the size of their box. In many cases, you might use a Canvas in the center of the screen and have it react to the scrollbars.

Events!

Anyone who has developed user interfaces for modern windowed environments like the Apple Macintosh or machines running Microsoft

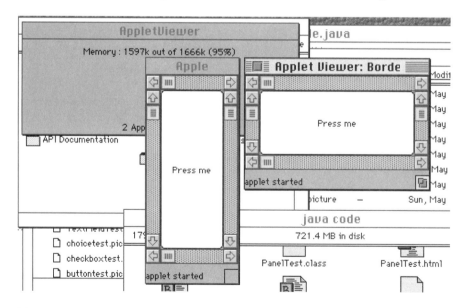

Figure 11.13. Here are two versions of the BorderLayoutTest applet. Notice how the central Button object shinks or grows to fit the box. Some components will do this while others won't.

Windows knows that the *event* is the fundamental center of the program. A user interface program doesn't process data; it waits for events and then reacts to them. Naturally, you'll need to do the same thing if you want your applet to interact with the user. If you're just animating some little set of pictures, there isn't any need to read this section, but if you're going to be asking the user for information, then you need to understand how the AWT responds to events.

The description of the AWT and the components in this chapter have provided a good glimpse of how you can modify methods like `handleEvent` and `action` to intercept events and take action when they occur. These two methods are called whenever a `Component` object receives an event. If you want to create a method that will receive all of the events for an applet, then you include a new version of `handleEvent` in your subclass of `Applet`. If you want to change how an individual component reacts, then you would create a subclass of that component and add your own version of `handleEvent` to that class.

The code beginning on page 197 shows how to create your own `handleEvent` *for an applet.*

The events are actually objects from the class `Event` and they carry the information inside a number of different variables. Here are the variables that you can access:

`target` This contains a `Object` pointing to the component that received the event. It may be a `Scrollbar` or a `Button`. You can filter the events by testing this `target` variable with either the `equals` method or the `instanceof` method.

`when` A `long` integer containing a time stamp for when the event occured.

`id` This contains an `int` that describes the type of action. These integers are defined as static variables (constants) in the class `Event`. A description of them follows this description of the regular variables in the class.

`x` If the event comes with an x coordinate, this `int` holds it.

`y` If the event also comes with a y coordinate, this `int` holds it.

`key` An `int` that represents which key was pressed if it was a keyboard event.

`modifiers` Another `int` that holds the state of the modifier keys like the Shift key or the Alt key.

clickCount When MOUSE_DOWN events are signalled, this holds the number of clicks that began the event. 1 is a single click and 2 is a double click. Many user interfaces distinguish between these numbers.

arg The API calls this an "arbitrary argument."

evt If you link events together in a linked list as the OS might do if they come in quickly, this points to the next event in the list.

There are two possible ways to filter the events that called into handleEvent. You can either do it by the type of action, which is stored in the id field, or you can check the type of the target. In many cases, you'll need to do both. Here's a list of the types of static variables that are defined in the Event class. The id field will hold one of them.

WINDOW_DESTROY When the life of a window comes to an end, this is event appears.

WINDOW_EXPOSE   If a window is brought to view, this event is reported.

WINDOW_ICONIFY   Windows can be put out of the way as icons. If the user does this, then this event is generated so you can take the appropriate action.

WINDOW_DEICONIFY   If a window is recreated, this event takes hold.

WINDOW_MOVED Should a window be dragged across the screen, you can react to it by filtering for this event.

KEY_PRESS When a key is pressed, this event is generated. Note that a different event, KEY_RELEASE will follow.

KEY_RELEASE The followup event to KEY_PRESS. You should note that it is often important to distinguish between the click down and the click release in a mouse event because the mouse can move between these events. While this can't happen with the keyboard, you might use these two events to allow a key to toggle some action. For instance, some programmers change the on-line help information when a modifier key like the Shift key is pressed.

KEY_ACTION   Actions are different from events and these actions are generated when a key is pressed.

KEY_ACTION_RELEASE This action comes when the key is released.

MOUSE_DOWN When a mouse button is pressed down, this event will appear. Note that it is often considered bad user interface programming form to react to the mouse button going down. You should wait until it comes up to allow the user to change his mind by moving the mouse to a benign part of the window. You should provide some visual feedback, however, to the user on the down click. Highlighting a button or changing a radio button is acceptable.

MOUSE_UP When the mouse comes up, this event is generated and you should finalize any action started by the mouse click.

MOUSE_MOVE When the mouse moves, this event arrives with the new coordinates.

MOUSE_ENTER When a mouse's cursor is first dragged into a component's bounding box, then this event is created. It will show the x and y coordinates of where the mouse entered. A common response to this event is changing the on-line help to describe the component under the cursor.

MOUSE_EXIT When the cursor leaves the component, this event appears carrying the x and y position the last time the cursor was in a component.

MOUSE_DRAG This is similar to MOUSE_MOVE, but it is generated when the mouse button is down.

SCROLL_LINE_UP Clicking in a scrollbar's "up" arrow is supposed to add one notch to the scrollbar's unit. This Scrollbar component does this automatically. This event lets you add your own actions to accompany the change.

SCROLL_LINE_DOWN This is generated when the "down" scrollbar arrow is clicked.

SCROLL_PAGE_UP If you click in the part of the scrollbar that lies between the thumb or slider and the "up" arrow, then the Scrollbar component will add an entire "page" value to the value of the scrollbar. You can also get in on the action if you watch for this event.

SCROLL_PAGE_DOWN   The "page down" section lies between the slider and the "down" arrow. If a click occurs there, this event is generated.

LIST_SELECT   If someone selects an item in a list, this is activated. Note that if they double-click, then it will also generate an action.

LIST_DESELECT   If a list item is deselected, then this is event comes down the queue.

ACTION_EVENT   Action events are a subset of events that are passed on to the action method. You might want to only filter these significant events instead of testing for each mouse movement.

LOAD_FILE   If a file is loaded, then this is called.

SAVE_FILE   Should a file be saved, then this is called.

GOT_FOCUS   If there is more than one text input field on the screen, then the keyboard actions can only be directed at one of them. This is the one with the focus. This event is generated if the mouse clicks on a field activating it.

LOST_FOCUS   If the focus goes somewhere else, this event is called. You might use this to process the data in the field in the background to test to see if it is valid.

The id field will hold one of those values indicating what event happened. Naturally, the values in the id and the target should match. It wouldn't make sense for a SCROLL_LINE_DOWN to come in the id field when the target points to a Button object.

If a KEY_PRESS event is generated, then the key field will contain an integer pointing to a particular key and the modifiers field will contain pointers describing which modifier keys are down. Some of the keys have special values that are defined by static variables in the Event class. They are:

HOME The Home key, which is often used to return a cursor to the beginning of a line.

END The End key, often used to move a cursor to the end of a line of text.

PGUP The Page Up key should move you up a document by an entire page.

PGDN The opposite of PGUP.

UP The up arrow used in cursor manipulation and games.

DOWN The down arrow.

LEFT The left arrow.

RIGHT The right arrow.

F1 **through** F12 The function keys F1 through F12. Note that not all keyboards support all these keys.

If you want to test the value of the modifier field, then you should AND the modifier field with one of the following masks : SHIFT_MASK, CTRL_MASK, META_MASK, or ALT_MASK. You can also test these by executing one of the methods: shiftDown, controlDown, or metaDown.[3]

How to Filter Events

The most macho way to filter events is to write your own version of handleEvent. This method is called when every type of event occurs and it must be ready to intercede. But this may be overkill in some situations. If you build a fairly complicated user interface, you may be able to rely upon the basic behavior in the AWT to handle the user's actions. The TextField and TextArea components will handle almost all of the important interactions on their own. But you still might need to grab particular actions. Then you can use more specific methods like action or mouseDown to handle only these specific actions.

Mouse Event Routines

Here's a list of some of these "smaller" mouse methods that you can also subclass if you only have specific needs:

mouseDown Called when a mouse button is pressed down.

---

[3]My version of the API documentation doesn't list an altDown method, but one might be added for the sake of completeness.

mouseUp Called when the mouse button is released.

mouseMove Started up when a mouse is moved with the button up.

mouseDrag Called when a mouse is moved while the button is down.

mouseEnter When a mouse enters a component, this is called.

mouseExit When a mouse leaves a component, this is called.

These mouse methods are called when the corresponding mouse events are generated. There is a one-to-one connection between events like MOUSE_DOWN and the call to the mouseDown function. Normally, the standard version of handleEvent for the applet would grab the mouse click and parcel it out to the mouseDown function. If you subclass this mouseDown method, you can grab the click without rewriting handleEvent.

All of the mouse methods described above take three parameters and return a boolean like this template:

```
public boolean mouseDown(Event evt, int x, int y){
  // Some code to do stuff.
  return true;
}
```

The Event object should have id set to MOUSE_DOWN, but you can also access information about any target or the time the event was generated. The x and y values are the coordinates of the click.

Here's an example of how to use a mouse routine. This one watches for any dragging action when the mouse button is down. If it occurs, it stores the coordinates in an array that is used to paint a comet-like tail behind the mouse.

```
import java.awt.*;
import java.applet.*;
public class mouseFollowCode extends Applet {
  final int ShadowLength = 15;
  int[] xx = new int[ShadowLength];
  int[] yy = new int[ShadowLength];
  int now = 0;
  public void init(){
    for (int i=0; i<ShadowLength; i++) {
```

```
      xx[i]= 0;
      yy[i]= 0;
    }
  }
  public boolean mouseDrag(Event evt,int x, int y){
    now++;
    if (now>=ShadowLength) {
      now=0;
    }
    xx[now]=x;
    yy[now]=y;
    repaint();
    return true;
  }
  public void paint(Graphics g){
    int i = now;
    Color c = Color.blue;
    do {
      g.setColor(c);
      g.drawString("X",xx[i],yy[i]);
      c=c.darker();
      i++;
      if (i>=ShadowLength){ i=0;}
    } while (i!= now);
  }
}
```

You can see what the tail looks like in Figure 11.14. Note that there are two tails in this image. One is the current tail behind the mouse and the other is a leftover tail that is being erased step by step. Another solution is to create another method subclassing mouseUp that would erase the array and make the comet tail disappear.

Key Events

There is also a collection of event routines that respond to keyboard actions. This collection of methods in the applet AWT are called for each keyboard action; they are the keyDown and keyUp methods. They are called when the corresponding KEY_PRESS and KEY_RELEASE events

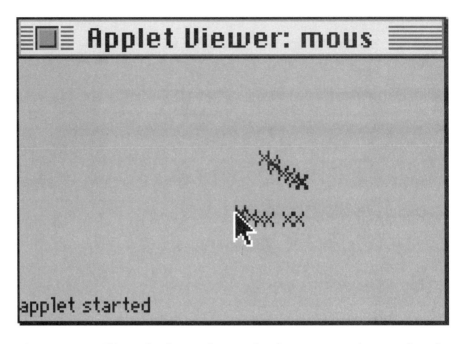

Figure 11.14. This code shows the result of a program that watches for mouseDrag events and records them, creating a tail behind the mouse every time that it is moved while the button is down.

are generated. Here are two templates you might use to subclass these methods:

```
public boolean keyDown(Event evt, int key) {
return true;
}
public boolean keyUp(Event evt, int key){
return true;
}
```

Events and Panels

You can create arbitrarily complex collections of Panels and Containers and they will each filter the events. The boolean value returned by an event-handling routine does not need to be pegged to be true at all times. In reality, it should only be set to be true if the current routine has handled the event successfully. Most of the examples in this book do that. In fact in most cases, if you're defining a method to handle an event, you're going to want to return true.

When you start building nested contraptions, however, there may be times when you want certain elements to ignore events and let some other part of the code collect them. At this time, it is important to understand just how the events flow. When an event is generated, the AWT begins with the component that was the focus of the event. If it is a mouse click, then it is the component under the mouse. If it is a keyboard event, then it is the TextField that is currently in focus. Often, the handleEvent for that component will do the right thing and return a true. If it doesn't, the AWT tries the next component that contains the current component. This will probably be a panel. It proceeds up this chain until it reaches the Applet, which is the final Panel in the chain.

On occasion, the component's local version of handleEvent might do something with an event and then return false to give the enclosing Panel a crack at the event. The Scrollbar, for instance, will need to redraw itself and change the position of the slider if someone clicks on a part of it. But it will also pass along its event to the handleEvent of the enclosing Panel because that Panel may contain another object that needs to react to the change.

Page 219 shows how to pass up events from different classes that might not fall in a direct chain. You may need to do this if you need to pass information between two objects in different parts of the hierarchy.

A good way to understand how the events flow in the AWT is to add your own debugging routines to the code. This next example, EventTest, builds up several panels of AWT widgets and informs you when certain events occur. The standard Panel is replaced by a custom subclass, MyPanel, that will report all calls to handleEvent. Not all events will arrive there and you can gather some information about the nature of the events in AWT by playing. Figure 11.15 shows what the panels look like.

```
import java.awt.*;
import java.applet.*;
class Converter {
  public static String IdToString(int id){
    switch (id){
    case Event.MOUSE_DOWN:
      return "MOUSE_DOWN";
    case Event.MOUSE_UP:
      return "MOUSE_UP";
    case Event.MOUSE_MOVE:
```

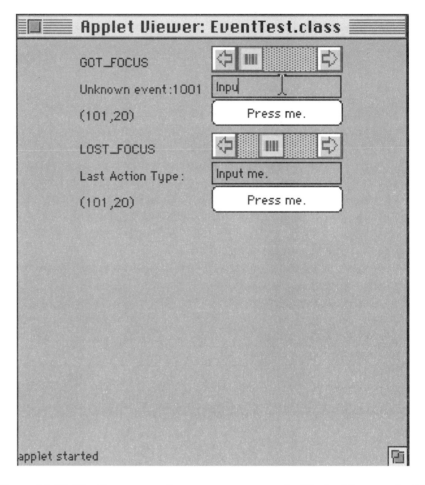

Figure 11.15. The EventTest class creates two panels filled with several widgets that generate events when they're manipulated. You can use this to watch how the AWT's event mechanism behaves.

```
    return "MOUSE_MOVE";
case Event.MOUSE_DRAG:
    return "MOUSE_DRAG";
case Event.MOUSE_ENTER:
    return "MOUSE_ENTER";
case Event.MOUSE_EXIT:
    return "MOUSE_DOWN";
case Event.KEY_PRESS:
```

```
        return "KEY_PRESS";
      case Event.KEY_RELEASE:
        return "KEY_RELEASE";
      case Event.KEY_ACTION:
        return "KEY_ACTION";
      case Event.KEY_ACTION_RELEASE:
        return "KEY_ACTION_RELEASE";
      case Event.SCROLL_LINE_DOWN:
        return "SCROLL_LINE_DOWN";
      case Event.SCROLL_ABSOLUTE:
        return "SCROLL_ABSOLUTE";
      case Event.SCROLL_LINE_UP:
        return "SCROLL_LINE_UP";
      case Event.SCROLL_PAGE_UP:
        return "SCROLL_PAGE_UP";
      case Event.SCROLL_PAGE_DOWN:
        return "SCROLL_PAGE_DOWN";
      case Event.GOT_FOCUS:
        return "GOT_FOCUS";
      case Event.LOST_FOCUS:
        return "LOST_FOCUS";
      default:
        return "Unknown event:"+id;
    }
  }
}
class MyButton extends Button{
  public MyButton(String s){
    super(s);
  }
  public boolean handleEvent(Event e){
    System.out.println("Button event:"+e.id);
    return super.handleEvent(e);
  }
}
class MyPanel extends Panel {
  Label l1,l2,l3;
  Scrollbar s;
  TextField t;
  MyButton b;
```

```
    public MyPanel(){
      super();
    }
    public void init(){
      setLayout(new GridLayout(3,2));
      l1=new Label("Last Event Type:");
      l2= new Label("Last Action Type:");
      l3=new Label("Last Event Location");
      add(l1);
      s=new Scrollbar(Scrollbar.HORIZONTAL, 1,10,1,100);
      add(s);
      add(l2);
      t=new TextField("Input me.");
      add(t);
      add(l3);
      b=new MyButton("Press me.");
      add(b);
    }
    public boolean handleEvent(Event e){
      l1.setText(Converter.IdToString(e.id));
      l3.setText("("+e.x+","+e.y+")");
      return super.handleEvent(e);
    }
    public boolean action(Event e, Object arg){
      l2.setText(Converter.IdToString(e.id));
      return super.action(e,arg);
    }
  }
  public class EventTest extends Applet {
    MyPanel p1,p2;
    Label l11,l12,l13,l21,l22,l23;
    public void init(){
      p1=new MyPanel();
      p2=new MyPanel();
      p1.init();
      p2.init();
      add(p1);
      add(p2);
    }
  }
```

Windows and Dialog Boxes

The Java AWT is not limited to displaying information inside of an applet Panel. You can also create stand-alone windows that will display information if you need to organize your data in this way. There are standard windows from the Frame class and more restricted versions from a class called Dialog. Both are subclasses of Container so you can treat them just like another place to add components.

There are several methods that can help you manipulate windows. resize takes the new width and height of the window. move will reposition the upper lefthand corner to a new x and y location. The method show will display the window and hide will close it. When the window is initially created, it is hidden. There are also a method, isShowing, that returns a boolean value.

Here's some simple code that will create a window and display it.

```java
import java.awt.*;
import java.applet.*;
class MyWindow extends Frame {
  Button b1,b2,b3,b4;
  Label l;
  int Count=100;
  public MyWindow(String s){
    super(s);
    init();
  }
  public void init(){
    b1=new Button("Add One");
    b2=new Button("Add Five");
    b3=new Button("Subtract Ten");
    b4=new Button("Close Window");
    l=new Label(Integer.toString(Count));
    add("North",b1);
    add("West",b2);add("East",b3);
    add("South",b4); add("Center",l);
    show();
  }
public boolean action(Event e, Object arg){
    if (e.target instanceof Button) {
```

```
        if (e.target.equals(b1)) {
          Count=Count+1;}
        else if (e.target.equals(b2)){
          Count = Count + 5;}
        else if (e.target.equals(b3)){
          Count = Count - 10;}
        else if (e.target.equals(b4)){
          hide();}
        l.setText(Integer.toString(Count));
      }
      return true;
    }
  }
public class WindowTest extends Applet{
  Frame w;
  public void init(){
    w = new MyWindow("My Window");
    w.resize(300,100);
    // You must give the window a size!
  }
}
```

BorderLayout *is the*
default layout for a
Frame *object.*

There are several important details to note about this code. First, there is a separate handleEvent routine written for the MyWindow class. Creating a Frame object is perfectly easy, but if you want it to respond to events or change the way that it draws, then you need to add its own handleEvent method.

Windows can present a major security hole. Figure 11.16 shows the window with its four buttons created by this code. In the Macintosh version of the Applet Viewer from Sun, the window looks no different from an ordinary window. If I chose to put up a password dialog box, then some user might input their password. In this case, there is no way to tell the difference between a window created by trusted software running on your local machine and windows created by an incoming Java applet. Some versions of Java include special warning messages in windows that can remind users that it was created by the applet. This should be the default for the Java AWT.

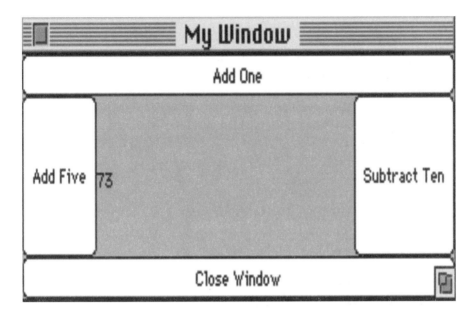

Figure 11.16.

Dialog Boxes

Dialog boxes are windows that are supposedly more transient than standard Frame objects. You would create them whenever you needed immediate information from the user, not when you wanted to leave information floating on the screen. Most dialog boxes warn of errors or ask for immediate input that can guide the flow of the program. These are usually *modal* dialogs, which is a term derived from the word "mode." When this dialog appears on the screen, the system is put into a special "mode" that will only respond to clicks in the dialog box. There are also nonmodal dialog boxes.

There are two major constructors for the Dialog class:

Dialog(Frame f,boolean b) This takes the Frame of the window generating this dialog box. An applet can't create a dialog; only a free-floating window can do it. If the boolean, b, is set to be true, then it is a modal dialog. Otherwise it is nonmodal.

Dialog(Frame f, String s, boolean b) The string, s, is used to set up a title bar for the dialog. If it isn't there, then there is no title bar.

One major debate in GUI design was whether an interface should be "modal." Generally, "nonmodal" GUIs are less confusing because they always behave the same way.

The dialog created with this constructor may look different than one created with the other constructor.

If you create a dialog using these constructors, you can manipulate it with the same methods that work with the Frame class. resize will change the size, and you must execute it or the dialog will be microscopic. move changes its location while show will reveal it and hide will close it.

This code demonstrates how to create your own dialog boxes. Note that a separate class called MyDialog was created to grab the events. If I did not do this, the events from pushing button b5 would be lost. This is an effective way to pass them on. Figure 11.17 shows how this looks on the screen.

```java
import java.awt.*;
import java.applet.*;
class MyDialog extends Dialog{
  Frame big;
  public MyDialog(Frame f, boolean b){
    super(f,b);
    big=f;
  }
  public boolean action(Event e, Object a){
    big.action(e,a);
    return false;
  }
}
class MyWindow extends Frame {
  Button b1,b2,b3,b4,b5;
  Label l;
  int Count=100;
  TextField t;
  MyDialog d;
  public MyWindow(String s){
    super(s);
    init();
  }
  public void init(){
    b1=new Button("Change Label");
    b2=new Button("Write Fred");
```

```
      b3=new Button("Write Barney");
      b4=new Button("Close Window");
      l=new Label(Integer.toString(Count));
      add("North",b1);
      add("West",b2);add("East",b3);
      add("South",b4); add("Center",l);
      show();
      d=new MyDialog(this, true);
      b5=new Button("Okay");
      t=new TextField("New Label");
      d.setLayout(new GridLayout(2,1,50,50));
      d.add(new Label("Enter new term:"));
      d.add(t);
      d.add(b5);
      d.resize(200,100);
      d.move(50,75);
    }
public boolean action(Event e, Object arg){
    if (e.target instanceof Button) {
      if (e.target.equals(b1)) {
        t.setText(l.getText());
        d.show();}
      else if (e.target.equals(b2)){
        l.setText("Fred");}
      else if (e.target.equals(b3)){
        l.setText("Barney");}
      else if (e.target.equals(b4)){
        hide();}
      else if (e.target.equals(b5)){
        l.setText(t.getText());
        d.hide();
      }
    }
    return true;
  }
}
public class DialogTest extends Applet{
  Frame w;
  public void init(){
```

```
    w = new MyWindow("My Window");
    w.resize(300,100);
       // You must give the window a size!
  }
  public boolean handleEvent(Event e){
    System.out.println(e.target);
    return true;
  }
}
```

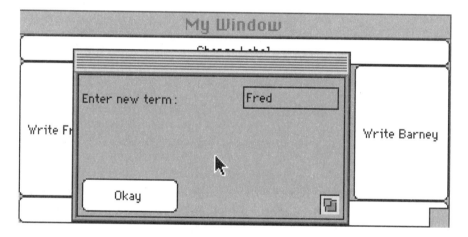

Figure 11.17. The DialogTest creates a dialog box on the screen for a window.

File Dialogs

If you want to display a scrolling list of files available to the user, then you can call upon the class FileDialog. This class is useful if you're using Java to write code for a system, but it really doesn't do much if the code will be run on a distant HTML browser. This is because the security model for Java will block the code from accessing files, for good reasons.

There are two constructors for the class:

FileDialog(Frame f, String s) Creates a file dialog and uses s for a title.

`FileDialog(Frame f, String s, int i)` The additional integer controls whether the action button in the dialog is labeled "open" or "save." If you are using the box to look for a new file to open, then pass `FileDialog.LOAD` as the integer parameter. If you want to save a file, then pass in `FileDialog.SAVE`.

Menus

Windows can come with menus if you need them. All you have to do is create them and add them. There are four major classes that do the work: `MenuBar`, `Menu`, `MenuItem`, and `CheckboxMenuItem`. First you create a `MenuBar` object. To bind it to a window, you execute `setMenuBar`. Then you create objects from the class `Menu` and add them to the `MenuBar`. Finally, you can add objects from `MenuItem` or `CheckboxMenuItem` to the `Menu` objects to give the users something to choose.

MenuItem is a subclass of MenuComponent. CheckboxMenuItem is a subclass of MenuItem.

If you want a standard menu choice, then you would add an object from the class `MenuItem`. The objects from the class `CheckboxMenuItem` contain an additional check mark next to the item on the menu. It will turn on and off each time the item is selected. If you need to check the status of a checkbox item, then you execute `getState`. You can change it with `setState`.

Two major methods, `enable` and `disable`, will turn on or off either specific menu items or entire menus. If something is disabled, then it is shown in light gray and the user can't select it. No events or actions are generated either.

Finally, if you need to add a separation bar, just add the text "-" and the AWT will automatically turn this into a bar. Here's some sample code that shows how to add a menu bar to a window. Figure 11.18 shows how it looks.

```java
import java.awt.*;
import java.applet.*;
class MyWindow extends Frame {
  Button b1,b2,b3,b4;
  Label l;
  int Count=100;
  MenuBar mBar;
  Menu m;
  CheckboxMenuItem cb;
```

```
public MyWindow(String s){
  super(s);
  init();
}
public void init(){
  b1=new Button("Add One");
  b2=new Button("Add Five");
  b3=new Button("Subtract Ten");
  b4=new Button("Close Window");
  l=new Label(Integer.toString(Count));
  add("North",b1);
  add("West",b2);add("East",b3);
  add("South",b4); add("Center",l);
  show();
  mBar=new MenuBar();
  m = new Menu("Changes");
  m.add(new MenuItem("Five"));
  m.add(new MenuItem("Seven"));
  m.add(new MenuItem("Eleven"));
  m.add(new MenuItem("-"));
  cb=new CheckboxMenuItem("Positive");
  m.add(cb);
  mBar.add(m);
  setMenuBar(mBar);
}
public boolean action(Event e, Object arg){
  int value;
  String s;
    if (e.target instanceof Button) {
      if (e.target.equals(b1)) {
        Count=Count+1;}
      else if (e.target.equals(b2)){
        Count = Count + 5;}
      else if (e.target.equals(b3)){
        Count = Count - 10;}
      else if (e.target.equals(b4)){
        hide();}
      l.setText(Integer.toString(Count));
    } else if (e.target instanceof MenuItem) {
```

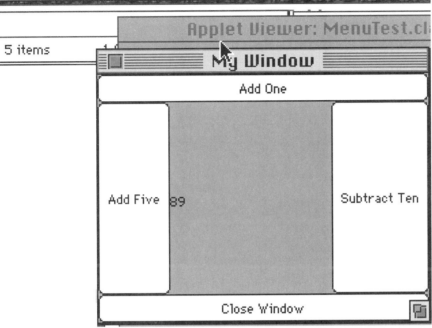

Figure 11.18. The menu for the window is added to the end of the regular menu bar on a Macintosh. Other versions of the API may place the menu directly on the window. Some differences will continue to exist in a cross-platform world.

```
if (cb.getState()) {
  value = 1;
} else {
  value = -1;
};
s = (String)arg;
if (s.equals("Five")){
  Count = Count + value * 5;
} else if (s.equals("Seven")){
  Count = Count + value * 7;
} else if (s.equals("Eleven")){
  Count = Count + value * 11;
}
```

```
            l.setText(Integer.toString(Count));
    }
    return true;
  }
}
public class MenuTest extends Applet{
  Frame w;
  Dialog d;
  public void init(){
    w = new MyWindow("My Window");
    d = new Dialog(w,"My Dialog",true);
    w.resize(300,100);
      // You must give the window a size!
  }
}
```

Summary

The Abstract Windowing Toolkit is one of the most important parts of the Java Developer's Kit. You can create a smart user interface with only a few short statements. This makes programming easy, and it minimizes the size of the code that must travel across the Net when someone fires up an applet.

Some of the most important lessons of this chapter are:

- The basic unit of the AWT is the Component object.

- The layout manager is responsible for placing the components in the browser's window. You can choose from a variety of layout managers that behave differently.

- The layout manager's intelligence can handle the layout problems in a complicated browsing environment.

- The set of components includes sliders, checkboxes, radio boxes, text input fields, and buttons.

- You can filter events by subclassing the handleEvent routine.

Chapter 12

Java Guts

You can do a good job programming Java without knowing much about what happens inside, but you can do a better job if you understand how the mechanism operates. This chapter describes how Java code is converted into something that runs on a chip. It also illustrates how security is handled.

The inside of Java is an interesting combination of features designed to ensure security while running efficiently. The basic Java code that programmers learn is compiled into byte code that few people learn or see. This byte code is designed to be relatively simple and machine-independent. If you want to implement Java on a new machine, you don't need to write an entire Java compiler, you only need to write a byte code interpreter.

The structure of the byte code is designed to restrict the operation of the code and prevent it from doing harm. Stopping trouble is relatively easy on one level, but quite difficult on another. For instance, there is no byte code that will erase all of the files. These destructive capabilities have been left out of the language.

But preventing all calamities is a substantially more complicated proposition. The designers must somehow be certain that all possible combinations of instructions will not produce a situation where the incoming Java applet can seize control of the host machine. Several bugs have been discovered[1] and they've all been plugged. There is no reason to be certain, however, that all bugs have been removed.

Understanding the guts of the Java system is an option that many Java programmers might not want to take for several reasons. First, there is no real reason for learning it. While some people still program their computers in assembly language, there is no clear indication that writing your own byte code will offer great speedups. There may be opportunities, but there could also be potential problems. Each Java-capable browser will check the byte code of an incoming class to determine whether it meets a set of rules. While the compilers can be designed to never generate code that will break these rules, you might not be as clever. Or, perhaps more correctly, you might be too clever and break a few Java browsers. The rules are still not well understood and the ground may shift.

The second reason you might want to ignore the guts is because they're subject to change. The syntax of the language described in this book is probably close to the final standard for the language. The details of the AWT class language will change with time, but most of the syntax should stay fixed. Changing it is too difficult. But the insides of the compilers and the runtime environments are still in flux. At the time of this writing, most Java-capable browsers completely interpret the code. In the future, just-in-time compilers will convert the byte code into native code for the local processor. These internal details can easily change with time and it is entirely likely that many implementations will handle these details differently.

Nevertheless, knowledge is power, and understanding what happens inside can often help in the strangest ways. Many bizarre bugs can only be solved if you understand the entire process from top to bottom. The rest of this chapter will describe the Java byte code system and explore Java security.

Byte Code

The Java byte code is a simple, abstract stack machine. This may be familiar to programmers who have written their own compilers or played around with the guts of simple languages like Adobe's PostScript. All of the information is kept on a simple stack. New data

---

[1]For a good beginning, see the work of Drew Dean, Edward Felton, and Dan Wallach.

is pushed onto the stack and other operations grab the information they need to work directly from the stack.

Each code, which is only a single byte, asks the interpreter to perform some simple task. Some of the jobs, like arithmetic, use the stack. For example, the code iadd tells the interpreter to pull the top two values from the stack, add them, and put the result back on the stack. There are also simple instructions that will push new values onto the stack, pop values off of it, or branch to some new code based upon the value on the top of the stack.

Some instructions come with operands. The instruction bipush comes with a single byte operand. This is considered a signed, 8-bit value and is converted into a 32-bit value which is the size of all data on the stack. There are other operands for pushing different sizes of data onto the stack and finding certain variables in memory and loading them onto the stack.

Much of this should be easy to understand. The expression a=b*b+c*c might get translated into byte code that looks like this:

```
iload 14 dup imul iload 15
dup imul iadd istore 17
```

The iload operation will load a local variable onto the top of the stack. The parameter (either 14 or 15), determines which variable to load. There are 256 possible local variables that can be defined for each procedure or method. The compiler gives them numbers and then the interpreter is responsible for finding a location in memory in which to place them.[2]

The dup instruction will simply copy the top value on the stack and the imul instruction will multiply the top two values and put the answer back on the stack. The iadd instruction will add the two of them together and the istore instruction will put the result back in local variable 17.

If you haven't experienced a stack machine before, work through the code above to understand the simplicity and power of the model. It should be clear why many compiler designers use this to help convert

---

[2]The memory locations are obviously not made directly available because this could lead to a security hole. Nevertheless, several people have noted that most Java interpreters do the obvious thing and simply store the local variables in the order that they're defined. This weakness allows you to store a certain pattern of consecutive bytes in memory. Jumping to it is another story.

the more complex structure of a higher-level language like C into the lower-level machine code.

Data in Byte Code

The structure of the stack machine goes a long way toward explaining the overall structure of the byte code hidden inside a Java .class file, but there is more to writing code than pushing elements on and off a stack. Data comes in different types and Java allows you to bind the data into objects. Implementing the more complicated data structures offered to Java programmers requires more than pushing and popping data.

There are four types of data. The first is called the *constant pool* and it holds all of the constants defined for a particular class. If you initialize a variable with a line like double i=3, the value 3 will be placed in a constant pool and given an index. It might be the 17th value. The instruction ldc2w is followed by two bytes that give a 16-bit index into the constant pool. The long integer is taken from there and pushed onto the stack.

Looking up objects in the constant pool is a two-step process. The two bytes give an index that is later resolved to an actual pointer to data. This can be time-consuming, so many instructions that access the constant pool come with _quick variants that cache the result of finding the item in the pool. When an instruction, say, looks for item 5 in the constant pool, an actual pointer is determined. Then the instruction is replaced by the _quick variant that can access the cached pointer. The second time the instruction is encountered, the constant lookup is only a one-step process.

The second step involves *local variables*, and these include all of the local values that are temporarily defined for a method. These are also given as indices and the interpreter of the byte code is responsible for finding some spot in memory to keep them. This will almost always be another stack. The collection of local variables is often called the *stack frame*.

The third type of data is the object. Objects are usually stored as *handles*, or pointers to pointers that determine the location of the data. If you create a new instance of an object, the byte code interpreter will allocate the memory for the object and create two pointers, call them p1 and p2. p1 will point to the location in memory that holds p2 and in turn p2 will point to the x bytes of memory that holds the data of the object. The value of p1 is stored in the local variable that will hold the particular object. This double dose of pointers is used to speed garbage collection and aid in memory management. If there was some reason to move all of the x bytes in an object, then only the value of p2 would need to be changed. There would be no need to scan through all possible variables looking for p1s. That is, there could be many different copies of p1 floating throughout the local variables, but there is only one copy of p2.

The instructions `getfield` and `putfield` access the different fields inside the objects. The object itself is placed on the stack. The name of the field and the class of the object is stored in the constant pool and the index to this constant is placed in the two bytes that follow these commands.

Classes are specified in the constant pool by their names. A browser will try to load a class by asking the distant HTTP server to produce the file name.class.

Accessing the fields takes two steps thanks to the dynamic nature of Java. First, the two bytes are combined to find a class name and field name for the object in the constant pool. Then the description of this class and the field is looked up separately. This can change from time to time and so this lookup must be accomplished each time the code is run. This will produce an offset in the field that is then used to pull the data onto the stack.

The fourth kind of data is the array, which is a special type of object. There are special instructions for creating an array and accessing the elements inside of it. The basic instruction, `newarray`, will construct an array filled with the types specified by the one-byte operand. For instance, the byte 4 specifies boolean values in the array. The size of the array is specified by the top value on the stack. The instruction `iload` will take an index and an array object reference from the top of the stack and then check to make sure that the index is valid before pushing the integer from that location onto the top of the stack. The instruction `anewarray` will create a new array of objects. The two-byte operands that follow this instruction point to a class name in the constant pool.

Types

Most of the types are determined at compile time, not run time. There are, for instance, four different byte codes for addition: `iadd`, `ladd`, `fadd`, and `dadd`. These stand for operations performed on the four basic numerical types: integers, long integers, floating-point values, and double-precision floating-point values.

In many cases, there are multiple byte codes for most of the operations depending upon the type of the data. There are eight operations for accessing arrays because arrays can hold boolean values, bytes, shorts, and chars as well as integers, long integers, floats, and doubles. These are converted into regular values if they're pushed on the stack.

This multiplicity of instructions means that many of the 256 possible byte codes are already taken.

Determining the type of objects at compile time can simplify the byte code and make the execution quicker. It would be a major drag if the byte code interpreter needed to determine the type of each stack item before adding or manipulating it. But this can also lead to deception. A hacker could edit the byte code directly to change the types of the operations and access data that is not permitted. The Java interpreters check the byte code to make sure that it doesn't mismatch types and write long values to short memory locations.

Objects and Methods

Accessing objects and calling their methods is the most complicated part of the Java byte code world. Pushing and popping values from a stack is relatively straightforward and the sequence of instructions can be determined at the time the Java program is compiled into byte code. But objects and their methods are dynamically bound. That means the Java interpreter must find the object's class description at run time. This adds flexibility, but as you will see, it can fill the execution with plenty of time looking up class descriptions.

Whenever a new object is created, an object's field is accessed, or a method is invoked, the class and the field or method is stored in the constant pool. The class loader is responsible for making sure that this class is brought into memory and made ready to go. This class might be stored locally with the rest of the code from the browser or it might be stored remotely at a Web site.

When a method is called, the constant pool contains a *method signature*, which is a unique name for the method. Each class has a method table that contains a list of signatures and a pointer to the code that should be run when the method is invoked. The interpreter takes the signature and scans down the table looking for a match.

Clearly this lookup process can be tedious, and it is made more complicated by the fact that Java offers inheritance. If you invoke a method like foo, the interpreter must walk up the class hierarchy until it finds a version of foo to run. The current object might have completely inherited this method from a parent class.

There are four byte codes for invoking methods that match all of the four types of methods: invokevirtual, invokenonvirtual, invokestatic, and invokeinterface. These will all operate slightly differently after they look up the method signature. For instance, invokevirtual uses the runtime type or class of the object. invoke nonvirtual determines this type at compile time and saves a bit of trouble. invokestatic calls a static method determined by the class name.

Obviously, the search for a method signature can be somewhat complicated and time consuming so Java has a feature that can speed it up. There are four other versions of these method-invoking byte codes with the extra name _quick appended to them. This speeds the time of looking up signatures in the constant pool, but it doesn't solve the problem of searching out the method signatures in the tables.

This method calling is probably the most time-consuming part of Java and it may be most responsible for slower run times. Java code may run at 3 to 5 percent of the speed of a version written in C because the process of switching between methods or procedures is so table-intensive. A just-in-time Java byte code compiler can solve some of these problems.

This is why it is important to mark methods as final if you possibly can. The compiler will recognize that they can't be replaced and try to in-line them whenever possible. This can produce long methods that do little calling. Just in-lining a method in a loop can be a significant time savings.

Memory and Garbage Collection

The Java byte code interpreter is responsible for managing the memory and making sure that it is reused effectively. This is mainly done as a security precaution. Giving the user the ability to write in any arbitrary location of memory can be a real disaster on machines like the PC or the Macintosh because they offer no protection. So Java fetches the information for you and brings it to the stack.

The memory management function, however, has the potential to remove lots of bugs. In my personal experience, over half of the serious bugs I've encountered were produced when either I or another programmer did not handle memory with care. Sometimes not enough memory was allocated. Other times it was reused incorrectly.

Java's runtime interpreter will reclaim memory through a process known as *garbage collection*. That is, it will scan through memory looking for objects that are no longer needed and remove them. Each running thread comes with a set of frames for each of the methods that have been invoked. If a local variable in one of these threads points to an object, then the object is still in use. The garbage collector scans through all of these frames and marks all of the objects that are still in use. An object is also considered in use if any of these objects contains a field that points to an object. This scanning continues through the list and there are complicated algorithms that defend against circular data structures.

After that, it scans through the list of objects and finds the unused objects. These are marked for a two-step death. First, Java invokes the object finalize method. This is called at the end. Then it removes the memory from use. Occasionally, it will copy all of the objects to one part of the memory to make one big free block.

The Java garbage collector normally runs as a separate thread scanning the internal lists of objects. It is quite efficient and the extra overhead may be as low as 3 percent of the scanning time. If you need to run the garbage collector by yourself, you can call System.gc(). You may only need to do this after you destroy a large data structure filled with interconnected objects.

Java Security

Java's designers undertook a great task when they decided to make the Java system "secure." At the very least, the term "secure" is ill-defined and can mean many things to many people. Some people may discover that Java allows them to play certain types of tricks that its designers never considered. If Java is going to be truly secure, then either the designers are going to have to provide a very thorough definition of what Java can and can't do, or they're going to have to restrict the system in very fundamental ways.

At this writing, no one is really sure exactly what Java can and can't do. There is a strong list of forbidden items, but there is still great debate about the edges. For instance, some people would want to restrict Java applets from communicating with anything on the Net. This would prevent a rogue applet from doing things like sending crank e-mail or doing worse damage all from a remote platform. Others would like their Java applets to freely access information from throughout the network. This would allow them to gather data from multiple Web sites and do neat things with it. But suddenly these applets with open access to the Net can do many things.

Balancing the options available to applets is bound to cause friction. Some will consider the ability to communicate with arbitrary machines on the Internet to be a feature, but others would see it as an open channel for data leakage. One popular solution is to constrict the ability of an applet to speak with all but the host that launched it on the Net. This limits both the server and the client side of this transaction and it is not clear if much is gained. The entire Internet is quite insecure and Java applets can exploit weaknesses in systems like the DNS with impunity.

These are just some of the examples that confront Java system designers as the Java language develops over time. Fixing these problems will be an ongoing process and the language designers will tweak the language specifications. Some parts will be relatively fixed while others will be open to change and modification. The Java designers aren't giving up on security in any sense, but they're recognizing just how complicated it can be.

Basic-Level Security

Java does several things at a basic level that contribute to restricting the ability of applets to cause any damage. These features:

Restrict Access You can't ask your Java applet to open a file or write to the local disk because there is no command for it. All of these are accomplished by `private` methods and the incoming applet code can't invoke them. Anything that is vaguely dangerous is prohibited.

Control Access to Pointers Some people have commented that in this book I shouldn't use the word "pointer" to describe variables that hold objects. This argument is fair because these variables are not pointers in the same sense that C creates pointers. You can't access the value of the pointer or do something arbitrary like add 4 to it. Java won't let you touch them. This prevents you from setting them to some arbitrary spot in memory and writing away.

Still, these variables act like pointers. If you set x=y and then you modify some field in y, the same field in x will also change. You must remember that these are objects and the variables hold pointers to them. I find it is just easier to call them pointers.

Control Access to Strings In C, strings are just pointers to blocks of memory. The last item in the string is specified with a null character (0). This technique has been the source of more bugs and security holes in UNIX than any other I can think of. People are constantly running over the space allocated to hold the string and writing on other parts of the memory. The famous Internet "worm" used this trick to overwrite the stack.

Java doesn't let you access strings in this way. You must request individual characters with an array-like reference system. It checks to make sure that you aren't requesting data past the end of the string.

Control Access to Arrays C also treats arrays as it does strings—they're also just pointers. Java treats them as objects and fetches the individual items for you after testing to make sure that you're requesting something within bounds.

Ensure Type Safety If x holds an object from class foo, then you can't write code like x=x*x because the multiplication is not defined for the class of objects. Java watches the type of operations to ensure that they don't violate any type restrictions. This type surveillance is also the basis for controlling access to the pointers.

Incidentally, Java does have some places where types are modified on the fly. You can add a floating-point number to an integer, but Java will do the necessary conversions to ensure that this is done safely. It will not convert pointers into integers. Also, many objects can be "added" to a string through the "+" operator because they are converted into a string with the toString method.

Some argue that having two forms of Java (source code and byte code) needlessly complicates things and that security holes can be introduced when the translation between the two is not perfect.

Verify Byte Code The Java compiler checks the types and prevents unauthorized method calls, but it does not have the final word. It converts all of the source code into byte code and there is nothing that can prevent a scurrilous hacker from modifying the byte code. Java verifies that all of the operations are type safe and there are no unauthorized function calls when the byte code is first loaded. This check must be repeated with every array access, however, because the arrays can hold objects, not just simple types like integers.

These basic defenses against rogue applets can be quite effective. In theory, the applet should be prevented from doing anything it isn't explicitly allowed to do. In practice, the system must be designed to actually make this happen, and this can be quite frustrating. It is quite common for complicated systems to have unintended side-effects that can prove devastating. Searching for these takes a long time.

Some people argue that the Java designers should construct a formal description of the language's semantics and then formally prove that certain dangerous operations are impossible. The supporters of this approach believe that this is the only way to be certain that security holes don't exist. But the detractors suggest that a formal proof is really something entirely different from the software that is running it. Something may be true within the internal logic of the proof but incorrect in the software implementation because of a difference between the assumptions in both arenas.

It is certain, however, that the security of the system can benefit from a longer look at the fundamental assumptions about the language. A formal proof may not guarantee a perfect implementation, but it can reveal problems in the assumptions and these can be valuable. Also, a dedicated search for security holes can also reveal more problems. Netscape, one of the companies that has included a Java interpreter in its HTML browser is offering rewards to people who discover holes. This should encourage more to search.

ClassLoader **and** SecurityManager

There are two major classes that are part of the Java run-time system and have the responsibility of system security: ClassLoader and SecurityManager. The ClassLoader will pull in classes from either the local file system or from across the network and establish these classes in their own name space. This is important because a Java interpreter might load several different applets from different places around the Net. There is no reason why there couldn't be name conflicts. The ClassLoader keeps them separate and ensures that they don't bump into each other.

The SecurityManager works hand in hand with the class loader to control the actions of classes that are installed. It checks the byte code and makes decisions about which methods can and can't be invoked. If an applet is running in a browser like Netscape which forbids incoming applets from accessing the disk, then the SecurityManager stops any calls to access the disk.

Applets are generally forbidden from creating a subclass of either of these classes. Netscape and the Java Applet Runner both forbid the creation of new versions of these classes to prevent confusion. If you could do it, then you might be able to start up your own versions of the local classes and gain access to the file system or the Net.

More details about how to use these classes to create your own security model are really beyond the scope of this book. You can read the API documentation and other material distributed by JavaSoft.

Applet Do's and Don'ts

All applets are not created equal. Nor are all classes. The current versions of Java Applet Runner treat incoming applets with a much higher degree of scrutiny than the applets or classes that are pulled in off the local disk. Netscape is more circumspect. If you happen to load an .html page filled with applets, then these will be treated as if they came over the Net.

Applets that come in from the Net come from AppletClassLoader which is a subclass of ClassLoader. It uses its own SecurityManager to ensure that the applets can't access the local disk or make network calls to any machine other than the one from which it came. The AppletClassLoader passes the byte code through the byte code verifier that ensures that types are always respected and no strange or illegal typecasting is attempted.

Frank Yellin wrote a paper describing the byte code verification process. You can read a copy at http:// www.javasoft.com/ sfaq/verifier.html

Trusted applets that come in from the local file system, however, get a much kinder reception by the Java Applet Runner. They are not subject to being tested by the byte code verifier. They can access the file system to read or write files. They can also execute processes and load libraries. It's a much nicer existence.

The Java design team made this distinction to allow people to use Java as more than a tool for animating stuff on Web browsers. It is meant to be a full system-level language, and that means being able to do system-level things. The HotJava browser was written in Java using all of these capabilities.

Past Security Holes

While I was writing this book, newspapers like *the Wall Street Journal* frequently reported the discovery of Java security holes. This section describes some of the most important ones in the hope that readers can get an appreciation for the subtle problems facing the system designers. Most of the information in this section was gathered from the text of a paper by Drew Dean, Edward Felton, and Dan Wallach, some of the researchers who have discovered some of the most interesting holes.

The most basic attacks are "denial of service" attacks, and these are still not fixed in the Java system. A rogue applet can shut down a browser simply by grabbing all of the memory space in a huge data structure that remains in use. Or it could spawn many different threads that hog the CPU cycles. Java does not defend against these types of attacks because it does not ration system resources. Most of the computers that run Java (Win95 and MacOS) don't have preemptive multitasking operating systems, so Java would need to implement all of this security on its own. The Thread manager does some of this, but cannot stop attacks.

Telescript, the agent language system from General Magic (Mountain View, CA), does offer the ability to control the CPU cycles used by agents.

These "denial of service" attacks, however, are sort of minor. There are plenty of badly designed Web sites on the Net that fill their pages with large GIFs and complicated layouts. If someone writes an applet that hogs the system resources, then people won't return. Also, it is impossible to defend against inadvertent system hogs. An endless loop or a bad program can also suck up all of the resources.

More important security breaches can access the file system or the memory of the client machine that loads an applet. Some of the problems might be more properly described as UNIX security holes because they exploit weaknesses in the UNIX system running the Java applet. If you ran the same applet on a Macintosh or PC, the hole would not exist. Some parts of the AWT, for instance, do not check the first character of the name of the file. The UNIX path resolver would thus be invoked and it could give the AWT program access to any file on the system. This is a simple example of the types of oversights that might not be caught by a proof because no one anticipated it. These holes, however, are easy to fix.

Another similar problem arose with Java's original system for controlling the access to the Web by using the DNS system. Imagine you want to restrict the applet to communicating with the machine that sent it. The problem is that many domain names on the Internet correspond to several machines. www.bigcompany.com might point to five machines because the company gets so much Net traffic that it needs five machines to handle it. The DNS allows many IP addresses (the four-byte values) to be bound to each name to handle cases like this.

There is an additional problem. Ideally, a Web site administrator might want to set up one machine that would be responsible for servicing the applets out on the Web. It might hold a special database or run some special processes. This might be called java.bigcompany.com. So the initial implementation of the JDK and the Netscape browser would fetch the IP addresses for the source of the data and the desired destination and check to see if there was an intersection.

Here's a hypothetical attack that exploits this hole and assumes that the bad guy has access to the DNS server that will produce the IP addresses. This is fairly easy to do. If you're going to place a rogue applet at hypothetical.com,[3] then you can probably gain access to its DNS server. The original applet comes from www.hypothetical.com and wants to access java.hypothetical.com. So the Java interpreter calls up the DNS and gets this list for www.hypothetical.com: 1.2.3.1, 1.2.3.2, 1.2.3.3, and 1.2.3.4. Then Java looks up java.hypothetical.com and gets this list: 1.2.3.4, 99.99.99.1. Since 1.2.3.4 is present in both lists, the Java interpreter allows the connection.

The danger is that the Java applet can now connect to 99.99.99.1, and this could be a machine from behind a firewall that blithely trusts all connections sent to it. If this machine has holes in its OS like the infamous UNIX Sendmail hole, then the Java applet could then begin to exploit them. It can send any packets it wants to the address. This hole has been fixed, but it illustrates how complicated it can be to control the access to the network.

One potential solution is to keep an audit trail of all IP accesses. This would not stop illicit activity, but it would make it easier to detect it afterwards.

A deeper problem confronts some browsers like HotJava. This is a WWW browser for the Web that was written in Java by Sun. The idea is that the basic byte code interpreter can be ported relatively easily to new machines and when that is done, the HotJava program will run successfully. This is all a good idea, but it can inadvertently open up more information to the rogue applets. All of the data is stored in Java

---

[3]hypothetical.com and bigcompany.com are meant to be hypothetical companies. It is getting increasingly difficult to identify names that don't correspond to actual companies. If someone registers these names, you should not assume that there is any correspondence. They're fictional.

variables and while it is supposed to be private, if any hole can give the applet access, the data is predigested.

If someone forgets to make something `private`, then the danger is even greater. Dean, Felton, and Wallach show how to place a proxy server that will intercept all communication between the HotJava browser and the Web. This is ordinarily done as a security measure, but it can also be used to eavesdrop on someone's browsing habits. A Java applet running in HotJava could access this proxy information on its own and set up a proxy connection to any arbitrary machine— including the machine of any enemy.

The Source Code/Byte Code Schism

There are many potential problems hidden in the fact that the Java source code is translated into byte code, but the byte code has different semantics than the source code. The compiler may catch some offending bugs, but the byte code may let them sail right on by. For instance, Dean, Felton, and Wallach discovered that this code would not compile, but the byte code interpreter would accept the byte code that corresponds to it:

```
class MyLoader extends ClassLoader MyLoader()
try super(); catch (Exception x)
```

This code will create a new class loader that is not completely initialized because Java generates a `SecurityException` whenever an applet tries to create an instance of the `ClassLoader` class. This exception would be caught by the enclosing `try` block, not passed up the system chain where it would ring alarm bells. The byte code verifier has now been changed to block any calls to `super` that are enclosed in a `try` block.

This is important because the class loaders make decisions about matching names to classes and their types. It would be quite easy to have a rogue class loader that would pull in two versions of a class. One might be an unprotected version of a system class that would access variables. This unprotected version would define these variables as `public` and the rogue class loader would substitute this version.

There are deeper problems with the byte code. Checking the type of the variables in the Java source code is relatively easy to do. Each line is independent, and if a line says a=b+c, then you can easily check that a,b, and c are the right type. The byte code, however, is simpler and this makes the checking more complex. If Java loads something from the local variable pool, it must make sure that the variable will always be the same type. This can be a complicated exercise and some people are skeptical that it can be made perfect.

More Bug Information

This book is a static production. Once it goes to press, I can't update the manuscript to include more information about the latest security bugs. Here is a list of several Web sites that you'll want to examine to get more thorough and more up-to-date information about the status of Java security. Also, people who are serious about understanding the guts of Java and keeping track of weaknesses will want to be certain to turn to these sources. This book is aimed at the beginning Java programmer, not the security researcher.

http://ferret.lmh.ox.ac.uk/david/java/bugs/ David Hopwood has found several important problems in the type system. He maintains a good survey of many Java bugs on his home pages.

http://www.cs.princeton.edu/sip/ The Safe Internet Programming project at Princeton University maintains a deep collection of papers and bug reports about Java and many of the other Internet scripting languages like JavaScript. The News section and the FAQ are an excellent introduction to the topic.

http://catless.ncl.ac.uk/Risks This URL lets you access the very excellent comp.risks forum moderated by Peter Neumann. The forum deals with many things that can go wrong between computers and the people who love them. But it is also treated as a fairly official place to put public announcements about important bugs and holes. The most significant Java holes should be announced here.

http://www.math.gatech.edu/mladue/HostileApplets.html Mark Ladue has maintained a collection of hostile applets that can do nasty things like kill off other applets, starve the machine, or crash it. It's a scary collection and Sun has "declared war" on the applets in it. There may come a day in the future when all of these holes are patched and none of the applets will be able to work their wicked ways.

Summary

Java is an effective system for distributing software across the Net, but its designers made several important decisions in order to enforce security protocols. The language is strongly typed and the memory is entirely controlled by the local Java interpreter. The combination of these two ideas is a very good foundation for building a secure system.

There have been a number of minor bugs found in the Java implementations that have been distributed by Sun. As of this writing, Sun has fixed all of the known problems, but there has not been any large-scale recall program to remove old versions from the Net. If you plan on running Java applets with either a browser or an applet runner, you should make sure to watch for the latest versions in order to maintain security.

Will Java always be secure? The foundations are quite good, but it only takes one little hole to cause great damage. I believe that the overall strategy of the Java team is solid and well thought out, but I do worry that no one truly understands all of the details of building a system like this. It will be several years before anyone can speak confidently about the design of secure systems. I hope that Sun Java designers will be the ones who will be able to write definitive books about Java's design and include strong, logical arguments that bolster the confidence of all users. Until then, we can cross our fingers and be certain that the beginning is solid.

Chapter 13

Some Java Examples

This chapter offers some examples of Java applets that
you might want to use as the basis for your own projects.

Animating Components

For many people, the most compelling feature of the Java language is
the ability to create moving images on a distant Web browser. Flash
built Las Vegas and there is no reason why it can't build the WWW
and Java.

If you want to create animated images, you have a variety of different choices. Sun distributes several animated applets that you can use
verbatim for your experimentation. The `Animator` class was written
by Herb Jellinek and is distributed with the Java Development Kit.
You can use this code even if you don't want to learn how to program
in Java. The class is a great example of how you can let people specify
data using the parameters embedded in the HTML. You can set the
images, the time between the images, and the sound files that will be
played alongside. If you just need to drop an animated image into a
Web page, it might be a great idea to just use this applet and set the
parameters.

Another good example is the Tumbling Duke animating applet written by Jim Gosling. This shows the little Java mascot named Duke cartwheeling across the page. You can also replace the images used by this animator with your own by changing the parameters in the HTML file.

This section illustrates a component that displays an animated image. You might want to use this if you want to add some glitz to an AWT interface. This example shows how to create a three-component page with two buttons and the display section. Here are some of the most important details you should keep in mind when you write some of your own animating components:

If you use this component in your own code, you need to load the images in the applet itself. I chose this path because the method `getImage` is only defined in the `Applet` class. You can't run it directly from the class `AnimationComponent`.

You must set up your own thread to run the animation. Pushing the buttons will start and stop the thread.

This example uses two different pairs of start *and* stop. *One is for the class* Thread *and the other is for the class* AnimationComponent. *There should also be one defined for the Applet. This confusion is the downside of overloading.*

The thread in this example will run even if the applet is placed in the background when the page changes. Remember that the stop method for an applet is executed when the browser switches to a new page and the start method is executed when the browser returns. For the sake of simplicity, this example does not define new versions of these methods for `AnimTest`. As it stands, this thread does not use many cycles, so you probably won't notice this oversight.

This version simply animates images. In some cases, you might actually be building up the image from scratch by drawing a variety of different items on the page. If this building routine is computationally intensive it can really make the display look jerky. One solution is to use double buffering. You create a hidden image that accepts all of the drawing commands. When everything is finished, you flash this one image on the screen.

Here's some code that will build an offscreen image and another graphics page to do the painting:

```
Image i2=createImage(width,height);
Graphics hg=i2.getGraphics();
```

Now, if you execute your commands like drawText with hg, the results will be drawn in the image i2 which is not visible to the user. When the image is finished, you would execute:

```
g.drawImage(i2,0,0,this);
```

The GIF images used in this example are transparent GIFs. That means that one color from the GIF colormap is designated as invisible. When the GIF is drawn, the background of the current window is substituted. If you're going to create animated figures, you should create GIFs like these.

If you don't want the background behind the animated figure to be the same as the standard background, then you must override the update method. This method will normally clear the box of the component and fill it with the designated background. Here's what it usually does:

```
public void update(Graphics g){
  g.setColor(backgroundColor);
  g.fillRect(0,0,length,height);
  g.setColor(foregroundColor);
  paint(g);
}
```

If this background is a different color from the image, it will really make the screen flicker. First the eye sees a blank box of some color, then it is treated to a box filled with a different image. You definitely want to do this if you're showing movie images. Here's a better solution:

```
public void update(Graphics g){
  paint(g);
}
```

If your animation is particularly complex, but the motion is limited to small part of the image, then you might want to consider *clipping* the region. The method clipRect will restrict the drawing to a rectangle. This can speed up the graphics if transferring the entire image to the screen is significant drain on the system. Here's an example of a paint shell that is restricted to a rectangle:

```
public void paint(Graphics g){
  g.clipRect(top,left, length,height);
  paint(g);
}
```

Figure 13.1 shows the results using some of the cartwheeling images distributed with the Tumbling Duke applet. Here's the code:

```
import java.io.InputStream;
import java.applet.Applet;
import java.awt.*;
import java.net.*;
class AnimatingComponent extends Canvas implements
Runnable {
```

Figure 13.1. One version of `AnimTest` shown using one picture of Duke distributed with Sun's Java Development Kit.

```
// This can be included in an AWT application. That's
// why it extends Canvas.
Image[] Im;
  // What will be displayed.
int MaxImages;
  // From zero to MaxImages.
int DrawThisOne;
  // Which image to draw.
int WaitTime = 10;
  // The standard amount of waiting.
Thread SpinMe = null;
  // The thread that spins the show.
public void setWaitTime(int t){
  WaitTime = t;
}
public Image[] WhatToGet( int num){
  // Start off by loading these images.
  Im = new Image[num];
  MaxImages=num;
  DrawThisOne=0;
  return Im;
}
public void paint(Graphics g){
  if ((DrawThisOne<MaxImages) && (Im!=null) &&
(Im[DrawThisOne]!=null)) {
    g.drawImage(Im[DrawThisOne], 0,0,this);
  }
}
public void run(){
  while (true) {
    if (Im!=null) {
      DrawThisOne++;
      if (DrawThisOne>=MaxImages)
        DrawThisOne=0;
      repaint();
      try {
            Thread.sleep(WaitTime);
      } catch (InterruptedException e) {
        break;
      }
```

```
        }
      }
    }
    public void start(){
      if (SpinMe==null){
        SpinMe = new Thread(this);
        SpinMe.start();
      }
    }
    public void stop(){
      if (SpinMe!=null){
        SpinMe.stop();
        SpinMe=null;
      }
    }
}
public class AnimTest extends Applet {
    AnimatingComponent a;
    Button b1,b2;
    Image[] I;
    Label el;
    public void init(){
      setLayout(new BorderLayout());
      b1=new Button("Start");
      b2=new Button("Stop");
      add("North", b1);
      add("South", b2);
      a = new AnimatingComponent();
      add("Center",a);
      String nm = getParameter("ImageName");
      String ct = getParameter("HowMany");
      int count = Integer.valueOf(ct).intValue();
      String pa = getParameter("WaitTime");
      if (pa!=null) {
        int wt = Integer.valueOf(pa).intValue();
        a.setWaitTime(wt);
      }
      I= a.WhatToGet(count);
      for (int ii=0; ii<count; ii++){
```

```
      I[ii]=getImage(getDocumentBase(),nm+ii+".gif");
    }
  }
  public boolean action(Event e, Object arg){
    if (e.target instanceof Button) {
      if (e.target.equals(b1)) {
        a.start();}
      else if (e.target.equals(b2)){
        a.stop();}
      }
      return true;
    }
  }
```

Here's the HTML code that was used to fire up the applet:

```
<title>The Animator Applet</title>
<hr>
<applet code=AnimTest.class width=200 height=200>
<param name=ImageName value="T">
<param name=HowMany value=14>
<param name=WaitTime value=30>
</applet>
<hr>
<hr>
<a href="Animator.java">The source.</a>
```

Using the Net

One of the most contentious debates in the Java world is deciding how much access to the Net Java applets should have. The Netscape browser only allows them to connect with the source machine. The JDK from Sun comes with three different settings, one of which gives applets unlimited access. This example is intended to show how powerful even tiny applets can be.

This applet will compute the current value of a portfolio by connecting with a distant HTTP server, asking for a price quote for each stock, and then interpreting the HTML answer. This example uses the Quote company's server at quote.com, which currently offers free quotes for individual stocks. More complicated services are available from them on a subscription basis.

The process is very simple. If you want the current price quote for Microsoft (symbol: MSFT), you request a URL from the server of this form: `http://fast.quote.com/fq/quotecom/quote?symbols=MSFT`. The server returns something with HTML. You can parse this HTML to extract the price from the middle of it.

Java comes with the `java.net` package that includes a wide variety of routines that can be used to plumb the Net. You can run practically every protocol at either a high level (like HTTP or FTP) or at a lower socket level. This means that there is a wide variety of things that you can do if you want or need to do so. Many programmers are writing their applications in Java because they know that this will make the applications machine-independent.

This example shows the easiest way to set up a simple HTTP connection. You may want to do this if you want to load in pages and display them in the browser. This example merely reads them into a string by using a `StringBuffer`. Then it uses the `String` method, `indexOf`, to locate the right place in the HTML.

Here are some suggestions that you might want to use if you're going to be implementing something similar:

The one danger of this scheme is that it is fragile. If the company decides to change the structure of the layout, it might make no difference to a human, but it could crash the Java applet.

The code uses a separate thread to read in the data. This is because the Net can often be unpredictable. The data will arrive in bits and pieces. Although there really isn't anything else to this particular application, it is a good idea to get in the habit of using a thread to control these processes. If this application was extended to include a user interface built with the AWT, then you could continue to monitor that with the main thread of the applet while fetching the data with the other one.

The type `URL` is a class of objects that contains all of the information for a Uniform Resource Locator, but the data is broken up into its component parts. It isn't one string. The access protocol, say HTTP, is in one field of the object. There are a number of different constructors for the URL that take one or more strings.

The `InputStream` class is in the `java.io` package.

You start up a connection with the method `openStream`. It interprets the URL and starts up the connection using the protocol specified.

`InputStream` is an abstract class designed to make it easy to control incoming data. You simply ask for more data and it will provide it for you. In the background, Java may try to read ahead and use a buffer. The basic method for grabbing data is called `read` and it takes at least one parameter, an array of bytes. The method `skip(n)` will skip the next *n* bytes and `close` will close the stream. Most programmers won't want to work with simple `InputStream` objects.

The `DataInputStream` is a much more usable class. It includes the following methods with names that are perfectly descriptive: `readBoolean`, `readByte`, `readUnsignedByte`, `readShort`, `readUnsignedShort`, `readChar`, `readInt`, `readLong`, `readFloat`, `readDouble`, and `readLine`.

All of these commands throw exceptions from the class `IOException`. If the end of the file is reached, an exception from the class `EOFException` is tossed.

The streams in this example are set up in a chain. The simple `InputStream` fetches the data from the URL which passes it along to a `BufferedInputStream` which then hands it off to the `DataInputStream` that finally delivers the data as a line. This is not an example where typecasting is used to make one data structure, a stream, look like another one. There are literally three objects in memory connected in sequence. When you ask to read a line of data from the `DataInputStream`, it asks the `BufferedInputStream` for more data until it gets a complete line. The `BufferedInputStream`, in turn, asks the URL's `InputStream` that is actively monitoring the port.

There are also some fancy types of streams like `LineNumberInputStream` that comes with the method `getLineNumber` that returns the line number of the last stream. The class `PushbackInputStream` comes with the extra `unread` method that will push data onto the stream.

In practice, each stream runs in its own thread which allows the `BufferedInputStream` to build up the data in its own internal buffer. The pushing and pulling can be quite efficient if you put a `BufferedInputStream` in the middle.

The method `ExtractStockPrice` will find the stock price from the string using the method `indexOf`. This method is not found in the `StringBuffer` class so the string was converted. A better solution is to read the lines in and search them individually. There may not be the need to keep them around.

If an applet like this is going to have to run in a browser like Netscape's, it will need to be shipped from the `fast.quote.com`

site. Otherwise the connection won't be allowed. This may change
in the future because Netscape and the other browser companies
are actively considering more sophisticated models for access.

Here's the code:

```java
import java.awt.*;
import java.applet.*;
import java.net.*;
import java.io.*;
public class MyIndex extends Applet implements Runnable{
  String BaseURL="http://fast.quote.com/fq/quotecom/quote?
                  symbols=";
  Thread RunMe;
  StringBuffer MyBuf;
  String BufString;
  double PortfolioValue=0.0d;
  public void init(){
    System.out.println("Starting up.");
  }
  public void GetStockData(String symbol){
    // Get the data...
    URL GetMe;
    InputStream is;
    DataInputStream dis;
    String l;
    try {
      GetMe=new URL(BaseURL+symbol);
      is = GetMe.openStream();
      dis= new DataInputStream(new BufferedInput
                          Stream(is));
      MyBuf=new StringBuffer();
      l = dis.readLine();
      while (l !=null) {
        MyBuf.append(l);
        System.out.println(l);
        l = dis.readLine();
      }
    } catch (IOException e) {
      System.out.println("Error with IO");
```

```
    };
    BufString=MyBuf.toString();
  }
  public double ExtractStockPrice(String s) {
    // Call this to extract the price from the string s.
    int i,j,k;
    Integer a1;
    double answer;
    String sub;
    i=s.indexOf("LAST:");
    System.out.println("i="+i);
    i=i+5;
    // We're lucky that this is the first.
    j=s.indexOf("<B>",i);
    System.out.println("j="+j);
    i = j+3;
    j=s.indexOf(" ",i);
    System.out.println("j="+j);
    sub=s.substring(i,j).trim();
    System.out.println("Sub = "+sub);
    answer=Integer.parseInt(sub);
    System.out.println("We've found the first part:
                       "+answer);
    i=j;
    j=s.indexOf("/",i);
    sub=s.substring(i,j).trim();
    return(answer+(Integer.parseInt(sub))/8.0);
  }
  public void start(){
    if (RunMe == null) {
      RunMe= new Thread(this);
      RunMe.start();
    }
  }
  public void stop(){
    if (RunMe != null){
      RunMe.stop();
      RunMe=null;
    }
  }
```

```
public void run() {
  System.out.println("Starting up the running
                     routine.");
  GetStockData("MSFT");
  PortfolioValue+=100*ExtractStockPrice(BufString);
  GetStockData("INTC");
  PortfolioValue+=200*ExtractStockPrice(BufString);
  GetStockData("IOMG");
  PortfolioValue+=50*ExtractStockPrice(BufString);
  System.out.println("The Portfolio Value is:
                     "+PortfolioValue);
}
}
```

Chapter 14

JavaScript

This chapter introduces JavaScript, compares it to Java, and offers an extended example that is discussed line by line.

Java is not the only way to write programs that change the way that HTML behaves. Netscape developed a language called JavaScript that is a good option for many simple tasks. It was named LiveScript when it was being developed, but then through a miracle of marketing genius, it became JavaScript.

The language is a simple tool that is similar to other scripting languages like AppleScript or the UNIX shell scripts. The text is interpreted at the time it is run on a browser and there is no compiler involved that turns the language into a byte code. The language includes many bells and whistles, but it is not as heavily structured or as complete as Java. Many of the similarities are cosmetic and there are deep structural differences that will affect how you program with each. Although the two languages share a part of their name and a common syntax, you should not count on this being any more than a surface similarity. You need to learn both languages separately.

Most people will end up using Java for big projects and JavaScript for smaller ones. The strong structure of Java and its programming tools means that you can build and debug complex programs. The language comes with enough object-oriented features to make it possible for you to organize the details successfully.

JavaScript, on the other hand, is easy to spin up on the run. If you're creating an HTML page for someone, you can easily add the JavaScript language right in the middle of the HTML text. There is no need for a compiler or a separate development. If your program is short, this can be a quick way to implement it. If you need extended computation power or more sophisticated structure, then this simplicity may not give you the support you could get from Java.

Choosing between the two languages is bound to be a personal decision. There will be many cases when either would be a perfectly acceptable choice. Some people treat the selection of a computer language as a source of great debate and the existence of these two languages will provide plenty of fodder for such debate in the future.

The rest of this chapter will review the similarities and differences between Java and JavaScript in detail. Chapter 15 will describe the syntactic details that you need to build simple bits of code in JavaScript and Chapter 17 will offer several examples that you can use to learn more about writing JavaScript.

Similarities between Java and JavaScript

The two languages share many similarities despite the fact that they were developed largely independently. Most of the sameness is due to the fact that the programming population has come to expect certain standard features. These features aren't part of all new languages or revisions, but they are usually part of dominant languages like C++.

See Chapter 3 for Java syntax and Chapter 15 for JavaScript syntax.

Here's a list of the similarities between Java and JavaScript:

Syntax Both Java and JavaScript borrow heavily from C and C++. C and C++ are the most popular choices now, and making the basic syntax similar makes life easier for everyone. If you're going to have a loop in your language, you might as well imitate the C syntax since it is quite general.

HTML Usage Both languages are driven by the need of Web developers to ship runnable code across the network with a page marked up in HTML. The language designers were motivated by the need to keep the code small to save network bandwidth while providing enough power to produce flashy graphics and smart forms. The

Web is a very compelling platform and its needs will continue to drive both languages for the short term.

Object-Oriented Structure Both Java and JavaScript include object-oriented data structures. Java takes this to the extreme and requires everything to be an object. If you want to write any bit of code, you must first create an object and then add methods to it. JavaScript has a simpler approach and its object-oriented nature organizes the data and gives it structure. It is not an all-encompassing definition for the entire language.

Memory Management Both Java and JavaScript rely upon their host to manage memory for them. The programmer cannot allocate sections of memory at a whim and then manipulate it with abandon. This provides both some security to the host running the code and also offers some support to programmers, making their lives easier.

Security Both Java and JavaScript are "crippled" languages. You can't write arbitrary code that will have access to all of the secrets of the distant machine that has invoked the software.

Events Both Java and JavaScript can produce code that will react to events when they are run on a distant browser. If someone types a key or uses the mouse, either Java or JavaScript can intercept the event and respond to it.

These similarities should make it easier to learn to use both Java and JavaScript, but they have their limitations. You can't count on everything being the same in both languages because there are substantial differences that are described in the next section.

Java may be a Web designers' language now, but the designers obviously have greater ambitions. It may emerge as the standard language for all programming because it has the features to handle almost all system programming.

Differences between Java and JavaScript

The similarities are nice, but it's the differences that will keep you up late. There are deep differences between the languages that lurk underneath their C-like syntax and can cause you to make mistakes or introduce bugs. Here's some of the major points to remember:

Compiled vs. Interpreted Java is half-compiled. JavaScript is entirely interpreted at run time. The Java compiler may catch many potential bugs that might exist, but it can't catch all of the ones that might emerge when the program is run. JavaScript code is not tested until it is loaded in a browser. The Java compiler may find plenty of little problems of type incompatibilities that might cause a later crash.

Speed Java's compiler can produce better speed for the user. It still won't be as fast as native C code, but it may approach that rate in the future. Right now, the Java compilers produce a byte code that is a simplified abstraction of machine code. Each machine may interpret this byte code, but it can also convert it into native machine code. JavaScript, on the other hand, is completely interpreted. Although it may be possible to build some type of run-time compiler, such an approach is unlikely to happen. The tool is best suited for smaller programs and speed is not an overriding issue in these cases.

Devotion to Object-Orientation Java is completely object-oriented. If you want to create an integer, you must first create an object and then give that object an integer field. If you want to write a procedure, you must define it as an object's method and attach it to an object. The entire structure is very organized.

JavaScript, on the other hand, lets you define simple functions and use them without making them part of any object. Variables are freely defined and there are loose rules about their use. You can use objects if you want, but you don't have to.

Class Structure and Inheritance Java offers you the chance to create hierarchical class structures that effectively reuse code and make it easier to create complicated software. You can create classes and have the classes inherit behavior from superclasses.

JavaScript offers no classes or inheritance. You may create data objects and associate methods with them, but there is no formal structure dictated by a class system.

Typechecking Java requires you to specify the type of every piece of data. The compiler will not permit you to change the type of a variable on the fly. This allows the compiler to catch many potential errors and it forces the programmer to conform. Many people like this feature in a programming language, but many don't.

JavaScript doesn't do typechecking. There is no compiler, so JavaScript has less reason to require it. So you're free to write

x=14 and then later in the program write x="fred". This opens
the potential for errors if you accidentally run some function that
expects x to be an integer, but it also offers some freedom.

Delivery Java arrives at the host computer as a separate file filled with
byte codes. JavaScript is embedded inside the HTML. You can put
it in a separate file or you can simply place it inline.

Syntax Although there are many syntactical similarities, there are also
many differences. You need to end each statement in Java with a
semicolon, but you're free to just start a new line in JavaScript.
There are many other little differences that you must keep straight.

Each of these differences is important to keep in mind because they
can get in the way of writing good, clean code.

An Example

A good place to begin with JavaScript is with an example. This next
piece of code produces a simple form that asks you for your birthday.
Then it checks the data to make sure that what you input is valid.
Figure 14.1 shows how it would look in a browser.

The beginning of the code looks like standard HTML. The Java-
Script instructions are kept at the end. You can intermix the instructions
with HTML in any fashion. A point-by-point description of the code
follows.

```
<HTML>
<HEAD>
<TITLE> A Simple Form </TITLE>
</HEAD><BODY>
<p>
<H3> Birthday Greetings </H3>
<p>
To register for your free birthday greetings from
Omniglomerate, please enter your name and birthday.
When your special day arrives, we'll send you a
package of coupons for free Omniglomerate
products as our gift.
<p>
```

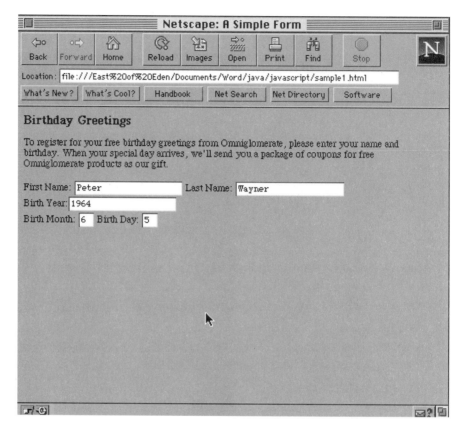

Figure 14.1. This is a form produced using standard HTML for forms. JavaScript code runs behind to check that the input is valid.

```
<p>
<FORM Name="Birthday">
First Name: <INPUT TYPE="text" NAME="Fname" VALUE="">
Last Name: <INPUT TYPE="text" NAME="Lname" VALUE=""><br>
Birth Year:<INPUT TYPE="text" NAME="byear" VALUE=""
onChange="checkYear(this.value)"><br>
Birth Month: <INPUT TYPE="text" NAME="month" SIZE=2
  onChange="checkMonth(this.value)"<br>
Birth Day: <INPUT TYPE="text" NAME="day" SIZE=2
onChange="checkDay(this.value, Birthday.month.value)">
</FORM>
```

```
</BODY>
<SCRIPT LANGUAGE="JavaScript">
<!--
function checkYear(number) {
  if (number<1850 || number>1997) {
    alert("Please use a real year between 1850
          and 1997.");
    return false;
  }
}
function checkMonth(number){
  if (number>=1 && number <=12){
    return true;
  } else {
    alert("Please use a number for the month between 1
          and 12.");
    return false;
  }
}
function checkDay(day, mn){
  if ( mn==1) {
    if (day>=1 && day <=31){
      return true;
    } else {
      alert("January has 31 days.");
      return false;
    }
  } else if ( mn==2) {
    if (day>=1 && day <=28){
      return true;
    } else {
      alert("February has 28 days.");
      return false;
    }
  } else if ( mn==3) {
    if (day>=1 && day <=31){
      return true;
    } else {
      alert("March has 31 days.");
```

```
      return false;
    }
  } else if ( mn==4) {
    if (day>=1 && day <=30){
      return true;
    } else {
      alert("April has 30 days.");
      return false;
    }
  } else if ( mn==5){
    if (day>=1 && day <=31){
      return true;
    } else {
      alert("May  has 31 days.");
      return false;
    }
  } else if ( mn==6) {
    if (day>=1 && day <=30){
      return true;
    } else {
      alert("June has 30 days.");
      return false;
    }
  } else if ( mn==7) {
    if (day>=1 && day <=31){
      return true;
    } else {
      alert("July has 31 days.");
      return false;
    }
  } else if ( mn==8) {
    if (day>=1 && day <=31){
      return true;
    } else {
      alert("August has 31 days.");
      return false;
    }
  } else if ( mn==8) {
    if (day>=1 && day <=30){
```

```
      return true;
    } else {
      alert("September has 30 days.");
      return false;
    }
  } else if ( mn==10) {
    if (day>=1 && day <=31){
      return true;
    } else {
      alert("October has 31 days.");
      return false;
    }
  } else if ( mn==11) {
    if (day>=1 && day <=30){
      return true;
    } else {
      alert("November has 30 days.");
      return false;
    }
  } else if ( mn==12) {
    if (day>=1 && day <=31){
      return true;
    } else {
      alert("December has 31 days.");
      return false;
    }
  }
}
// -->
</SCRIPT>
</HTML>
```

Here's a point-by-point discussion of the code that highlights many of the important features of JavaScript.

⟨**HTML**⟩ . . . ⟨**FORM**⟩ The top of the code is straight HTML. This book won't go into the details of HTML coding; it assumes that you know how to build simple HTML code. The language is not hard to learn, and if you're not familiar with it, you can probably pick up plenty simply by imitating the code written here.

⟨**FORM Name="Birthday"**⟩ The name of the form given here, `Birthday`, also defines a JavaScript object. You can refer to a form by this name as a field in the main object `document`.

First Name: The first two elements of the form do not interface with JavaScript. They're simply filler.

onChange="checkYear(this.value)" The text entry field for the birth year also includes this parameter. This tells the browser to execute this script whenever the data in this field is changed. In this case, the script invokes the function `checkYear` and passes it the data `this.value` which happens to be the data in the form. The function is defined later.

onChange="checkMonth(this.value)" This line also invokes a similar function to check the validity of the input. This function also isn't defined yet in the file. Netscape ignores what is actually in the script until it is executed. It is entirely possible that you could list an undefined function between the quotation marks. This would not be discovered until that particular form element was changed. Then an error box noting that the function couldn't be found would appear for the user. This is why it is important to check all parts of a JavaScript program because there is no compiler that will notice simple mistakes.

onChange="checkDay(this.value, Birthday.month.value)" The third form element with the name day invokes the function `checkDay` whenever it is changed. This function gets passed two parameters. The first one is the local value of the form, `this.value`, but the second is the data in the `month` field. This is specified with the text `Birthday.month.value` in hierarchical form.

⟨**SCRIPT LANGUAGE="JavaScript"**⟩ This tag indicates that scripting code is about to appear. The `LANGUAGE` parameter specifies that it will be JavaScript code. There may be other scripting languages that are accepted by browsers in the future.

⟨**!--** This starts a tag that will hide the script code from browsers that don't recognize JavaScript. This allows you to create pages that will appear fine to people who don't have a browser that can process JavaScript.

function checkYear(number) { A function is defined with the keyword `function` followed by the name and the list of parameters. You don't include the type of the data in the list of parameters. The bounds of the function are specified by the curly brackets.

if (number < 1850 || number > 1997) { An if statement in JavaScript consists of the keyword, `if`, a boolean statement enclosed in regular parentheses, and the code to be executed between curly brackets. The boolean statement can be made up of several clauses. In this case, the `if` statement executes if `number` is less than 1850 or greater than 1997.

alert("Please use a real year between 1850 and 1997."); This line places an alert box on the screen and delivers the message. In this case, it is notifying the user of an error.

return false; The function returns the boolean value `false`.

function checkMonth(number){ Most of the structure of this function is the same as the structure of `checkYear`.

} else { The `if` statements can also include `else` clauses.

function checkDay(day, mn){ This function will take two parameters and decide whether the day and month are consistent. If it isn't, it will raise an alert message. This function is essentially a collection of nested `if` statements mixed in with `alert` messages that notify the user of problems.

// --⟩ The end of the script is indicated by this tag. The first two characters, "//", are used by JavaScript to indicate a comment. That means JavaScript will ignore the rest of the line. HTML, on the other hand, doesn't recognize "//" as a comment so it will interpret it as the closing part of the tag that began long ago. A browser without JavaScript doesn't recognize this tag; it will ignore all of the code.

By this point you have probably identified many limitations in the code you've seen. For instance, there is no checking to make sure that the data in the fields are actually numbers. If someone types a letter into, say, the Birth Month field, it will generate a run-time error. Figure

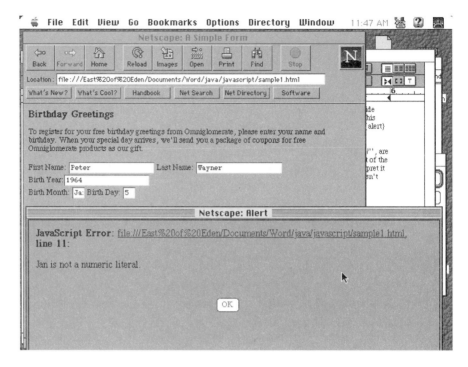

Figure 14.2. A sample of the run-time error that is generated when someone types the wrong type of data into the form in question.

14.2 shows what this would look like to the user. The program doesn't actually reset the fields if an error is detected. This example, though, is preliminary, and you'll learn how to protect against these problems in the future.

This sample code has only shown you how to create functions in JavaScript and to execute the functions when a form is activated. There are many other form items available and there are also many other things you can do with JavaScript. The next chapters will explore these topics.

Summary

This chapter introduces JavaScript and compares it to Java. There are significant differences. JavaScript is more an extension to HTML than a stand-alone programming language. Here's some of the more important lessons from this chapter:

- JavaScript allows you to embed scripting code inside HTML documents.

- The basic syntax is very close to Java or C.

- You can attach JavaScript code to run whenever an HTML form generates some events.

Chapter 15

JavaScript Basics

This chapter introduces the basic details of syntax and structure that you must learn to program in JavaScript. The chapter provides this information by comparing JavaScript to Java. The similarities and differences are spelled out.

The basics of JavaScript are very similar to the basics of Java. The syntax of both was borrowed heavily from C. In this chapter I'll go through these details again briefly. If JavaScript handles a process in the same way that Java does, a quick pointer is given. If there are differences, they'll be pointed out. The chapter is as much a comparison as a tutorial on how to create JavaScript code.

Syntax Similarities

Many of the similarities between JavaScript syntax and Java syntax can be summarized in this list:

Comments JavaScript will ignore everything between a "/*" and a "*/" as well as everything to the right of a double slash ("//").

String Literals You can enclose strings in double quote marks. If you need to include special characters like line feeds, you use the backslash followed by a character. The important ones are

"\n" for new line,

"\t" for tab,

"\b" for backspace,

"\\" for backslash,

"\r" for return,

"\'" for a single quote,

and "\"" for a double quote.

Boolean Literals Either `true` or `false`.

This hidden octal conversion has the potential for confusion! Be aware.

Integer Literals If you need to include an integer in your code, you should type it without a decimal point (14 or 42). If the number has a zero and an x as a prefix, then JavaScript will interpret it as a hexadecimal number (0x10 is the same as 16). If the integer starts with a plain zero, then JavaScript will assume it is in base 8, or octal. (010 is the same as 8).

Floating-Point Literals Floating-point numbers need a decimal point in them (1.1 or 15.0). If you use scientific notation, then you glue the exponent to the mantissa with an E, like this: 15.3E-2 or 1.59E69.

Names The names of variables, objects, and functions must conform to some simple rules. They can't begin with a number and they can't include spaces, hyphens or other obscure punctuation. Some characters like "#" or "_" are accepted. Also, keywords are excluded.

Arithmetic All of the basic arithmetic syntax is the same. 2+2 means two plus two. a*b means a times b. i++ means increment the variable "i" by one.

Test Operators The standard tests for equality ("=="), inequality ("!=") and difference (">","<","<=", or ">=") are available.

Boolean Operators You can AND (&&) and OR ("||") boolean values if you need to.

Precedence of Operators The precedence of the operators is the same as in Java, described in a table on page 34. Some of the operators like `instanceof` are not defined for JavaScript, but the ones that are follow the same rules of precedence.

String Concatenation The "+" symbol means string concatenation as well as numerical addition.

Curly Brackets Blocks of code are encased in curly brackets ("{" and "}"). These blocks are usually found in loops and decision statements.

`if-else` **decision statements** The `if` statement takes the standard C format:

```
if (x==0){
   // Do if x is zero.
}
if (y!=3) {
   // do if y is not 3
} else {
   // do if y is 3
}
```

`for` **Loops** The `for` loop takes the standard C format:

```
for (i = 3; i<100; i++) do {
   fred[i] = 0;
}
```

This code will execute the code in the first section of the loop header (i=3) at the beginning of the loop. After each time through the loop, it will test the second section (i<100) to determine whether to continue. This loop will stop when i is greater than or equal to 100. The last section (i++) is executed after each pass through the loop and it should ensure that the loop is progressing toward completion.

You can also use the for to iterate through parts of an object. See above.

`while` **Loops** The JavaScript `while` loop also looks like C or Java:

```
while (i<100) {
   // stuff
   i++;
}
```

`break` **Statement** If you want to jump out of the loop and begin execution with the first statement after the loop, execute a `break` command.

continue **Statement** If you merely want to skip the rest of the statements in the current iteration of a loop and begin again with the next increment, use continue.

return **Statement** If you create a function, the return statement will control what is passed back. Note, however, that you don't need to declare the type of what will be returned, but you must be consistent. If you return something on one path of execution, then you must return it on all paths.

Accessing Objects JavaScript also uses the dot notation to access the parts of objects. So if the document object has a field name, you can access it with the expression document.name. Many other aspects of dealing with objects, however, are different in JavaScript.

Object Creation Syntax You still use the new keyword to create a new object and you still use a function that does the creation. The expression a = new Array(3) will create a new object and call the Array construction function with the parameter 3. The syntax is essentially the same, but there are major structural differences that are described beginning on page 279.

Array Syntax JavaScript has arrays that are accessed by placing the index in square brackets like this: a[14]=32; a[111]=99. But there are major differences in how the arrays are created (described beginning on page 279).

Syntax Differences

The differences between JavaScript and Java are important to know because they can lead to errors. Here are some of the major ones.

Semicolons Java requires semicolons to separate statements; JavaScript doesn't. But you *can* use them if it makes you feel better.

Variable Definitions JavaScript is not strongly typed. That means you don't need to declare what type of data a variable will hold. You simply assign it like this:

```
x=10;
y="fred";
x=1.34;
y=2;
```

This code will run without problems even though the variables x and y are being loaded with different types of data. JavaScript determines the type automatically.

You can also make a variable local by placing the keyword var in front of it. If you do this, then the references to that variable name inside that function will all be local. They will not affect any global variable that has the same name. It is a good idea to use this tag whenever practical to avoid side effects.

Function Declaration In Java, you create a function by adding a method to a class. In JavaScript, you just create one like so:

```
function foo(bar1,bar2){
  var bar=bar1+bar2;
  document.write(bar);
}
```

This function will accept two variables and add them together. The types of the variables are not declared, and since the "+" operator works on both strings and numbers, this function will work in each of these cases:

```
foo("Hey ", "You!");
foo(2,3);
foo(2,"20");
```

For an explanation of why the last version will work, see the next section on typecasting.

Typecasting JavaScript will convert data between types if it needs to do so. The conversions between floating-point data and integers will probably seem natural to many people because computer languages often provide this automatically. But conversion between strings and numbers can be more confusing. JavaScript will try to convert between strings and numbers if it will get the job done.

Naturally, this may be confusing. If you try to multiply two strings, you will get a correct answer if the two strings contain numerical representations. So "21"*"10" will return 210.

This can lead to problems. Here's a sample JavaScript page:

```
<HTML>
<HEAD>
<TITLE> Lets do some type casting </TITLE>
```

```
<SCRIPT LANGUAGE="JavaScript">
<!--
function Test1(number){
  var num1=1
  var string1="2"
  document.write(string1+string1+num1+string1+num1);
  document.write('<br>');
  document.write(num1+string1+num1+number);
  document.write('<br>');
}
function Test2(number){
  var num1=1
  var string1="2"
  document.write(string1*string1*num1*string1*num1);
  document.write('<br>');
  document.write(num1*string1*num1*number);
  document.write('<br>');
}
Test1(10);
Test2(10);
//-->
</SCRIPT>
</HEAD>
<BODY>
</BODY>
</HTML>
```

The output on the screen looks like this:

```
22121
12110
8
20
```

In the function Test1, the plus symbol is interpreted as string concatenation, not numerical addition, and the numbers are converted into strings. In the second function, Test2, the multiplication has no alternative meaning. So the strings are converted into numbers and the values are multiplied together.

Some programmers will undoubtedly feel that this automatic conversion is an intelligent thing. If JavaScript can do something, it will attempt the conversion. Others will see it as an invitation for surprises and surprising errors. Both are correct.

Object Creation Objects must be created with an constructor function like in Java. When JavaScript encounters the new keyword before a function call, it will create a new object and pass it to the function. Inside the function, the keyword this will refer to the object. There is no general definition, however, of the type of the object or the fields it might contain. Nor is there any class structure that you can use to save time and effort through inheritance. If you want an object to have a field, you simply refer to it. These fields are called *properties*. Here's some JavaScript code with a sample constructor:

```
<HTML>
<HEAD>
<TITLE> Create Some Objects</TITLE>
<SCRIPT LANGUAGE="JavaScript">
<!--
function Person(birthyear, name, height){
  this.name=name;
  this.birthyear=birthyear;
  this.age=1996-birthyear;
  this.height=height;
  return this;
}
a = new Person(1953, "Bob", "75");
document.write(a.name+" is "+a.age+ " years old.");
//-->
</SCRIPT>
</HEAD>
<BODY>
</BODY>
</HTML>
```

This JavaScript code will print out Bob is 43 years old with the document.write command. The function Person acts as a constructor and you refer to all of the parts of the object through the dot notation. If you want to add fields, you just create them. They're added automatically to the object.

Arrays If you build an array in Java, you must declare both the type of the objects that are held in the array and the size of the array.

Arrays in JavaScript are objects that serve as a collection of objects with numerical labels. You still reference them by placing this numerical label between square brackets, but you need to create them differently. You must explicitly create the object with a constructor function. Here's an example:

```
<HTML>
<HEAD>
<TITLE> Lets do some array play </TITLE>
<SCRIPT LANGUAGE="JavaScript">
<!--
function Array(len){
  this.length=len;
  for (i=1;i<=len;i++){
    this[i]=0;
  }
  return this;
}
function PrintArray(arr){
    for (i=1; i<=arr.length; i++){
    document.write(arr[i]);
  }
}
a = new Array(4);
a[1]="Fred "
a[2]="is "
a[3]=114;
a[4]=" years old."
PrintArray(a)
//-->
</SCRIPT>
</HEAD>
<BODY>
</BODY>
</HTML>
```

When this runs, it will print the message Fred is 114 years old. on the browser's screen.

The array is explicitly created like an object with the new command. The most important difference is that JavaScript arrays start with position 1, *not* 0. The zero-th position is used to hold the length.

You can access it, but you will corrupt the length. Be aware that you could inadvertently cause a bug by executing a[0]=14. You might think you were storing the value 14 in the zero-th position of the array and you would be correct. But you would also be overwriting the length of the array. If you passed the array to some function that accessed the length, like PrintArray in the example, then you could cause a crash.

Providing Output In Java, you have the opportunity to draw directly in a box on the browser. If you want to create animations or make cool pictures, you're free to do whatever you feel like programming. In JavaScript, you're constrained by the browser. If you want to send out information, you must imitate a document fed to the browser from a server. That means you will probably want to embed HTML codes inside the text if you want to format it at all.

Java comes with the AWT that offers you the ability to create user interfaces and widgets. JavaScript offers you all of the power of whatever version of HTML is running on the browser. This is certain to become more complicated as people begin to add more and more functionality of the markup codes used with HTML.

Summary

This chapter has listed some of the most important similarities and differences between Java and JavaScript syntax. Some of the functional differences are significant and potentially confusing. JavaScript's ability to do typecasting and conversion on the fly can be quite useful, but they're very different from Java's regimented approach to enforcing strong types. The other great difference is the way that output is sent to the user. Java uses the AWT, which is quite similar to the standard user-interface object libraries distributed with many traditional programming languages. JavaScript offers HTML.

Here's a step-by-step summary that boils down all of the similarities and differences into a guide for creating JavaScript code:

- Start with an HTML page with the standard tags defining the <HEAD> and the <BODY>.

- Place the script between <SCRIPT> and </SCRIPT> tags. The <HEAD> is the best place for the script.

- Indicate the language of the script in the tag like this: `<SCRIPT LANGUAGE="JavaScript">`.

- Hide the script code from non-JavaScript-ready browsers with the faux-tags: `<!--` and `-->`.

- Declare functions with the `function` keyword followed by the name of the function and a list of the parameters enclosed in parentheses.

- Use the standard Java or C syntax to manipulate the data. Remember that JavaScript interprets the code and will do typecasting if it achieves its end.

- There is no `main` routine for JavaScript. It simply executes the statements between the `<SCRIPT>` tags in order. If the code is a function definition, then execution is postponed until the function is called. Otherwise, JavaScript executes the statement immediately.

- You can output information to the screen with the `document.write` command.

This list is just an introduction to JavaScript. Chapter 16 describes the structure of the JavaScript object world. You must understand this if you want to manipulate some of the guts of the browser.

Chapter 16

JavaScript Objects

This chapter explores the way that you can create JavaScript objects and manipulate data using these objects. This is important because all of the browser information is in a hierarchy of objects. If you can find your way around this hierarchy, then you can change the appearance of the browser and execute functions that access this data.

The "object" is a central part of JavaScript used as a means to organize information and provide a hierarchy that keeps the data straight. The Netscape browser's information about forms, links, and colors of the visible documents is arranged in a hierarchy of objects that you can access from JavaScript. If you create your own forms, you can access the different elements in the form by searching through this collection of objects. If your document has anchors or links, you can access them through a central array. Almost anything you can do with a browser window can be done, redone, and undone by manipulating the objects.

The browser also comes with several JavaScript objects that act as bundles of functions. The `Math` object has a number of the standard mathematical functions bound to it as methods. If you want to compute the sine of a number, you type `Math.sin(3.1415)`. There are also built-in objects for dealing with strings, time, and dates.

This chapter describes how to create your own objects, how to access the standard Netscape object libraries, and finally how to manipulate the object hierarchy of the browser to create some truly neat displays.

Creating Objects

Objects are created by a *constructor* function. The individual fields in the object are known as *properties,* and they are created by simply storing information to them. Here are two examples:

```
function Location(longitude,latitude){
  this.longitude=longitude;
  this.latitude=latitude;
}
function Tree(genus, species, longitude, latitude){
  this.genus=genus;
  this.species = species;
  this.where = new Location(longitude,latitude);
}
```

The first constructor, Location, will build an object and add two fields to the object named longitude and latitude. They do not have to have the same name as the parameters. That is just a coincidence.

The second constructor takes four parameters and builds an object with three properties. The third property, where, is another object that is created by calling Location.

You create a new version of an object by prefacing the call to that function with the new keyword. This tells the JavaScript interpreter to create a new object that will go by the name this during the execution of the function. When the function is finished, the pointer to the object will be returned and assigned to whatever variable accepts it. In this case, the second constructor, Tree, sticks it in the property where.

The properties of the objects are accessed by using dot notation. This is recursive, so if you want to create a new tree, you might type t1=new Tree("Oakus", "tallus", 153.323, 42.939). The longitude of the new tree would be recovered with the notation: t1.where.longitude.

You can store anything to a property including a function. Some call this *binding* a method to an object.

Built-in Objects

Netscape's basic JavaScript interpreter comes with some predefined objects that act as collections of standard functions. These include Math, String, and Date objects.

Math Object

The Math object contains many of the standard mathematical functions. Some call this object a static object because it acts just like the static methods defined in Java. You don't need an instance of the object to invoke the method or function.

There are six "properties" or constants defined with the Math object. They are:

Math.E The famous number, e, whose decimal expansion begins 2.718.

Math.PI The famous number, π, whose decimal expansion begins 3.14159.

Math.LN10 In theory, $Math.E^{Math.LN10} = 10$. In reality, JavaScript gets as close as it can with a short approximation.

Math.LN2 In theory, $Math.E^{Math.LN2} = 2$. In reality, JavaScript gets as close as it can with a short approximation.

Math.SQRT1_2 In theory, $Math.SQRT1\_2 = \sqrt{\frac{1}{2}}$. In reality, JavaScript gets as close as it can with a short approximation.

Math.SQRT2 In theory, $Math.SQRT2 = \sqrt{2}$. In reality, JavaScript gets as close as it can with a short approximation.

You can use these values instead of defining the constants yourself and they'll appear in the best precision available to the local browser.

The methods include all of the standard mathematical functions:

Math.abs The absolute value.

Math.acos The arc cosine measured in radians.

Math.asin The arc sine.

Math.atan The arc tangent.

`Math.ceil` If x is positive, then `Math.ceil(x)` finds the smallest integer k so that $x - k \geq 0$. If x is positive, then `Math.ceil(x)` finds the smallest integer k so that $x - k \leq 0$. In both cases, *smallest* is measured by absolute value. `Math.ceil(51.2)` is 52 and `Math.ceil(-14.3)` is -15.

`Math.cos` The cosine.

`Math.exp` `Math.exp(x)` returns e^x.

`Math.floor` If x is positive, then `Math.floor(x)` finds the largest integer k so that $x - k \leq 0$. If x is positive, then `Math.floor(x)` finds the largest integer k so that $x - k \geq 0$. In both cases, *largest* is measured by absolute value. `Math.floor(51.2)` is 51 and `Math.floor(-14.3)` is -14.

`Math.log` The natural log.

`Math.max` The maximum of two numbers. `Math.max(14, 1010)` returns 1010.

`Math.min` The minimum of two numbers. `Math.max(14, 1010)` returns 14.

`Math.pow` `Math.pow(x,y)` returns x^y.

`Math.random` A pseudo-random number between zero and 1. It takes no arguments.

`Math.round` Finds the closest integer.

`Math.sin` The sine.

`Math.sqrt` `Math.sqrt(x)` returns $\sqrt{x}$.

`Math.tan` The tangent.

The transcendental functions return their data in the best floating-point precision available. The truncation functions return integers.

`String` Objects

JavaScript also has `String` objects that are created every time you put something between quotes. Here's an example:

```
x="My name is 'x' and I am a string."
```

Each string comes with one property, its length. You can access it like this:

```
document.writeln("The length of x is "+x.length+"
                 characters.");
```

Naturally, these objects come with plenty of built-in methods that you can invoke to manipulate them. If you typed x.toUpperCase(), you would convert x to an uppercase string. Here are the String functions:

anchor This converts x into an anchor. You would pass in one parameter that would define the data in the anchor. This sample code,

```
x="Label Definition"
document.writeln(x.anchor("definition_anchor"))
```

would produce this HTML string sent to the document:

```
<A NAME="contents_anchor">Table of Contents</A>
```

The link method also creates an anchor that can be used to jump to other pages.

big If you print out x.big(), you'll get the string <BIG>x</BIG>. This will be in a larger font.

blink If you print out x.blink(), you'll get the output <BLINK>x </BLINK>. This text will blink in a Netscape browser.

bold If you print out x.bold(), you'll get the output <BOLD>x</BOLD>. This text will be boldfaced in a Netscape browser.

charAt If you want to find out the character at position i in a string x, then use the command x.charAt(i). These are numbered between zero and $length - 1$.

fixed If you want the output to look like it was from a uniformly spaced font like the output between <TT> tags in HTML, print out x.fixed().

fontcolor   You can change the color of a string using the fontcolor method, which will essentially embed the text between the <FONT> tags with color attributes. Here's a quick example:

```
var x="Pete"
document.write(x.fontcolor("maroon") +" is maroon in
   this line.<br>") document.write(x.fontcolor("30F0A0")
      +" is the color with 30 for the red component, F0 for
      the green and A0 for the blue in hexadecimal.")
```

You can get the same results by spitting out the HTML:

```
<FONT COLOR="maroon">Pete </FONT> is maroon in this
   line.<BR>
<FONT COLOR="30F0A0">Pete </FONT>is the color with 30 for
   for the red component, F0 for the green and A0 for
   the blue in hexadecimal.
```

fontsize The fontsize method also embeds text in <FONT> tags with size attributes. Here's some code to illustrate:

```
var x="Pete"
document.write(x.fontsize(9) +" is nine point in this
   line.<br>")
   document.write(x.fontsize(24) +" is 24 point in
   this line.")
```

You can get the same results by spitting out the HTML:

```
<FONTSIZE=9>Pete </FONTSIZE> is nine point in this
   line.<br>
<FONTSIZE=24>Pete </FONTSIZE>is 24 point in this line.
```

indexOf   If you want to look for a substring y in x, you can use x.indexOf(y) and it will return the starting location of the first occurrence. If you type x.indexOf(y,z), JavaScript will start with position z.

italics If you want italics output, then x.italics() will be the same as placing the text between <IT> tags.

`lastIndexOf`   If you want to look for a substring y in x, you can use `x.lastIndexOf(y)` and it will return the starting location of the last occurrence. If you type `x.lastIndexOf(y,z)`, JavaScript will start scanning with position z.

`link`   If you want to create a link instead of an anchor, use the `link` command. Pass the URL for the HREF in the argument for the `link` function.

`small`   If you want small output, then `x.small()` will be the same as placing the text between `<SMALL>` tags.

`strike`   If you want strikeout text, then `x.strike()` will be the same as placing the text between `<STRIKE>` tags.

`sub`   You can create subscripts with this method. `x.sub()` will be produced as a subscript.

`substring`   You can extract the characters between character y and z with the function call `x.substring(y,z)`.

`sup`   You can create superscripts with this method. `x.sup()` will be produced as a superscript.

`toLowerCase`   To convert x to lowercase, execute `x.toLowerCase()`.

`toUpperCase`   To convert x to uppercase, execute `x.toUpperCase()`.

Some of these functions are mainly useful when you're using the `writeln` command to print out data on the browser in HTML. The rest are good for pulling apart and putting together strings. Although the `+` operator is not officially a part of the object, it is the way that you concatenate strings.

`Date` **Objects**

JavaScript provides several standard methods for dealing with times and dates so you can interface cleanly with the Internet. You might want to use these methods to access the clock of the machine that is running the browser or simply to keep the data straight. These methods are all part of the `Date` class.

There are three major ways that you can use the constructor for `Date` objects. If you pass it no parameters, it will grab the current time.

If you pass it a string, it will parse the string assuming it fits this pattern: *month day, year hours:minutes:seconds*. "June 5, 1964" would be parsed correctly and zeros would be added in for the time. The third major way is to pass in numbers like this:

```
x=new Date(year, month, date, hours, minutes, seconds)
```

All of these will produce the same class of object with the information stored in the same format.

The properties for the `Date` class should be accessed indirectly through methods. Here's a list of methods that you can use to change a `Date` object like x:

getYear   x.getYear() returns the year of x

getMonth   x.getMonth() returns the month of x.

getDate   x.getDate() returns the day of the month of x. That is, 1, 2, 3, etc.

getDay   x.getDay() returns the day of the *week* of x. That is, Monday, Tuesday, etc.

getHours   x.getHours() returns the hours of x.

getMinutes   x.getMinutes() returns the minutes of x.

getSeconds   x.getSeconds() returns the seconds of x.

getTime   x.getTime() returns the number of milliseconds between January 1, 1970, and x.

getTimezoneOffset   Finds the amount of time in minutes between the current time x and Greenwich Mean Time (GMT). This will access a variable that may or may not be set correctly in the operating system.

setYear   x.setYear(1964) sets the year of x to 1964.

setMonth   x.setMonth(2) sets the month of x to March. 0 is January.

setDate   x.setDate(23) sets the day of the month of x to 23. 0 is *NOT* the first day.

setHours   x.setHours(13) sets the hour of x to 1 pm.

`setMinutes`   `x.setMinutes(32)` sets the minutes of x to 32.

`setSeconds`   `x.setSeconds(14)` sets the seconds of x to 14.

`toLocalString`   `x.toLocalString()` returns a string with the time in the format *mm/dd/yy hh:mm:ss*.

`toString`   `x.toString()` is slightly different than `toLocalString`. It spells out the names of the month and day.

`toGMTString`   `x.toGMTString()` puts x into the standard Internet time string which is based upon GMT.

Two of the `Date` methods don't require a string to act. They're accessed by placing the `Date` keyword in front of them. They are:

`Date.parse` If you want to convert a string of the format `"Month Day, Year hh:mm:ss"`, this method will convert the string into the number of milliseconds between the time represented by that string and the "beginning" of computer time, January 1, 1970.

`Date` This will also return the number of milliseconds since January 1, 1970, but it takes up to six parameters specifying in order the year, the month, the date, the hours, the minutes, and the seconds.

Extra Functions

Several extra functions that are an important part of the JavaScript collection of built-in methods are usually described with the rest of the built-in objects, even though they aren't referenced in that way. One is called `eval`, but you don't refer to it as `class.eval` or `objectname.eval`. The rest of these functions may be quite useful.

`eval` If you have a string such as `"6+9*8"`, you can evaluate this string like this: `x=eval("6+9*8")`. x will end up with the integer 78. This is a powerful function that can do plenty of things. Much of LISP's exceptional functionality emerges because it can build up arbitrary programs and then evaluate them.

`parseInt` JavaScript already has a convention that allows you to write integers as either decimal, octal, or hexadecimal numbers. `parseInt` allows you to convert arbitrary numbers in arbitrary bases. `parseInt("123",4)` will convert the string `"123"` into the correct integer by assuming that it is base 4. In this case, the value is 27.

parseFloat This takes a string with a floating-point representation of a number and converts it into a number, but it will not do so at an arbitrary radix. It will handle scientific notation. So parseFloat("1.23") will return a floating-point number with the value 1.23 in it.

escape Converts a character into the ASCII representation in ISO Latin-1 encoding that is commonly used when passing odd characters in HTTP requests. So if you ask for a URL, the ampersand turns into the string "%26".

unEscape Reverses the escape function. The percent notation is converted back into something useful, in other words, ASCII.

Netscape's Insides as Objects

Much of the guts of the Netscape browser are exposed to the JavaScript programmer. All you need to do is learn Netscape's object hierarchy and you can begin to fiddle with documents, their links, the overall color scheme, and almost anything else you might want to change.

Each object in this hierarchy has *properties*, *methods*, and *event handlers*. If you want to modify the way that a certain part of the display looks or acts, you must find the correct object that represents it and change a property or execute the right method. The event handlers are scripts that are called whenever the right event happens. You can define event handlers if you want to do so.

The basic hierarchy is shown in Figure 16.1. The window object is the top level. Each window displays a document which is one property of the object. The history property of the window describes what other documents have appeared in the past. The current document's location in cyberspace is encoded in the location property.

There is also a property known as self. This points to the current window and is included because the scoping rules are centered around the document. If you leave off an object designator, JavaScript will assume that you mean the document. The property window acts the same as self. The top property points to the topmost window in the browser. The parent property is defined if the window is contained as part of a set of frames.

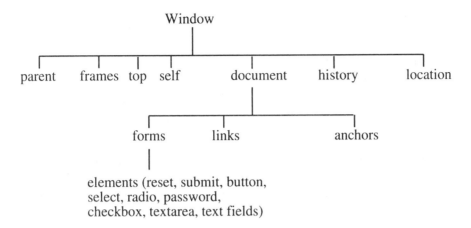

Figure 16.1. This is the hierarchy of objects hidden inside of a Netscape browser. For example, if you want to examine the links, you would look for the document object inside of the window. Inside of the document would be the links object that contains all of the data on links.

One property known as frames is an array with a pointer to all of the frames contained in the current window. Each frame may display a different document and it may have its own history. The objects in a frame are also windows, but windows may not be frames.

The document object is the most important object for most work. If you want to display information to the user, you'll be writing it directly to this object. It has two major arrays as properties, links and anchors, that list all of the hot links on the page. The forms array contains any of the input devices that are available to the user. If you want to access the information typed by a user, you need to get at an object in the forms array.

Each of the levels in this hierarchy have many different local properties that you can use to change details like color or selection. Understanding all of the levels might not be necessary to do a few simple things with the browser, but mastering everything may be a good idea. JavaScript has plenty of idiosyncrasies that are slowly being worked out and smoothed over. The revisions for PR2, the latest version of the Netscape browser at the time of this writing, include many simple fixes that make programming easier. More are sure to come with time.

Each of the sections here will deal with the individual parts of this hierarchy and provide a summary of their properties and methods.

The `window` Object

The `window` object is the most encompassing object from the Netscape browser. Its main job is to hold a `document` object, keep track of the past through its `history` object, and understand its relationship with other frames and windows spawned by the browser through its `self`, `top`, and `parent` pointers. Here is a list of the `window` object's properties:

`defaultStatus` The status bar on the bottom of the window will display this information to the user. You may change it, but this is the default value that is shown if you haven't made any changes.

`frames` An array that contains a list of all of the frames in the current window. Each of these frames is also another window so there is the opportunity for much recursion.

`length` The length of the `frames` array.

`name` The name of the window. When you create a window, you might give it a name that will allow you to refer to it by name. If you name a window `Fred`, you can access the object by name. `Fred.frames` points to the array of frames inside `Fred`.

`parent` If the window is a frame, this is the window that holds it.

`self` You must use this to refer to the current window. The `document` is assumed to be the center of attention so any method calls are assumed to belong to the `document` object.

`status` You can send a special message. This is usually used with the `onMouseOver` event handler. If the mouse moves over an item, then the status bar can change to display some help information describing what an item might do.

`top` The topmost window.

`window` Another self reference.

`document` The object containing all of the information being displayed.

`frame` The frame for the window.

`location` This contains all of the information about the URL that produced the information being displayed, that is, the name of the host running the data, the protocol used to get it, the IP address, the port, and other details.

Here's a short example of how to access one of the properties at the window level. This code will temporarily display a status message in the bottom of the browser. When it is clicked, the message "I'm a status message." appears at the bottom of the browser.[1] The result of this code is shown in Figure 16.2.

```
<<HTML>
<HEAD>
<TITLE> Create Some Objects</TITLE>
<SCRIPT LANGUAGE="JavaScript">
<!--
 function overElement(){
 self.status="I'm a status message.";
}
self.defaultStatus="I'm just a placeholder."
document.write("I'm just being written.");
//-->
</SCRIPT>
</HEAD>
<BODY>
<H2>This is HTML</H2>
This information is displayed through the body tags.
<FORM>
<INPUT TYPE="button" NAME="Hi" value="Click Me" onClick=
    "overElement()">
</FORM>
</BODY>
</HTML>
```

Most of the other properties are objects themselves and must be unpacked. Here's an example of some code that will iterate through the different properties of an object and display them for you. This is a good technique to use for debugging or learning about new parts of the object hierarchy. The command for will loop through the items in the object me and place each one in turn in the variable prop.

---

[1]Note that low-class browsers don't offer status!

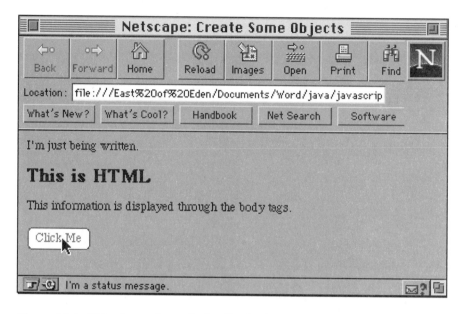

Figure 16.2. This shows the code for displaying a status message. In this case, Netscape has replaced it with its own message "I'm a status message."

```
<HTML>
<HEAD>
<TITLE> Create Some Objects</TITLE>
<SCRIPT LANGUAGE="JavaScript">
<!--
 function showLocation(me){
  document.write("</DL>");
  for( var prop in me){
    document.write("<DT>"+prop+" <DD> "+me[prop] + "<br>");
  }
  document.write("</DL>");
 }
document.write("I'm just being written.");
//-->
</SCRIPT>
</HEAD>
<BODY>
<H2>This is HTML</H2>
This information is displayed through the body tags.
```

```
<FORM>
<INPUT TYPE="button" NAME="Hi" value="Click Me"
onClick="showLocation(self.location)">
</FORM>
</BODY>
</HTML>
```

The results are displayed in Figure 16.3, but most of the properties for the location in this example are blank. This is because the HTML file was only processed locally, not over the Net.

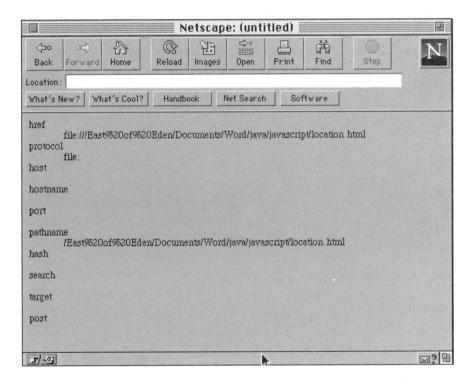

Figure 16.3. This window displays the different properties of the object `self.location`.

The document **Object**

The most important object for most applications is the document object. This object contains all of the information about what is being displayed in a particular window or frame at any one time. You can manipulate the details in this document to respond to the user in the proper way and customize the display.

Here are the properties of the `document` object:

Note that you can simply refer to the `document` *object without adding a prefix like* `self` *that modifies it. JavaScript will act upon the currently active document.*

`alinkColor` This is the color used to display the active link being selected in the document. You can set this color to be any combination of red, green, and blue by concatenating three hexadecimal representation of the bytes. So the command `document.alinkColor= "#40A8F3"` will produce a milky blue-green color with the red set to be 40 on a scale of 0 to FF, green set to be A8, and blue set to be F3.

`anchors` This is an array containing all of the anchors on the page. You can access them and modify them if you need to change where a link will go.

`bgColor` The background color for the window.

`cookie` The *cookie* is a persistent object that hangs around on the client's machine. If someone loads a page, it will give you access to information that was stored the last time your source code ran there. This is an ideal way to customize the pages for people. You might want to highlight the parts of the document that have changed since they last looked at the document.

`fgColor` The foreground color for the window.

`forms` An array pointing to all of the forms on the page. You can access them by name.

`lastModified` The date the page was last modified according to the server.

`linkColor` The color of links.

`links` An array pointing to all of the links on the page.

`location` The location object that contains all of the information about where this data came from.

`referrer` Who pointed to this page.

title The title that is displayed on the top of the title bars. You can
set it by placing it between the tags <TITLE> and </TITLE> and
change it if you want.

vlinkColor The color of the links that have already been *visited* and
are stored in a cache.

Changing the Colors

Here's a quick example of how to change the colors on the page if
someone clicks on a button. Clicking the button will toggle the background color.[2]

```
<HTML>
<HEAD>
<TITLE> Create Some Objects</TITLE>
<SCRIPT LANGUAGE="JavaScript">
<!--
flip=0;
 function changeColors(){
  if (flip==0){
     document.bgColor="#1050A0";
     flip = 1;
  } else {
     document.bgColor="#A09000";
     flip = 0;
  }
 }
//-->
</SCRIPT>
</HEAD>
<BODY>
<H2>This is HTML</H2>
This information is displayed through the body tags.
<FORM>
```

---

[2]Unfortunately, the options for setting all of the colors don't always seem to work.
The foreground color, fgColor, doesn't seem accessible in the current beta version of
the Macintosh version of the Atlas PR 1 used to prepare this document. The repainting
code needs to be fixed, as it probably will be before you read this book.

```
<INPUT TYPE="button" NAME="Hi" value="Click Me"
onClick="changeColors()">
</FORM>
</BODY>
</HTML>
```

Manipulating the Anchors and Links

The anchors and the links are stored in two arrays, anchors and links. The anchors are any place in the software that the <A> tag is found. The links are limited to the anchors that come with the parameter HREF="*some URL*". So plain anchors that might be used to name a location in a page will only appear in the anchors array, but the anchors that contain hot links to other locations will appear in both anchors and links.

Both arrays begin with zero and end with item length-1. The anchors array doesn't seem to hold anything at this time. The items in it are filled with null pointers. The Netscape documentation says that the main purpose for providing the array is to allow a programmer to check to see if a particular anchor exists. You can't really do much else with it. This may change in the future.

The links array contains all of the information about the link including details like URL, path, and the protocol.

Here's some code that accesses the two arrays.

```
<HTML>
<HEAD>
<TITLE> Create Some Objects</TITLE>
<SCRIPT LANGUAGE="JavaScript">
<!--
 function showAnchor(me){
  document.write("Showing:"+me);
  document.write("<DL>");
  var i = 0;
  for( var prop in me){
    document.write("<DT>"+i+":"+prop+" <DD> "+me[prop]
    + "<br>"); i++;
  }
  document.write("</DL>");
 }
```

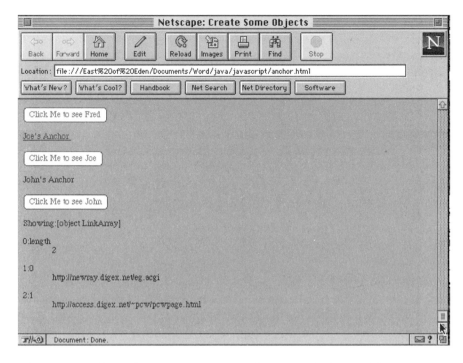

Figure 16.4. The code generates three anchors, two links, and three buttons. Pressing the corresponding button reveals information about the anchor.

```
//-->
</SCRIPT>
</HEAD>
<BODY>
<H2>This is HTML</H2>
This information is displayed through the body tags.
<A Name="Fred" HREF="http://newray.digex.net/eg.acgi">
    Fred's Anchor </A>
<FORM>
<INPUT TYPE="button" NAME="F1" value="Click Me to see Fred"
onClick="showAnchor(document.links[0])">
</FORM>
<A Name="Joe" HREF="http://access.digex.net/~pcw/
    pcwpage.html"> Joe's Anchor
</A>
```

```
<FORM>
<INPUT TYPE="Button" NAME="J1" value="Click Me to see Joe"
onClick="showAnchor(document.links[1])">
</FORM>
<A  NAME="John"> John's Anchor </A>
<FORM>
<INPUT TYPE="Button" NAME="J3" value="Click Me to see John"
onClick="showAnchor(document.anchors[2])">
</FORM>
<SCRIPT LANGUAGE="JavaScript">
<!--
showAnchor(document.links);
//-->
</SCRIPT>
</BODY>
</HTML>
```

If you run the code, you can examine the contents of the links array by clicking on the corresponding button. If you click on the button for the final anchor with codename John, you'll get null.

There are *two* scripts tags in this HTML file. The first one contains the defintion for the function showAnchor. The second passes this script the object document.links. Figure 16.4 shows some of the information displayed on the screen after the second script is run. Notice how the output of this function is nicely formatted? There is a toString function defined for the object that will format the data in the links object.

Figure 16.5 shows what happens when you click on a button. There are many properties to the links object and each is listed individually.

Using the Cookie

Java can't write files to the system, but JavaScript can leave information behind.

Netscape provides a way for your JavaScript program to save information locally. You might want to use this to record information about the last time that a user stopped at the page so you can update the data. This is the canonical usage, but I'm sure that people will come up with clever plans that may cache information about chess games locally. Netscape also suggests that fee-based Internet services might want to store access information in the cookie to simplify logging and billing.

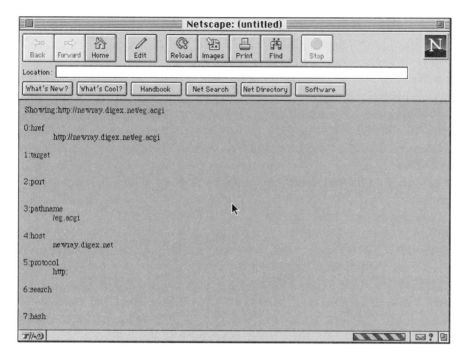

Figure 16.5. Here are the properties of the links item found by clicking on the button.

The cookie is deeply embedded in the Netscape HTML protocol. Each URL may have a corresponding cookie stored on the user's local disk. If the user requests that URL again in the future, Netscape will also ship along a copy of the cookie to the HTTP server. If the server wants Netscape to store a cookie, it can tell the local version of Netscape to do so and the user won't even know that the information is there unless they poke around in the hidden files. Naturally, some folks find the concept potentially dangerous because it is a threat to the large degree of anonymity supposedly built into the Internet.

Netscape suggests that each local browser will store no more than 300 total cookies and each is a string that can be no longer than 4K bytes long. Each domain or server is further limited to 20 total cookies. If the limit is exceeded, Netscape will start erasing the least recently used cookie. Clearly this may be a problem if a user is a big Net user because you might find that your cookie was deleted. At this time, you just can't guarantee that your cookie will be there when you return, so you should only use it to cache local information that can be regenerated.

JavaScript can also access the cookie and modify it. It is available as the `cookie` property of the `document` object. Although you could write arbitrary things to this string object, you must obey the standard cookie format so that Netscape can file and retrieve the cookie for you.

The cookie is a string that consists of a number of tags that are separated by semicolons. A tag consists of the name of the tag, the equals sign, and the data. You retrieve the data by searching through the string for the name of the tag. There are several important tags that must be found at the beginning of the cookie so Netscape can access them. These are:

expires This is the date the file can be erased. If it is not set, then the cookie will disappear when the browser is shut down. This date must be in the format:

> `Wdy, DD-Mon-YY HH:MM:SS GMT`

That is, it is the format created when you take a `Date` object and apply the `toGMTString` method to it.

domain This is the name of the domain that will have access to this object. If the current document is loaded from `www.foo.com`, then it will have access to all cookies with domains like `www.foo.com` or `foo.com`. It will *not* have access to cookies from domains like `www2.foo.com` or `random.slash.com`. Note you can't use top-level domains to pass information indiscriminantly. You can't set a domain to be `com` or `org.uk`. You must include another level.

path You might want to control which cookies are valid for which URL. If you want a particular cookie to work for all documents, then you would set it's path to be "/". If you want one cookie to work for all documents with paths that begin with `/fred`, then you would set to be `/fred` and it would match documents like `/fred/list.html` or `/fredsdir/home.html`.

secure If this tag is present, the data in the cookie will only be sent to servers when the HTTPS protocol is encrypting all of the data.

You're probably going to want to develop your own tags to store some information. You must be aware that these tags can contain no spaces, commas, or semicolons. You can convert a string that might be problematic into a safe string with the function escape. This function replaces dangerous characters with escape code sequences (i.e., %20 for a space). They can be converted back with noEscape. If you need to find an object, you must search the entire string looking for the matching tag. The function GetCookieTag shows how it can be done. In this case, the document.cookie behaves just like a long string.

Rolling Your Own Documents

The document object comes with five important methods bound to it: open, close, clear, write, and writeln. These allow you to build new documents and fill them with text. The functions all do what you would expect. open begins a new document in the browser. write and writeln insert text into it. close shuts the document and clear will empty it.

This sample text shows how it can be done in an extra window:

The window object was described starting on page 294.

```
<HTML>
<HEAD>
<TITLE> Create Some Text</TITLE>
</HEAD>
<BODY>
<SCRIPT LANGUAGE="JavaScript">
<!--
function Hello(){
  msg = window.open("","Fred","toolbar=no,width=200,
    height=100");
  msg.document.write("<H2> Welcome to HTML text </H2>");
  msg.document.write("<br><br> You can write to the screen
    with HTML. <br>");
  msg.document.close();
  msg.document.open();
  msg.document.write("<H2> Welcome to HTML text  2</H2>");
  msg.document.write("<br><br> You can still write to the
    screen with HTML.
<br>");
  msg.document.close();
}
Hello();
```

```
//-->
</SCRIPT>
</BODY>
</HTML>
```

Figure 16.6 shows the output from this code. You'll notice that only the second document is visible. The first one flashed on the screen and then disappeared. It was closed and replaced when a new one was opened.

Figure 16.6. This is an extra window filled with the second document.

If you're planning on simply outputting customized text into the main browser window, then you shouldn't rely upon the close method. It will happen automatically. If you execute close yourself, then you stand the chance of jeopardizing the execution of the remainder of the script. I crashed the Netscape browser several times while experimenting with the close function. The code sample above opens and closes a document twice in a separate window. This code failed repeatedly when I tried the same trick in the browser's main window. Beware.

The open method takes an optional parameter that will set the MIME type of the document being displayed. It defaults to text/html as you can see in all of the examples. Here's the list of options:

text/html The default is useful when you want the browser to handle the formatting chores for you. You can embed tags like <BR> in the text and the browser will do the work of making it fit. Naturally, you should make sure that it conforms to the HTML standard.

text/plain No HTML formatting. In this case, the write and the writeln work quite differently. The writeln method starts a new line. Use this MIME type to do plain formatting.

image/gif If you can spit out the format of a .GIF file from a JavaScript program, more power to you.

image/jpeg The same goes double for the JPEG format.

image/xbm The bit maps are somewhat easier.

x-world/plugin There are many different plug-ins that might be included with a Netscape browser. Some of the most important ones might be the VRML displayers. You can easily create 3D models of objects on the fly and push them into a VRML displayer.

There are many different uses for the method of opening a window and writing a document to it. If the document is not one of the standard plug-ins then the browser will ask users if they want to save the file. This is one way to write a file to the user's disk, if the transaction is approved.

Forms as Objects

The form object is probably the most important one for any JavaScript programmer. If you're going to be writing JavaScript, you'll often want to interact with the user. The form object is where the information is stored. If you want to get the information typed into a text input box, then you'll need to dig into the forms array, which is a property of the document object.

Most forms are created by including HTML code for the form inside the document. This may be explicitly written out as plain HTML text inside the file or it might be generated on the fly by a function that might use the cookie to personalize the form. In either case, the <FORM> tag opens the form and the </FORM> tag closes it. There may be several forms on a page and each one is given an entry in the forms array. You can access them with the commands like document.forms[1].

Before JavaScript, most forms were tied directly to the distant server. The initial <FORM> tag included the ACTION parameter that you would give a URL that will receive the information in the form. When the user pressed the ubmit button, the data in the form would be sent to this URL, which was a CGI script designed to process it. This method will continue to be used extensively because many Web applications involve communications between the user and the server.

JavaScript, however, offers the chance to do much more work locally. You can attach JavaScript code to be executed when the objects in a form are changed. These scripts are embedded in the tags defining the different parts of the form like the <INPUT> tag. If you want to execute a function like checkNumber when someone inputs a value in a field, you might create code that looks like this:

```
<FORM NAME="First">
Name:
<INPUT TYPE="text" Name="UserName" VALUE="" SIZE=20
onChange="checkNumber(this.value)>
</FORM>
```

This code would create a form with a single text entry field. The form object would be accessible in two ways. You could either refer to it as document.forms[0] if it was the first form to appear in a document, or you could simply call it document.First. When a form is created, it is inserted as a property of the document object if a name is given.

The <INPUT> tag sets up the item. The parameters for VALUE and SIZE should be familiar to anyone who's created forms in HTML. They set the initial contents of the form and the number of visible characters respectively. The Name parameter gives a name for the input field object so it can be referenced as a property of the form object. That means you can access the object with the term document.First.UserName.

The onChange parameter embedded in the tag points to a string that will be executed when the form element is changed. This happens whenever the user types something new into the text box and then switches the focus to another part of the form. When that happens, the string is evaluated as a JavaScript program. In this example, it invokes a function checkNumber and passes it a single parameter this.value. The this points to the form element that generated the event, document.First.UserName. The value is the property that holds the contents of the element.

The form object also comes with an array that points to each of the elements of the form in turn. In this example, document.First.elements[0] would also point to the text input field.

The different properties of the form element can be summarized as follows:

elements This array contains one object for each input element that is part of the form.

length The number of items in the elements array.

action This is a string that gets its value from the ACTION parameter/attribute that usually can be found in the <FORM> tag creating the form. This is the URL that will receive the data when the user presses the Submit button or JavaScript executes the submit method attached to the form object.

encoding Each <FORM> tag often specifies a ENCTYPE for the form that specifies how the data from the form will be returned to the distant server. This string holds the data.

method There are two ways that form data can travel: GET or PUSH. This is a string that holds one of these two values.

target When the data comes back from the form it may go into the same window or a different window. This string holds the contents of the TARGET parameter/attribute included in the <FORM> tag.

submit This is the only method attached to the form object. It is equivalent to letting the user press the Submit button.

You can create your own forms by stringing together a number of different elements that will be described in the following pages. Each of them comes with its own set of events that will trigger scripts to run. They also have different collections of ways to change their values.

The `button` Element

You can add a button to a form by inserting code like this in between the <FORM> and </FORM> tags:

```
<INPUT type="button" Name="Bob" Value="Click Me" onClick=
    "BobClick()">
```

`Name` sets the name for the element. This would allow you to access the element directly by name with an expression like `document.forms[0].Bob`. The text `Click Me` will be displayed on the button's face. When it is clicked, the JavaScript function `BobClick` will be executed.

The `name` and `value` are properties for the button object that hold the initial values specified in the <INPUT> tag. You can access them directly with a statement like:

```
document.forms[0].Bob.value="Please, Click Me"
```

The button element is pretty easy to use because there is no internal state. You should be aware that there are two special types of buttons, `reset` and `submit`, that define buttons with special predefined actions.

The `reset` and `submit` Elements

You can add a special button to a form for either resetting the form or submitting it to a server by inserting code like this between the <FORM> and </FORM> tags:

```
<INPUT type="reset" Name="Fred" Value="To Reset Default
Values" onClick="FredClick()">
<INPUT type="submit" Name="Joe" Value="Register Me"
onClick="JoeClick()">
```

The parts of these special button tags behave exactly like the parts of the ordinary button element. You can access these values through the same `name` or `register` properties.

You might want to simulate either of these buttons if you want to write your own code for submitting the form. This code will not use the standard routine from the Submit button. Instead it will first blank out the first element in the form. You might want to do this for security reasons. Then the standard `submit` method is invoked.

```
function MySubmit(){
  document.form[0].element[0].value = "<deleted>";
  document.form[0].submit();
}
<FORM>
<INPUT type="button" Name="Bob" Value="Submit" onClick=
    "MySubmit()">
</FORM>
```

The checkbox Element

If you want to add a checkbox to a form, you can do it by inserting HTML code like this between the <FORM> and </FORM> tags:

```
<INPUT TYPE="checkbox" NAME="Eileen" VALUE="Left" CHECKED
onClick="CheckOne()">
```

This tag will create a checkbox in the form. It will not display any text to identify what the box will do. It is your responsibility to insert that information in the HTML before the element. As you might expect by now, the NAME parameter/attribute will specify the name of the object and you can use it to retrieve the object from the form object. If the CHECKED code word is found, then the box is initially checked when it is first displayed. Otherwise it appears unchecked. Also, the JavaScript in the string attached to onClick will execute whenever the checkbox is changed.

The VALUE parameter/attribute acts differently here. In the button element, it would specify what would be drawn on the screen. In this case, the value will be returned with the other form data to be parsed by the CGI.

If you need to determine whether the element is checked, then you can test the checked property. This is a boolean that works well in if-then statements.

The hidden Element

When the FORM system was created for HTML, the designers wanted to include some way that people might pass information back with the form. Let's imagine that the central server passed out a form to a user and it wanted to keep track of who returned the information and how long they took to do it. One easy way to do this is to embed an element like this between the <FORM> and </FORM> tags:

```
<INPUT TYPE="hidden" Name="StartTime" Value="12:45:03">
```

When the form is returned, it will include the substring StartTime =12:45:03. This is a neat way to customize forms in a hidden way.

If you do add such an element to the form, then you can access the data in the usual fashion. document.forms[0].StartTime.value points to the string "12:45:03".

The radio Element

If you want to add a radio button to a form, you can do it by inserting HTML code like this between the <FORM> and </FORM> tags:

```
<INPUT TYPE="checkbox" NAME="Choice" VALUE="Six" CHECKED
onClick="CheckOne(0)"> <H6> Six of One. <H6> <br>
<INPUT TYPE="checkbox" NAME="Choice" VALUE="HalfDozen"
onClick="CheckOne(1)"><H6> One Half Dozen <H6> <br>
<INPUT TYPE="checkbox" NAME="Choice" VALUE=
          "OneTwentyFourthOfAGross"
onClick="CheckOne(2)"><H6> One Twenty-Fourth of a
        Gross<H6> <br>
```

This will create three radio buttons that function in a group. They all have the same NAME. The browser will ensure that only one of the three will remain checked at any one time. When the submit button is pressed, only one value will be returned with the Choice tag.

The items in the radio group are arranged inside an array. You can access the individual elements with expressions like: document.forms [0].Choice[0] or document.forms[0].Choice[1].

The select Element

You can create a pull-down menu or a scrolling list of selectable items by using the select element in your form. Here's an example:

```
<SELECT
  NAME="Poison" SIZE=20 MULTIPLE
  onChange="PourMe(this.index)">
<OPTION>  Claret
```

```
<OPTION SELECTED> Port
<OPTION> Scotch
<OPTION> Armagnac
</SELECT>
```

The NAME field identifies the element in the form and the SIZE field sets the number of characters in the width. The MULTIPLE keyword indicates that the user is allowed to choose many different items. Many browsers display MULTIPLE versions in a scrolling list and those without multiple choices as a pull-down menu. The various options are identified by separate <OPTION> tags.

This example has one JavaScript event handler: onChange. There are two other ones that you might want to use. onFocus is executed when the element is made the focus of the form by a mouse click and onBlur is run whenever the focus is lost.

If you need to access the information bound up in a select object, you have plenty of choices. The most important property is the options array, which contains one element for every option available to the user. The length property contains the length of this array. Each option object has five properties:

defaultSelected If this is true, then the option is considered selected when it is displayed.

index The index value of the current object, that is, where you can find it in the options array.

selected If this is true, then it is currently selected. This can change with each interaction.

text A string holding what is displayed.

value What is sent along to the server if the form is submitted when this option is selected.

The text and textarea Elements

You may want the user to input some text into the form. A text element as shown in this example will let you do it:

```
<H6>Name:</H6>
<INPUT TYPE="text" Name="UserName" Value="Type Name Here"
        SIZE=60
```

```
onChange="CheckName(this.value)"><br>
<H6>Rank:</H6>
<INPUT TYPE="text" Name="Rank" Value="Type rank Here"
          SIZE=60
onChange="CheckRank(this.value)"><br>
<H6>Serial Number:</H6>
<INPUT TYPE="text" Name="SNum" Value="Type Serial Number
          Here" SIZE=60
onChange="CheckSerial(this.value)"><br>
```

This will create three text areas that display 60 characters. Their intial value is set by the value parameter/attribute. When the user types something new in a field like UserName, then the data in this string, document.form[0].UserName, changes to reflect it.

There are four different event handlers for the text area, but only one is used in this example. onChange will be executed whenever the data in the form element is changed. onFocus will be run when an element is clicked in and the text form receives the focus where the keyboard clicks will go, and onBlur is run whenever the focus moves elsewhere. Finally, onSelect will be called whenever someone selects something in the field.

There are also three methods that you might want to call. focus will bring the focus to one element and blur will take it away. The select routine will take two parameters specifying the beginning and the ending of the text selection.

The text element will only produce a one-dimensional text input field. There are times when you might want to create a multi-lined input field. In this case, you'll want to use the very similar textarea. Most of the details are the same. Here's an example:

```
<H6>What's your story:</H6>
<TEXTAREA Name="homework" ROWS=10 COLS =60
onChange="CheckExcusethis.value)">
Type your first excuse right here.
</TEXTAREA>
```

All of the methods and event-handling routines for the textarea element are the same as the text element. The major difference is that the initial information is put outside the tag. The uses for the ROWS and COLS parameters/attributes should be obvious.

Summary

This chapter explored many of the basic objects that are part of the JavaScript environment. If you want to change the appearance or interact with the forms, you'll need to understand this heirarchy. The important lessons are:

- You can create your own objects to keep your data straight, but you don't need to do so.

- The libraries of basic functions are stored as objects with useful methods. Math, String, and Date are the most important.

- The data loaded from the web (the URLs, HTML files, images) is all stored in one big heirarchy of objects. You can traverse this tree if you need to change something.

- Forms are the most important use for JavaScript. You can access the parts of the form and react to changes using the basic JavaScript functions.

Chapter 17

A JavaScript Example

This chapter offers a good example of how you can build a complicated form with JavaScript that will update itself.

Tax Computations

This section shows a very simple JavaScript version of the 1040EZ tax form that U.S. citizens can use to pay their taxes if their tax flow is not too complicated. I have used a very nice version written by Dave Koblas from HomePages, Inc. (415-903-5353) as a beginning. My version is significantly simpler because I removed much of their nice HTML structure. What is left is some simple JavaScript code that will present a form and do calculations. If a user types in a number and then moves to a new form element, JavaScript will execute the routine `compute` to fill in the necessary form elements.

If you need to write a form, you can use this as an example of how to begin. You might also want to check out other examples from `www.homepages.com`. Here are some other suggestions:

The most complicated part about writing JavaScript code is keeping track of types. I've often cursed the system simply because it would not provide type checking and thus the deep bugtracking help. That's often why I prefer Java.

The code here provides some basic computation. The routine `compute` will pull the values out of the form, remove any nonnumerical characters, and then do some basic arithmetic. When the final numbers are known, it puts the value in the form.

Moving through a string is a complicated procedure in this version of JavaScript. This construction of extracting one-character substrings was borrowed from the HomePages version. Perhaps future versions of JavaScript will provide brackets so you can access a string like you do in Java.

This code is not guaranteed to produce any accurate information for the IRS. Nor should it be considered to be professional tax preparation help. Consult your tax professional if you intend to use this code for anything other than an example for how to create a simple form in JavaScript.

```
<html>
<head>
   <title>JavaScript 1040 </title>
</head>
<body>
<br>
<SCRIPT LANGUAGE=JavaScript>
<!-- hide this script tag's
function checkNumber(obj)
// From HomePages, Inc. version.
{
        var str = obj;
        if (str.length == 0 ||  str == "" ||  str == null) {
              return false;
        }
        for (var i = 0; i < str.length; i++) {
              var ch = str.substring(i, i + 1)
              if ((ch < "0" ||  "9" < ch) && ch != '.'
                  && ch != '$' && ch != ',') {
                    return false;
              }
        }
        return true;
}
function checkOut(obj)
```

```
{
        if (!checkNumber(obj)) {
                return 0.0;
        }
     var temp ="";
        for (var i = 0; i < obj.length; i++) {
                var tt = obj.substring(i, i + 1);
                if ((tt >= "0" && tt <= "9") ||  tt == '.') {
                        temp += tt;
                }
        }
        return parseFloat(temp);
}
function compute(input)
{
     wages = checkOut(input.form.tot_wag.value);
       interest = checkOut(input.form.int_inc.value);
       unemploy = checkOut(input.form.unemploy.value);
       ag = wages+interest+unemploy;
    input.form.adj_g_inc.value = ""+ag;
    input.form.std_ded.value=""+ 6400;
    var ti=ag-6400;
    input.form.taxing_inc.value=""+ti;
    var tw=checkOut(input.form.tax_withheld.value);
    var ei=tw+checkOut(input.form.eic.value);
    input.form.total_payments.value=""+ei;
    var tax = 0;
    if (ti>23350) {
      tax += (23350*0.15);
    } else {
      tax += ti*0.15;
    };
    ti = ti - 23350;
    if (ti>0) {
      if (ti> 33150) {
        tax += (33150 * .28)
      } else {
          tax += ti*0.28
      }
    }
    ti = ti - 33150;
```

```
if (ti>0) {
  if (ti> 61450) {
    tax += (61450 * .31)
  } else {
      tax += ti*0.31
  }
}
ti = ti - 61450;
if (ti>0) {
  if (ti> 138550) {
    tax += (138550 * .36)
  } else {
      tax += ti*0.36
  }
}
ti = ti - 138550;
if (ti>0) {
  if (ti> 138550) {
    tax += (138550 * .36)
  } else {
      tax += ti*0.36
  }
}
ti = ti - 138550;
if (ti>0) {
  tax += 0.396*ti
}
input.form.tax.value = ""+Math.round(tax);
 tax_withheld = checkOut(input.form.tax_withheld.
                          value);
    eic = checkOut(input.form.eic.value);
    payments = eic + tax_withheld;
    input.form.total_payments.value = ""+Math.round
                                      (payments);
    if (payments > tax) {
        input.form.refund.value = ""+Math.round
                                  (payments
                                   - tax );
        input.form.amount_owed.value = ""
    } else {
        input.form.amount_owed.value = ""+Math.
```

```
                                              round
                                              (tax -
                                              payments);
               input.form.refund.value = "";
          }
}
<!-- Hiding complete now. -->
</SCRIPT>
<FORM>
<h2>1040EZ</h2>
<br>
<h4> 1 </h4> Total wages, salaries, and tips. This should
             be shown in box 1 of your W-2 form(s). Attach
             your W-2 forms(s).
  <INPUT ONCHANGE=compute(this) NAME=tot_wag TYPE=text
             SIZE=15>
<br>
<h4> 2 </h4>Taxable interest income of $400 or less.
             If the total is over $400, you cannot use
             Form 1040EZ.
  <INPUT ONCHANGE=compute(this) NAME=int_inc TYPE=text
             SIZE=15>
<br>
<h4> 3</h4> Unemployment compensation (see page 14).
  <INPUT ONCHANGE=compute(this) NAME=unemploy TYPE=text
                SIZE=15>
<br>
<h4> 4 </h4>Add lines 1, 2, and 3. This is your <b>adjusted
             gross income</b>. If less than $9,230. see page
             15 to find out if you can claim the earned
             income credit on line 8.
  <INPUT ONCHANGE=compute(this) NAME=adj_g_inc TYPE=text
                SIZE=15>
<br><h4> 5 </h4>The standard deduction for a single adult
                is $6500.
  <INPUT ONCHANGE=compute(this) NAME=std_ded TYPE=text
                value=6500 SIZE=15>
<br>
<h4> 6 </h4>Subtract line 5 from line 4. If line 5 is
             larger than line 4, enter 0. This is your
             <b>taxable income.</B>
```

```
<INPUT ONCHANGE=compute(this) NAME=taxing_inc TYPE=text
            SIZE=15>
<br>
<br>
 <h4> 7 </h4>Enter your Federal income tax withheld from
            box 2 of your W-2 form(s).
 <INPUT ONCHANGE=compute(this) NAME=tax_withheld TYPE=text
            SIZE=15>
<br>
<h4> 8</h4><b>Earned income credit</b> (see page 15). Enter
type and amount of nontaxable earned income below.
 <INPUT ONCHANGE=compute(this) NAME=eic TYPE=text SIZE=15>
</TR>
<br>
<h4>9 </h4>Add lines 7 and 8 (don't include nontaxable
earned income). These are your <b>total payments</b>
 <INPUT ONCHANGE=compute(this) NAME=total_payments
            TYPE=text SIZE=15>
<br>
<h4> 10 </h4><b>Tax</b> Use the amount on <b>line 6</b>
to find you tax in the tax table on pages 29-33 of the
booklet. Then, enter the tax from the table on this line.
 <INPUT ONCHANGE=compute(this) NAME=tax TYPE=text SIZE=15>
<br>
<br>
<h4> 11 </h4><LI><B>Refund:</B> If line 9 is larger than
line 10, subtract line 10 from line 9. This is your
<b>refund.</b>
 <INPUT ONCHANGE=compute(this) NAME=refund TYPE=text
            SIZE=15>
</TR>
<br>
<h4> 12 </h4>If line 10 is larger than line 9, subtract
line 9 from line 10. This is the <b>amount you owe.</b>
See page 22 for details on how to pay and what to
write on your payment
 <INPUT ONCHANGE=compute(this) NAME=amount_owed TYPE=text
            SIZE=15>
</FORM>
```

Summary

This short example shows how to build a form and do some computations whenever someone enters data. JavaScript can be surprisingly powerful in these situations. Here are some of the lessons:

- First create a form using the standard HTML system. Give each element in the form a unique name.

- You can create several functions at the top of the form for calculating the results.

- Data can be extracted from an object with a function like checkOut. This can help eliminate bad input.

Index

Java and JavaScript Programming